DISCIPLE

UNDER THE TREE OF LIFE

Study Manual

The Writings • John • Revelation

Writers of
DISCIPLE: UNDER THE TREE OF LIFE
Study Manual

Richard Byrd Wilke
Julia Kitchens Wilke

Consultants to the Writers
William J. A. Power, Old Testament
Leander E. Keck, New Testament

DISCIPLE: UNDER THE TREE OF LIFE
Study Manual, copyright © 2001 by Abingdon Press
All rights reserved

Scripture quotations in this publication, unless otherwise indicated, are from the New Revised Standard Version Bible, copyrighted © 1989 by the Division of Christian Education of the National Council of the Churches of Christ in the USA. Used by permission. All rights reserved.

Scripture quotations containing the letters TEV in the reference are from the *Good News Bible: The Bible in Today's English Version*—Old Testament: Copyright © American Bible Society 1976; New Testament: Copyright © American Bible Society 1966, 1971, 1976.

Scripture quotations containing the letters NIV in the reference are taken from the *Holy Bible, New International Version*. Copyright © 1973, 1978, 1984 International Bible Society. Used by permission of Zondervan Bible Publishers. All rights reserved.

Maps and tree art by **Nell Fisher;** other illustrations by **Mitch Mann;** cover design by **Mary M. Johannes.**

Nellie M. Moser, Senior Editor; Mark Price, Development Editor; Katherine C. Bailey, Production Editor; Linda O. Spicer, Secretary; Ed Wynne, Design Manager.

For more information about DISCIPLE or DISCIPLE training seminars, call toll free 800-251-8591 or 800-672-1789.

02 03 04 05 06 07 08 09 10 — 10 9 8 7 6 5 4 3 2

DISCIPLE

Contents

DISCIPLE

As You Continue DISCIPLE

You come to DISCIPLE: UNDER THE TREE OF LIFE having completed study of at least DISCIPLE: BECOMING DISCIPLES THROUGH BIBLE STUDY. Indeed you may have completed study of all three of the earlier phases of DISCIPLE. So you know the expectation in terms of time and discipline—thirty to forty-five minutes of daily reading and notetaking, reflecting and praying six days a week, and participation in a two-and-a-half-hour weekly group meeting for thirty-two weeks. The study manual format is familiar to you as well.

So you are not new to DISCIPLE, nor is DISCIPLE new to you. But you are *starting anew*. And in DISCIPLE that means you will read Scripture passages as if you are reading them for the first time, and the notes you take will come from that new perspective.

Reading Scripture Aloud

Each daily assignment in UNDER THE TREE OF LIFE calls for reading Scripture aloud. Choose a time and place for daily study where you will not disturb others as you read aloud and where you will feel comfortable—not self-conscious—and free to express yourself as you read. Poetry and symbolic language in this study's Scripture appeal both to eye and ear. The amount of Scripture to be read daily varies from day to day and week to week, and the passages to be read aloud also vary in length daily and weekly. Maintain the discipline of daily study so you have time to prepare thoroughly and completely.

Study Manual Format

Two continuing sections in the study manual format have new titles: "Fruit From the Tree of Life" for the commentary section and "Marks of Faithful Community" for the discipleship section. Both sections usually are read on the sixth day of study, and both call for written responses.

Notice that "Marks of Faithful Community" does not include the word *the* before the word *faithful*. The message in this title is that faithful community is not an institution but a way of *being*. And the "Mark of Faithful Community" that appears in the margin beside this section always begins with the words *"Being faithful community, we. . . ."* The content of "Marks of Faithful Community" is the response arrived at by viewing "Our Human Condition" through Scripture. These two sections always are to be considered together.

Two new elements in the study manual format represent special emphases in this study—"Psalm of the Week" and "The Radical Disciple." "Psalm of the Week" provides occasion for living daily in the biblical text and is intended to lead participants into a deeper life of prayer using Psalms as a guide. The "Psalm of the Week" is to be prayed aloud daily during study, and weekly in the group session. Suggestions for experiencing the "Psalm of the Week" pay attention to feelings as well as words.

"The Radical Disciple" focuses on thoughts and actions relevant to the weekly theme that require stretch in terms of commitment to discipleship. The "Psalm of the Week" and "The Radical Disciple" sections belong within the context of faithful community. Whether praying the psalm or taking steps toward radical discipleship, participants know they are not alone—the community is there.

The brief prayer psalm, a familiar element in the study manual format, continues and functions as before. Always it comes from a psalm different from the "Psalm of the Week."

"The Radical Disciple" section will not always appear in the same place in the study manual format. Its emphasis will determine where it is placed in each lesson. Content varies—sometimes calling for action, other times calling for reflection.

Scripture in the study manual comes mainly from the New Revised Standard Version, though occasionally other translations are quoted. Using a variety of translations for comparing verses and passages will enrich study because subtle differences in wording can bring a passage to life. Consider using *Tanakh*, a Jewish translation of Scripture, for a fresh version of the Writings. Daily reading assignments occasionally include the Apocrypha, so you will need a study Bible with the Apocrypha.

UNDER THE TREE OF LIFE Scripture

UNDER THE TREE OF LIFE concentrates on the Writings—Ruth, 1 and 2 Chronicles, Ezra, Nehemiah, Esther, Job, Psalms, Proverbs, Ecclesiastes, Song of Solomon, Lamentations, and Daniel. Torah, Prophets, and Writings make up the Hebrew Scriptures. Writings include all the books not in Torah or the Prophets.

New Testament Scriptures include the Gospel of John; 1, 2, 3 John; James; Jude; and Revelation.

Scripture in this study speaks to both heart and head and carries the reader toward the climax of the message and completion of the promise.

DISCIPLE

THE
WRITINGS

FAMILY

"Ruth said,
'Do not press me to leave you
    or to turn back from following you!
Where you go, I will go;
    where you lodge, I will lodge;
your people shall be my people,
    and your God my God.'"

—Ruth 1:16

1 Redeem the Inheritance

OUR HUMAN CONDITION

Maintaining family is hard work. Family is constrictive, demanding, and not always convenient for us. Caring for others can be exhausting and painful. Staying connected is not easy. It's all we can do to look after ourselves.

ASSIGNMENT

Read the whole book of Ruth at one time. Use a fresh translation—Today's English Version; *Tanakh,* a Jewish translation; the Contemporary English Version; or others. Enjoy the beautiful story. Then read again—including the Introduction—slowly and carefully, appreciating allusions, hidden meanings, social and religious context.

Day 1   Ruth 1–4 (the story)
Day 2   Ruth 1 (Ruth and Naomi in Moab); Judges 3:12-30 (tension between Israel and Moab); Psalms 13; 77 (prayers for deliverance)
Day 3   Ruth 2 (Ruth meets Boaz); Leviticus 19 (be holy); 23:9-22 (appointed festivals); Deuteronomy 24:10-22 (laws to protect the poor); Psalm 69 (prayer for deliverance)
Day 4   Ruth 3 (family loyalty); Genesis 38 (Judah and Tamar); Psalm 103 (thanksgiving)
Day 5   Ruth 4 (Boaz marries Ruth); Deuteronomy 25:5-10 (redeem the inheritance); Jeremiah 32:1-15 (Jeremiah buys a field); 1 Chronicles 2:1-17 (descendants of Judah); Matthew 1:1-17 (Ruth, ancestor of kings); Psalm 111 (hymn of praise to the Lord)

Day 6   Read and respond to "Fruit From the Tree of Life" and "Marks of Faithful Community."
Day 7   Rest

PSALM OF THE WEEK

For thirty-two weeks, every day, every week, we will live in the Psalms. We will join our voices with the faith community that stretches across the centuries and reaches around the world. Pray Psalm 146 aloud each day this week.

PRAYER

Pray daily before study:
    "LORD, make us prosperous again,
        just as the rain brings water back
            to dry riverbeds.
    Let those who wept as they planted their crops,
        gather the harvest with joy!" (Psalm 126:4-5, TEV).

Prayer concerns for this week:

Day 1   Ruth 1–4 (the story)

Day 4   Ruth 3 (family loyalty); Genesis 38 (Judah and Tamar); Psalm 103 (thanksgiving)

Day 2   Ruth 1 (Ruth and Naomi in Moab); Judges 3:12-30 (tension between Israel and Moab); Psalms 13; 77 (prayers for deliverance)

Day 5   Ruth 4 (Boaz marries Ruth); Deuteronomy 25:5-10 (redeem the inheritance); Jeremiah 32:1-15 (Jeremiah buys a field); 1 Chronicles 2:1-17 (descendants of Judah); Matthew 1:1-17 (Ruth, ancestor of kings); Psalm 111 (hymn of praise to the Lord)

Day 3   Ruth 2 (Ruth meets Boaz); Leviticus 19 (be holy); 23:9-22 (appointed festivals); Deuteronomy 24:10-22 (laws to protect the poor); Psalm 69 (prayer for deliverance)

Day 6   "Fruit From the Tree of Life" and "Marks of Faithful Community"

Olive Tree

DISCIPLE

FRUIT FROM THE TREE OF LIFE

The rabbis had no trouble including Ruth in the Bible. The story is too compelling, too instructive to leave out. But they did have trouble deciding where to put it. Should it be placed after Judges, since its historical context is "in the days when the judges ruled"? The Septuagint, a Greek translation of the Old Testament, and the Christian Bible put it there. But the oldest texts, and the Hebrew Scriptures today, place it in the Writings—the third part of the Hebrew Bible— right after Psalms, Proverbs, Job, and the Song of Songs (Song of Solomon), perhaps because of its themes of sadness and love, but more likely because it provides the near miraculous link in the genealogy of David and Solomon.

Dating the writing of Ruth is nearly impossible, for it floats through Hebrew history, a love letter with a timeless message. The book of Ruth is a perfect place to begin our study of the Writings, for Ruth looks at the harsh realities of everyday life and tries to teach us how to live.

In the story, ordinary people like us, folks struggling with the mundane affairs of life—food, family, work, marriage, babies—figure out a way to survive. Each person has a role to play—Elimelech, Naomi, Mahlon, Chilion, Orpah, Ruth, Boaz, even the unnamed relative. But the key actor, the one working quietly behind the scenes, is the Almighty God of covenant who does not forget or abandon. The story of Ruth is one of the world's great narratives. Enjoy it. Let its teachings creep quietly into the corners of your mind.

A Family Tragedy

The story begins in tragedy. In five sentences we learn of famine, pasture and crop land cracking and blistering in the sun. We watch the young family pack a few belongings and, like millions of other refugees, walk away from their homeland in search of sustenance. They walk through the mountains, cross the Jordan River, and wind up as farmers in the sometimes friendly, sometimes hostile, land of Moab. Husband and father, Elimelech, dies, leaving Naomi to care for their two sons, Mahlon and Chilion. The sons marry Moabite women, but before they have children, the young men die. The name Mahlon can mean "sickly" and Chilion, "weakness." Naomi walks back and forth to the graveyard. She must have shared the thoughts of Job:

"I desire to argue my case with God. . . .
Why do you hide your face,
and count me as your enemy?" (Job 13:3, 24).

We can imagine that like the psalmist, Naomi is not afraid to let her cry of anger and her wail of grief explode toward God. Who else but God is to blame for famine, barrenness, and death?

"How long, O LORD? Will you forget me forever?
How long will you hide your face from me?

How long must I bear pain in my soul,
   and have sorrow in my heart all day long?
How long shall my enemy be exalted over me?"
   (Psalm 13:1-2).

Naomi says she came out "full," with a husband and two sons; she returns "empty."

Now, three landless, childless widows face one another in desperation. In an agricultural economy, what was a woman without land or male protector to do? Our story hinges on whether God will look after these seemingly Godforsaken women.

To Stay or Go

The family had its roots in Bethlehem, owning a piece of land inherited from father to son for generations. Bethlehem means "house of bread," but sometimes the pantry was bare. Some farmers had fields of barley and wheat, but farming in the hills southwest of Jerusalem, with marginal rainfall, was more suited for grazing than for crops. Remember, Ruth and Boaz's descendant David was a shepherd, not a farmer. Bethlehem was David's hometown (1 Samuel 16:18). The angels announced the birth of Jesus to shepherds near Bethlehem. It must have been soul-wrenching for Elimelech and Naomi to abandon the family plot of ground, leave a dried-up pasture, and move away.

They went to Moab, where a Semitic people, distantly related to them through Abraham and Lot, grazed sheep and goats and raised some grain and fruit. They settled in the area east-southeast of the Dead Sea, a plateau that rises rather abruptly to about three thousand feet above the Jordan Valley. That quick rise catches some moisture, allowing some twelve to sixteen inches of annual rainfall in an area of about forty by twenty-five miles. Today, with irrigation, this land now in Jordan produces abundant fruit, vegetables, and grain.

Naomi, now in midlife, recognizes she cannot provide security for her "daughters." She contemplates security the only way she knows how—by giving them husbands, offspring, land. She presses the thought to its ludicrous limit. Even if she were to marry, bear sons and start over, it would be too late. All that remains is for them to split up, each go home and throw herself on the fringes of family, community, and the providence of God.

Orpah—the name can mean the beautiful curve in the back of the neck—loves her mother-in-law, but she does the logical thing. Urged by Naomi, she goes back to her own village, to her people, looking after her own welfare. Like the near-relative later in the story who almost, but not quite, redeems the family, Orpah turns the back of her neck.

Ruth faced the same decision. To go home would mean some semblance of security. To go with an elderly widow, a woman emotionally exhausted, to a land Ruth had never seen,

DISCIPLE

was risky. What if the town rejected them? Where would they live? What would they use for resources? What if Naomi died? But in her heart, Ruth must have asked herself also, What if Naomi trudged back to Bethlehem alone? How could the older woman make it, physically, emotionally, financially by herself? She would be helpless. She needed somebody. She needed family.

How far are we to go in trying to save the family?

_____

_____

Ruth's vow of loyalty rings across the centuries like a silver chime:
"Where you die, I will die—
    there will I be buried" (Ruth 1:17).
Ruth's lyrical words of love are from a foreign-born daughter-in-law to her mother-in-law as they bonded, daughter and mother. Don't gloss over "there will I be buried." At a death, family members placed the body in the ground without embalming it. After the body had decomposed, they gathered the bones and placed them in an ossuary, a chest for bones, or in a pile on the floor of the family tomb. The bones of persons who died far away could be brought back to the family ossuary or tomb and thus be "gathered" to their ancestors (2 Kings 22:20). Ruth declares that her bones will rest with Naomi's bones forever.

Ruth gave a sacred oath. She uses the word "Yahweh," calling on the God of Israel (Ruth 1:17). Ruth declares total religious, national, and family loyalty to Naomi and her people. The God of covenant was at work. Bereft of sons, Naomi had a daughter.

But tired and grief-stricken Naomi responds to her old friends in Bethlehem with words stripped of hope. Naomi means "pleasant" or " sweet," but she says, call me "Mara," which means "bitter." The word is an allusion to the bitter water at Marah found by Moses and the Hebrew people when they were wandering in the wilderness (Exodus 15:23-25). God through Moses turned bitter water into sweet. Now, claims Naomi, God has done the reverse, turning sweet into bitter.

A Glimmer of Hope

Naomi thought of herself as bereft, empty; but she was not as empty as she thought. Resources were at hand—community, family, the compassionate teachings of the covenant God, and a daughter standing beside her—but Naomi seems to hold on to her bitterness. Suddenly, in the darkest hour, a glimmer of hope. Naomi's return home has come "at the beginning of the barley harvest" (Ruth 1:22). The barley harvest, earliest and first harvest, symbolizes hope. The people began praying for rain in the fall; the harvest was an answer

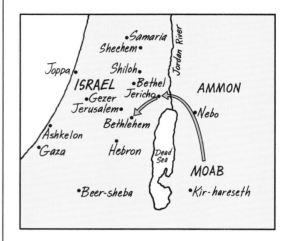

Ruth and Naomi probably traveled north through Moab, through the hills and across the Jordan River, through Jericho, and then southwest to Bethlehem, where they arrived in early spring at the time of the barley harvest.

to prayer. Ruth and Naomi arrived home, to "the house of bread" when food was once again available. Ruth went to work in the fields as a gleaner.

Family and hired hands harvested: men and boys, women and girls—wielding the sickles, tying and stacking. Torah instructed them to leave broken heads of grain, loose straws, random scattering, forgotten sheaves, some hard-to-cut barley or wheat growing in the corners of the field, to leave it for the poor, the widow, the orphan, the stranger (Deuteronomy 24:19-22). Why does the covenant call for protection of the poor? Why does Torah demand a safety net under the impoverished? Because the "Father of orphans and protector of widows is God" (Psalm 68:5). The poor were "family" members of the covenant community. Remember, says Torah, you were all once poor slaves in Egypt. We're together in this thing called life.

"As It Happened"

Now there's a storyteller's phrase! Was it luck that Ruth entered Boaz's field at sunup? The reader knows better. Somehow the providential hand of God is in that phrase, "as it happened." A kinsman! Boaz was a relative of Elimelech. God the Redeemer often needs a human helper, hands to carry out providential care. Naomi and Ruth needed a family member who cared.

Following the Exodus, each family was given a piece of land, but time and chance, greed and hardship had taken their toll. Some people got rich, and some got poor. God expects compassion, demands that the community care for its own, even care for the stranger. But do people always do it? Did they always do it in Bethlehem? Obviously not. Where were family and friends in the earlier drought when Elimelech, Naomi, and their two sons needed them? The prophet Isaiah, during the monarchy, pleaded for repentance:
"Wash yourselves . . .
cease to do evil . . .
rescue the oppressed,
defend the orphan,
plead for the widow" (Isaiah 1:16-17).
Boaz warned Ruth about other fields where workers might harm her or drive her off. "Keep close to my young women. . . . I have ordered the young men not to bother you" (Ruth 2:8-9). Later Naomi also warns, "You might be bothered in another field" (2:22). People have a tendency to look out only for themselves.

Every word indicates that Boaz, like Naomi, is of middle age. Both give advice; both speak and act with the assurance of older people. Both call Ruth "my daughter" even though she must be 25 or 30. Naomi and Boaz might be midforties or older—old for the times. Had Boaz ever married? Was he a widower? He was generous with his grain but cautious with

Barley, one of two staple grain crops in biblical Israel, was more abundant and cheaper than wheat and was the main food of low-income people. The barley harvest was the earliest harvest. The "sheaf of the first fruits" (Leviticus 23:10) waved at the beginning of Pentecost was a barley sheaf. The scroll of Ruth is read aloud on Shavuoth (Feast of Weeks) because the story's setting is the time of the barley harvest.

DISCIPLE

his emotions. Ruth had to be the one who proposed marriage (3:9-11).

Ruth's speech and actions are youthful, eager, respectful, enthusiastic. Boaz is careful, thoughtful, in command, deliberate. His foreman takes pains to tell his boss that Ruth never sat down, never stopped bending over—"without resting even for a moment" (2:7). The reader remembers another woman, Rebekah, who ran to water the camels of Abraham's servant when he was looking for a wife for Isaac (Genesis 24:10-21). We wonder if Boaz thought of Rebekah. Apparently God likes people who do their part. Boaz did.

When Ruth makes the act of proposal, Boaz uses a phrase seldom found in the Bible. He calls her a "worthy woman" (Ruth 3:11). The phrase is the exact Hebrew wording translated in Proverbs as "a capable wife"—a quite unusual phrase in the Bible.

"A capable wife who can find?
She is far more precious than jewels" (Proverbs 31:10).

Appealing to the Law

At Naomi's urging, Ruth dresses up, puts perfume behind her ears, and lies at Boaz's feet (Ruth 3:3-4). Her act is romantic, but it is primarily formal and legal. Ruth, a Moabite daughter-in-law to the widow of Elimelech, is laying claim to his inheritance—and to a relative of Elimelech that even Naomi's active mind had not remembered. Ruth is proposing, but she is reaching.

To what are the women appealing? To a practice called levirate marriage. This religious and civil law was embedded deeply in Israel's tradition, going back to the time of the patriarchs. Formalized later in the law of Moses, levirate marriage simply meant that if a man died childless, his brother should marry the widow and give her a child. By that simple family act, the dead brother's name would not be blotted out; the inheritance would not be lost (Deuteronomy 25:5-10). Complications came when the brother refused or died. Further complications developed if the brother was a child, or if there was no brother at all. What about a cousin, or uncle, or father-in-law? Torah doesn't say. Undoubtedly rabbis made countless theoretical and practical interpretations. Somebody was challenged; somebody was sued; somebody was embarrassed. The sandal episode began as an act of shame but evolved into a formalized legal act like the filing of a deed (Deuteronomy 25:7-10; Ruth 4:7-11).

But no court in the land would demand that Boaz be responsible for Ruth. That's the point. Boaz lived above the legal requirements. Just as Tamar is remembered for pushing the levirate law beyond boundaries to save the family (Genesis 38), so Boaz and Ruth are revered for going the second and third mile. Remember that Naomi had the levirate law in mind when she talked of birthing other sons, but even she had

The next-of-kin, sometimes called the "kinsman-redeemer," is identified by the Hebrew word *go'el* (*ga'al*), which means redeemer, redeem, redemption. The next-of-kin had an obligation to buy back (redeem) any family land that had been sold or lost, and that obligation extended to buying back family members sold as slaves. In Ruth the obligation of the *go'el* included the right of levirate marriage.

not contemplated the distant relative. The safety net worked because Ruth and Boaz showed the lovingkindness that resides in the heart of the covenant God.

God's *Hesed*

God's nature is *hesed* (also *chesed*), lovingkindness or steadfast love. The constant refrain in Psalm 136 is God's "steadfast love endures forever." Boaz compliments Ruth for showing steadfast love to Naomi (he has heard the gossip in the village) (Ruth 2:11). Now he proceeds to show *hesed* himself, "May the LORD reward you for your deeds," and refers to God "under whose wings you have come for refuge." Later when Ruth boldly lifts the cloak and sleeps at Boaz's feet, it is the wings of Boaz that become the wings of God.

Recall a time when a member of your family or of another family went beyond the call of duty.

Ruth birthed the baby, but you would have thought Naomi did it. The Moabite daughter-in-law who had been childless in her earlier marriage, now with middle-aged husband Boaz, places the baby in Naomi's arms. The village women shout "Blessed be the LORD" and claim that Ruth is worth more to Naomi than seven sons. Most of all, they recognized that this baby was the Lord's doing. The women named the baby Obed, who became the father of Jesse, who became the father of David, who became king. Ruth, a Moabite and a foreigner, grandmother of kings. God's providence!

So the story of Ruth moves through Jewish and Christian thought, gently reminding us that the covenant God wants to sustain us, aids the family in its struggle to survive, challenges us to sacrifice for one another, and invites us to include the outsider who may turn out to be the saving link in our destiny.

MARKS OF FAITHFUL COMMUNITY

Disciples take family seriously, giving high priority to family responsibilities, even extended family, often at considerable sacrifice. On occasion, we reach outside family to include others who may not be blood relatives. Disciples also seek social and political structures that strengthen family life.

Name your priorities that strengthen your family life.

Being faithful community, we take family seriously, giving high priority to family responsibilities, even extended family, often at considerable sacrifice. We reach outside family to include others.

DISCIPLE

What threatens relationships of lovingkindness in families?

Jealousy, competition

How does your experience of faithful community strengthen or weaken your family's cohesiveness?

What determines the effort and/or the sacrifice you are willing to make to maintain connections with extended family?

Identify some of the inconveniences that keep us from including the outsider in our family life.

What actions and attitudes overcome barriers of inconvenience?

THE RADICAL DISCIPLE

What family matters need your attention? Is there addictive behavior? Abuse? Failure to communicate? Need for reconciliation? Secrets that should be confronted? Financial problems? Isolation and loneliness? What would be the cost in time, energy, money?

IF YOU WANT TO KNOW MORE

The name commonly used for the Jewish version of what Christians call the Old Testament is *Tanakh* (TNK). *T* stands for *Torah* (the first five books of the Bible), *N* for *Nevi'im* (the Prophets), and *K* for *Kethuvim* (the Writings). These three divisions of the Jewish Bible probably reflect the stages in the development of the canon: Torah by about 450 B.C., Prophets by about 100 B.C., and Writings by about A.D. 90.

The Writings comprise a miscellaneous collection of books: wisdom books—Psalms, Proverbs, and Job; five books grouped as "five scrolls" or *megilloth* for use in festival liturgy—the Song of Songs, Ruth, Lamentations, Ecclesiastes,

The study manual uses the familiar designations B.C. and A.D. Occasionally the video presenters use the scholarly designations B.C.E. (Before the Common Era) and C.E. (Common Era). Think of the term *Before the Common Era* as that time in history when our religious ancestor, Judaism, existed but Christianity had not yet come into being. The *Common Era,* then, is that time in history when Judaism and Christianity began to share history together. The term *common* here means "shared."

and Esther; the apocalyptic book of Daniel; and historical narratives—Ezra, Nehemiah, and First and Second Chronicles. The canonical order of the Writings was not finalized before the late Middle Ages, thirteenth or fourteenth century A.D., though the five-scroll collection was known as much as two centuries earlier.

The Hebrew Bible

TORAH	THE PROPHETS	THE WRITINGS
Genesis	Joshua	Psalms
Exodus	Judges	Proverbs
Leviticus	1 and 2 Samuel	Job
Numbers	1 and 2 Kings	Song of Songs
Deuteronomy	Isaiah	Ruth
	Jeremiah	Lamentations
	Ezekiel	Ecclesiastes
	Hosea	Esther
	Joel	Daniel
	Amos	Ezra
	Obadiah	Nehemiah
	Jonah	1 and 2 Chronicles
	Micah	
	Nahum	
	Habakkuk	
	Zephaniah	
	Haggai	
	Zechariah	
	Malachi	

The Five Scrolls—*Megilloth*

Each of the five scrolls is read in the synagogue during a particular Jewish festival. The scrolls are arranged according to the order of the festivals.

The Song of Songs—Pesach (Passover)
Ruth—Shavuoth (Pentecost)
Lamentations—Ninth of Av (commemoration
of the destruction of the Temple)
Ecclesiastes—Sukkoth (Booths)
Esther—Purim

For more information on the Writings, consult Bible handbooks, Bible dictionaries, and general articles in Bible commentaries.

HERITAGE

"Say to my servant David: . . . I declare to you that the LORD will build you a house. When your days are fulfilled to go to be with your ancestors, I will raise up your offspring after you, one of your own sons, and I will establish his kingdom. He shall build a house for me, and I will establish his throne forever."

—1 Chronicles 17:7, 10-12

2 The Dream Restored

OUR HUMAN CONDITION

Now, and who we are now, is what matters. We can't live in the past—in fact we want to be free of the past. Besides, people who look backward tend to sentimentalize the "good old days," offering us little of value for our own time. We want no claim on us by either the past or the future. Free to be, in the here and now! That's us.

ASSIGNMENT

This week and next we'll read the two books of Chronicles. How can we read sixty-five chapters in two weeks? As we might view a mountain range, not by counting the rocks but by gazing at the snow-capped peaks and sweeping across the landscape.

Day 1   1 Chronicles 1–6 (genealogy rooted in creation; descendants of Abraham, Judah—including David and Solomon, tribes east of the Jordan, and the Levites)

Day 2   1 Chronicles 7–12 (genealogies of northern tribes, descendants of Benjamin, people of Jerusalem after the exile, death of Saul, David anointed king)

Day 3   1 Chronicles 13–18 (bringing the ark of the covenant to Jerusalem, psalm of praise, God's covenant with David, David extends the kingdom)

Day 4   1 Chronicles 19–23 (David's wars, census and plague, preparation for building the Temple, Levites and their duties)

Day 5   1 Chronicles 24–29 (divisions of worship heads, military divisions, civil officials, and Temple personnel; plans for Temple to Solomon)

Day 6   Read and respond to "Fruit From the Tree of Life" and "Marks of Faithful Community."

Day 7   Rest

PSALM OF THE WEEK

As you read Psalm 132 aloud daily, think about your congregation and your place of worship. Recall the people who made possible your place of worship. Say a prayer for those who prepare it weekly for worship. Picture in your mind and offer thanks for people who passed on to you both a place and a heritage of faith.

PRAYER

Pray daily before study:
"Happy are those whom you choose,
    whom you bring to live in your sanctuary.
We shall be satisfied with the good things
    of your house,
    the blessings of your sacred Temple" (Psalm 65:4, TEV).

Prayer concerns for this week:

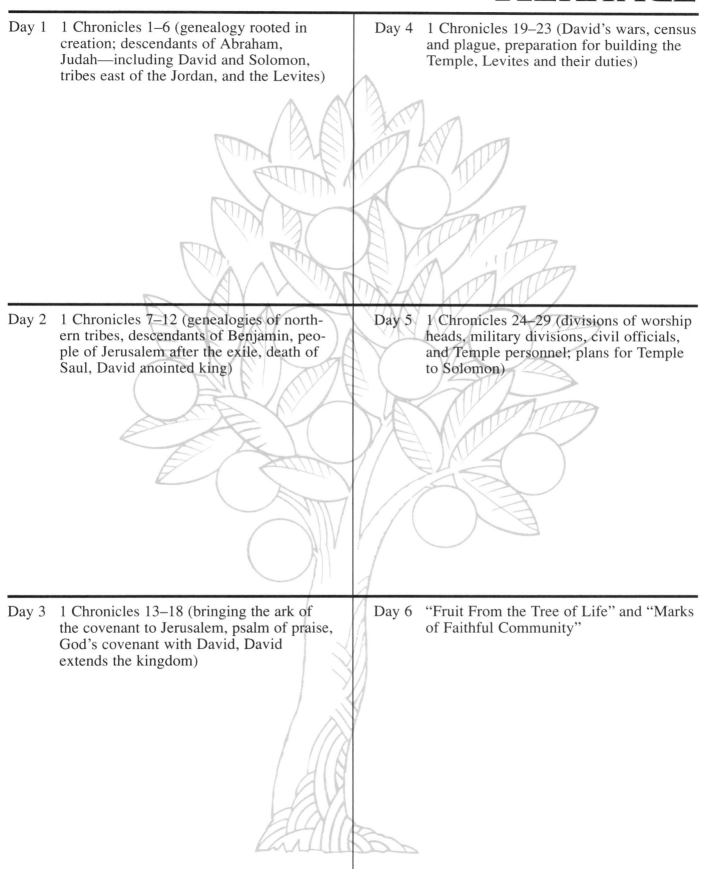

Day 1   1 Chronicles 1–6 (genealogy rooted in creation; descendants of Abraham, Judah—including David and Solomon, tribes east of the Jordan, and the Levites)

Day 4   1 Chronicles 19–23 (David's wars, census and plague, preparation for building the Temple, Levites and their duties)

Day 2   1 Chronicles 7–12 (genealogies of northern tribes, descendants of Benjamin, people of Jerusalem after the exile, death of Saul, David anointed king)

Day 5   1 Chronicles 24–29 (divisions of worship heads, military divisions, civil officials, and Temple personnel; plans for Temple to Solomon)

Day 3   1 Chronicles 13–18 (bringing the ark of the covenant to Jerusalem, psalm of praise, God's covenant with David, David extends the kingdom)

Day 6   "Fruit From the Tree of Life" and "Marks of Faithful Community"

Stylized Tree of Life

DISCIPLE

FRUIT FROM THE TREE OF LIFE

Originally one book, Chronicles was divided into two parts—First and Second Chronicles. The word *Chronicles* literally means "the events of the days." Many scholars think Ezra and Nehemiah are a continuation of the historian's work, making First and Second Chronicles, Ezra, and Nehemiah a four-volume history, though increasingly scholars see Ezra and Nehemiah as distinct. The Chronicler apparently wrote well after refugees began streaming back into Jerusalem from all other parts of the world, especially Judean exiles from Babylon.

Picture our scholar/historian at his desk, pen in hand, surrounded by manuscripts—histories, speeches, genealogies, government records, tax rolls, sermons, worship liturgies, psalms—carefully writing a theological version of Israel's history. Why should he labor so diligently? He wanted to remember the past, remember it in light of his own time. But he also pursued an agenda that we will unravel slowly. His selection of certain materials—and the omission of others—aims to put spring into the tired steps of his contemporaries, aims to dream a glorious future. Chronicles intends to inspire Israel once more to be a great people obedient to God.

The account begins with Adam (Creation). Why? Because Israel's faith is not grounded in a tribal god but in God the Creator of heaven and earth. Other nations—Babylonia, Persia, Greece—had their local gods, but the God of the Hebrews is God of the universe.

That's why we're given the children of Ishmael as well as those of Isaac, the genealogy of Esau as well as that of Israel (Jacob). Recorded are the people of Seir and the kings of Edom. By the time we focus on Israel's sons (1 Chronicles 2:1), we know we're living in a world bigger than the narrow land bridge between Egypt and Mesopotamia, a world of many diverse peoples, a world of the Diaspora. Into that world, the people of Israel are called to be faithful witnesses. Their place of worship, the Temple, was to be the focal point of Judaism everywhere. The Temple was not a tribal tabernacle but the house of holiness for the God of the universe.

The Family Tree

The genealogy spotlight shines on Judah. Judah was not the oldest of the twelve sons of Jacob; he was fourth, but from his loins came King David and King Solomon. And from David and Solomon came the Temple. The kingdom of David and the Temple lasted for four hundred years, and according to the Chronicler, would have lasted forever if the kings and the people had been faithful.

On occasion David's lineage hung by a thread. Tamar, Judah's Canaanite daughter-in-law, used the levirate marriage law to continue the family line. She birthed Perez, the second of twins and ancestor of David. Just think: The kingdom of

Scrolls such as the Chronicler would have used were made from a sheet of leather, parchment, or papyrus wound on wooden rollers and usually kept in a container.

David, the city of Jerusalem, and the building of the Temple hung on Tamar's action after her two husbands had died. Courageous Tamar—dressed as a prostitute; squatting by the roadside; calling to her father-in-law, Judah; and sleeping with him (Genesis 38). Providence and an act of faith maintained the family line. Ruth is not mentioned, but all Israel knew, when they read the phrase, "Boaz of Obed, Obed of Jesse" (1 Chronicles 2:12), that when the line was in jeopardy, God intervened—and a Moabite widow made David's birth line possible.

Jesse's two daughters are mentioned along with his seven sons (daughters are not usually included in genealogies); all are David's siblings (2:13-16). The elaborate genealogies have been building up to David. David is carefully noted as the seventh son, the youngest. The culture usually gave inheritance rights and power of position to the first son. As often happens, God reverses human expectations and strategies (1 Samuel 16:1-13).

David's sons are listed—even the places they are born. All were potential heirs to the throne. The mothers are named, often along with their nationalities—evidence of David's skill in making political treaties. Some of Solomon's innumerable sons are named—possible heirs to the throne. Special attention is given to the little tribe of Benjamin (1 Chronicles 8:1-28) because in earlier days, the fortified Jebusite, pre-Israelite city of Jerusalem was within its boundaries. King Saul, given little notice in Chronicles, came from the tribe of Benjamin.

Why does the Chronicler list the other sons of Judah? Because unity is a major theme. All Israel must be included. Unity brought divine approval and success to David and Solomon. Disunity brought divine disapproval, division of the kingdom, and disaster. Under David, the other tribes became supportive of Judah, the strongest tribe and the synonym for the Southern Kingdom. Most of the exiles who returned from Babylon were Judeans.

Did the exiles who straggled back to Jerusalem perceive themselves as insignificant, of no account in the vast Persian Empire? They had no army, held no national boundaries. They paid homage to foreign kings. Even the Temple and the walled city no longer frightened foreign forces. Were the people of Abraham now "nobodies"? The vast genealogies reminded the people they were "somebodies." Their people had names, tradition, heritage. They had descended from great heroes of the faith and once had lived in a unified, God-fearing community. They had deep roots. They could hold their heads high. They could become mighty again.

David the Ideal

In the old days the tribes of Israel had been victorious, "for they cried to God in the battle, and he granted their entreaty because they trusted in him." But when they "prostituted

This fragment of a pottery jug found in Mizpah dates from the period after 539 B.C. when Persia controlled Judah. The letters YHD stamped on it indicate the name Yahud, the Persian equivalent of Judah.

DISCIPLE

themselves to the gods of the peoples of the land," God brought destruction and exile upon them (1 Chronicles 5:20-26). Saul was disobedient and failed. "He was unfaithful to the LORD in that he did not keep the command of the LORD; moreover, he had consulted a medium, seeking guidance, and did not seek guidance from the LORD" (10:13-14).

Chronicles says the people did not "turn to" the ark of the covenant in the time of Saul (13:3). David, however, looked to God for guidance and to the people for advice: In Chronicles, David typically says, "If it seems good to you, and if it is the will of the LORD our God, let us . . ." (13:2). What a contrast to the arrogance of ancients kings; what a tribute to David's humility before the Lord. If consultation with God is the theme, consultation with the people is a subtheme and a sign of equity within the covenant community.

Omitted are David's adultery and Absalom's rebellion. Spotlighted is David, the shepherd concerned for his people, the king willing to listen to God's counsel, the psalmist making plans for God's house. No wonder the Chronicler proclaimed David's kingdom the ideal and the standard for restoration. If Israel would learn lessons from the past, the people again would be great. Even the dream of messiah drew on the example of the Davidic kingdom,

The fledgling kingdom of Saul and David had been built on a foundation of two hundred years of loosely-knit confederacy, a free association of twelve tribes held together as a people by tradition and religion. David transformed the tribal confederacy into a centralized government. He unified the military to include all Israel. He organized the priests and Levites for divine worship, elevating the Levites to high honor. His capture of Jerusalem was particularly ingenious. According to 2 Samuel 5:8, David's men entered the city by way of the water shaft. Jerusalem was a small, fortified Jebusite town, nestled in the mountains, on the border between the northern and southern tribes. Saul's headquarters had been at Gibeah, David's at Hebron. David moved the capital from the tribal town of Hebron (even though Abraham, Isaac, and Jacob were buried there) to the neutral, in-between city of Jerusalem.

David reached out to all Israel. He worked to gain God's blessing and the people's consent. He honored local customs and walked softly around tribal traditions. Carefully he moved the ark of covenant, sacred to all the tribes.

A Place for the Temple

Now watch this series of events: David had ordered a census of all able-bodied fighting men in the kingdom. Though not forbidden by the law, the act was perceived as a lack of faith that God would provide the fighting force when necessary. God punished Israel for the census; and "David said to God, 'I have sinned greatly. . . . take away the guilt of your servant. I have done a very foolish thing'" (1 Chronicles

21:8, NIV). Of the three choices God then gave him, David chose "pestilence on the land," and a plague fell on Israel, killing seventy thousand people. Seeing himself to blame, David walked up to Jerusalem, bought the threshing floor from Ornan (Araunah) the Jebusite, and offered official sacrifices. Religious people of all generations have been inspired that David purchased rather than seized the land, saying, "I insist on paying the full price. I will not take for the LORD what is yours, or sacrifice a burnt offering that costs me nothing" (21:24, NIV). The king's sacrifice was offered, the plague stopped, and the ground later became the site for Solomon's Temple.

David's Vision of Temple Worship

The Chronicler pays no heed to Exodus. He directs our interest not to Moses and the tabernacle but to David and the Temple. He mentions Moses, not to tell us of manna in the wilderness but to describe the distribution of land as a symbol of equity. He will inspire his readers by telling about Jerusalem, the Temple, the time of David and Solomon.

Moses and Joshua gave land to the other eleven tribes but not to the Levites. Levites were set apart to be priests of the people forever, supported by the tithes and offerings of the people. Levites were allowed to live in certain cities and to graze herds on public pasture lands (1 Chronicles 6:54-60). They were usually poor, sometimes sojourners, and when there was no Temple, often destitute.

When David's dream was realized and Solomon's Temple erected, some Levites were priests, overseeing the sacrifices at the main altar; others helped with worship, assisting with the sacrifices, singing psalms in the choir, playing instruments, and guarding the gate. David organized the priests and Levites into twenty-four groups or divisions. Every priestly person had his unique role. The worship personnel were prepared even before the Temple was built. David wanted worship to be done right. If Torah was to be obeyed, the festivals must be celebrated correctly.

Moses gave us the instruction of Torah. Isaiah and the prophets demanded justice and compassion. The Chronicler revels in Temple worship properly carried out and with attention to detail.

When the people of Israel were scattered into foreign lands, many Levites assisted the priests in remembering the high holy days, singing the psalms, offering prayers, teaching the Scriptures. Some returned under Ezra and Nehemiah to help rebuild the city and to serve in the Temple; others remained in the Diaspora, still emotionally related to Temple worship and spiritually empathizing with its sacred festivals. Guided by the Levites, Jerusalem's Temple worship gave spiritual unity and religious focus to Jews everywhere—even in places of prayer in distant cities.

This coin, minted during the Second Jewish Revolt (132–135 A.D.), bears an inscription in ancient Hebrew used a thousand years earlier and an impression of a lyre from the time of King David.

DISCIPLE

Concerned primarily with Judah, the Chronicler turns briefly to the northern tribes, mentioning genealogies and military lists (7) to show that all Israel served David gladly. He consistently speaks of unity: "So all Israel was enrolled by genealogies" (9:1); "all Israel gathered together to David at Hebron and said, 'See, we are your bone and flesh. . . . The LORD your God said to you: It is you who shall be shepherd of my people Israel. . . .' So all the elders of Israel came to the king at Hebron" (11:1-3). The elders, with one voice, acclaim David their shepherd king! Warriors showed up from everywhere, even from King Saul's kindred, to help administer justice and establish order (12). When we read First and Second Samuel, we know the political transition wasn't that smooth; but the Chronicler wants to emphasize spiritual unity, knowing it would be essential for Israel's survival. The Chronicler's point: Under Persian rule, the Jerusalem Temple offered welcome and unity to all Jews everywhere.

What is David's key contribution? Not his shepherd-king's heart, not his extension of the kingdom, not even his unification of the tribes of Israel. According to the Chronicler, David's remarkable and lasting gift was his vision of Temple worship. The pestilence David had caused by counting all Israel ended when David bought the threshing floor in Jerusalem to offer a sacrifice. From that moment on, King David dreamed of a central place of worship. He carefully moved the capital from Hebron to Jerusalem to prepare a central and neutral site between southern and northern tribes. He brought the ark of the covenant to Jerusalem, using only Levites the second time (15:1-3). In ecstasy, he danced in celebration, dressed in fine linen like the Levites and the singers (15:27). (He wore less clothes in 2 Samuel 6:20-22.)

The old king planned to fulfill his dream, so he consulted the prophet Nathan about the Temple. The prophet gave a perfunctory "yes" to his king, then after prayer, changed his mind. The task of building the Temple was reserved for David's son (1 Chronicles 17:1-15). But David's restless energy drove him to prepare, to lay up gold and silver (18:9-11), and to stockpile huge amounts of stone, lumber, and precious metals (22:2-5). His charge to Solomon was to build a house for the Lord and to faithfully keep the Law with wisdom and understanding (22:6-12). Of utmost significance are David's closing words to the whole assembly: "I have provided for the house of my God, so far as I was able" (29:2).

The Chronicler knows that while some people of Israel are in Jerusalem, many more are dispersed in other lands. He looks to the Temple, to Jerusalem, to holy worship, and harmonious obedience to the Law as the hope for Israel. David the king, drawn up from the past by the historian's pen, will inspire and encourage the people toward their God-given destiny. In unity and humility, consulting God and one another, faithfully obeying Law and Temple, they can restore the glory days of David.

MARKS OF FAITHFUL COMMUNITY

By appreciating God's action and human faithfulness in the past, we are inspired to move confidently into the future. We remember the faith we have inherited so we can go forward, unified and faithful.

What part of your religious heritage and identity do you draw on most for insight and strength for today?

_____

_____

What is the role of Scripture in shaping worship in your congregation?

_____

_____

How is Scripture shaping your personal obedience to God?

_____

_____

What past, pivotal events and decisions shaped your present congregation?

_____

_____

In what ways has your denominational heritage inspired and guided your congregation as a worshiping community?

_____

_____

THE RADICAL DISCIPLE

The radical disciple recognizes that a name always brings with it a heritage and a heritage always makes claims. To take the name *Christian* is to accept the heritage and the demands behind the name. To take the name *disciple* is to accept the requirements that go with the name. The radical disciple intentionally lives up to the name.

IF YOU WANT TO KNOW MORE

Keeping in mind what you have read about David in First Chronicles, read the more human account of David recorded in 2 Samuel 11–19.

NOTES, REFLECTIONS, AND QUESTIONS

Being faithful community, we value the power of memory and heritage to form us into God's worshiping people, obedient in the present and responsible to the future.

⎡ERIORATION

"If my people who are called by my name humble themselves, pray, seek my face, and turn from their wicked ways, then I will hear from heaven, and will forgive their sin and heal their land."

—2 Chronicles 7:14

3 Rise and Fall of Faithfulness

OUR HUMAN CONDITION

We pretend to be self-sufficient, able to live freely, without boundaries. We're drawn by the claim of culture that the right choice is having many choices, that the way to live fully is to have it all.

ASSIGNMENT

Get a feel for reasons some kings were "good" and others "bad." Note the consequences. Look for trends. Don't get bogged down in detail.

Day 1   2 Chronicles 1–5 (Solomon receives wisdom, builds and furnishes the Temple)

Day 2   2 Chronicles 6–9 (Solomon's prayer, dedication of the Temple, the queen of Sheba, death of Solomon)

Day 3   2 Chronicles 10–18 (the kingdom divided—Judah and Israel, good kings and bad kings)

Day 4   2 Chronicles 19–28 (more good and bad kings; goodness and prosperity, sin and punishment)

Day 5   2 Chronicles 29–36 (Hezekiah, the great Passover, invasion and defeat of Sennacherib, Josiah's reform, the book of the Law found, fall of Jerusalem, edict of Cyrus)

Day 6   Read and respond to "Fruit From the Tree of Life" and "Marks of Faithful Community."

Day 7   Rest

PSALM OF THE WEEK

As you pray Psalm 85 aloud daily, reflect on the needs both communal and individual that call for such a prayer. Pray the prayer as your congregation's prayer to God. What is being asked? What is being acknowledged? Why does your faith congregation need this prayer?

PRAYER

Pray daily before study:
"Turn to us, Almighty God!
Look down from heaven at us;
come and save your people!" (Psalm 80:14, TEV).

Prayer concerns for this week:

DETERIORATION

Day 1 2 Chronicles 1–5 (Solomon receives wisdom, builds and furnishes the Temple)

Day 4 2 Chronicles 19–28 (more good and bad kings; goodness and prosperity, sin and punishment)

Day 2 2 Chronicles 6–9 (Solomon's prayer, dedication of the Temple, the queen of Sheba, death of Solomon)

Day 5 2 Chronicles 29–36 (Hezekiah, the great Passover, invasion and defeat of Sennacherib, Josiah's reform, the book of the Law found, fall of Jerusalem, edict of Cyrus)

Day 3 2 Chronicles 10–18 (the kingdom divided—Judah and Israel, good kings and bad kings)

Day 6 "Fruit From the Tree of Life" and "Marks of Faithful Community"

Fig Tree

DISCIPLE

FRUIT FROM THE TREE OF LIFE

Solomon started strong and his power base was secure. Nathan, the tough old prophet, nominated him. Bathsheba, his mother, supported him (1 Kings 1:11-31). David, his dying father, confirmed him (1 Chronicles 28:5; 29:19). Though not the oldest, Solomon was named by those who counted. The Chronicler doesn't mention the jealousies and intrigue recorded in 1 Kings 1–2. The torch was passed from father to handpicked son. Israel gave endorsement (1 Chronicles 29:22-24).

Solomon's kingdom was built on David's military conquests and political alliances. He inherited a kingdom that stretched from the Euphrates River to the Gulf of Aqabah, from the blue waters of the Mediterranean to the blowing desert sands of Arabia. The young king was blessed with a peaceful political landscape. Nearby tribal enemies had been conquered, pushed back, or brought into alliances. Egypt was feeble, and Assyria was asleep, a century away from power. The sea-faring Phoenicians considered their empire to be the coastlands and the sea islands. Even the often powerful and hostile Philistines on the coast were broken and subservient.

Solomon began his reign with prayer, not pompous or political but powerful, from the heart. Facing a monumental task, he rightly prayed for wisdom and understanding. And since Solomon had asked only for wisdom, God promised fame and fortune as well (2 Chronicles 1:10-12).

David, prohibited by God from building the Temple because he was a man of war, left instructions to his son, a man of peace. Solomon fulfilled his father's dream, but he took the dream to a higher level. David had herded sheep; Solomon probably had sat at the feet of the sages. David fought alongside his men; Solomon visited with ambassadors from foreign lands. With expanded horizons, he embraced Phoenician architecture and artisans, the finest in the world. He imported the fabulous cedars of Lebanon and used state-of-the-art construction techniques.

Small by today's standards—ninety feet by thirty feet by forty-five feet—the Temple was so carefully crafted, so ornate, so cosmopolitan with Egyptian, Phoenician, and Canaanite influences, that it was the talk of the Mediterranean world. The Temple platform was a dramatic achievement—it's hard to build a level place in the mountains. It required a 150-foot retaining wall for support. Since only a few people could enter the Temple, the thousands of worshipers at the festivals stood in massive array in the courtyard. The entire area was known as "the Temple."

Across the years, the Israelites had built several shrines for worship—Shechem, Gibeon, Shiloh, Gilgal. But with the building of Solomon's Temple, Jerusalem became the site for Israel's worship. For the Chronicler, long after the Northern Kingdom breakaway, long after exile and destruction, long

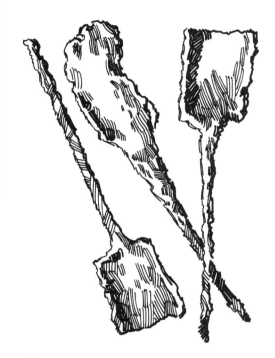

Three incense shovels, found near a stone altar at Tel Dan, date from the eighth century B.C. Leviticus 16:12-13 describes how the high priest used such shovels on the Day of Atonement. Huram-abi, the artisan who made the bronze incense shovels for the Temple, was the son of a woman from Dan (2 Chronicles 2:13-14; 4:11, 16).

DETERIORATION

after the return, the rebuilt Temple would be the center toward which every eye should turn, every prayer be said.

Shadows on Solomon's Greatness

Palestine is a crossroads—in war, a trampling ground for armies; in peace, a bridge for trade. Solomon bought chariots and horses from Egypt and sold them to the Hittites of Syria. He traded the olive oil, wheat, and barley of the Galilee for the cedar of Lebanon and the ivory of Africa. His seven hundred wives and three hundred concubines symbolized wealth and political savvy more than sexual prowess. His marriages sealed peace treaties and confirmed trade agreements.

Israel had no seaport, so Solomon captured the east coast of Sinai along the Gulf of Aqabah with what is now the port city of Elath, opening up trade to the Red Sea and the Indian Ocean. He turned to Hiram (or Huram) of Tyre to build his ships and train his sailors. Hearing of Solomon's wisdom and riches, the queen of Sheba came to Jerusalem to see for herself. Their huge exchange of gifts (2 Chronicles 9:9, 12) sealed a pact for commerce that linked North Africa and the Indian Ocean to the riches of the Mediterranean.

Chronicles idealizes Solomon, as it does David, but it does not hide the dark side totally. Even as we see Solomon's greatness, we hear hints of forthcoming tragedy. The king spent seven years building the Temple; he spent thirteen years building his own palace. He built a separate palace for his Egyptian queen twice the size of the Temple. To construct the Temple, he pushed the people hard. He increased the pressure for public works, demanding one month's labor in three from citizens. He turned foreign laborers into near slaves.

Worship was compromised. Most of Solomon's wives were foreign born. They brought treaties and dowries with them, but they also brought their gods and pagan religious practices. The king of Egypt gave the important western city of Gezer as a dowry to his daughter, Solomon's queen. No doubt, the Egyptian queen and other foreign wives taught reverence for household gods to their children, worshiped on the high places, ignored Jewish practices. Solomon mellowed, compromised, syncretized.

Solomon's Descendants

Disaster did not start with Rehoboam and Jeroboam, nor did it end with them. But in a critical moment in history, these two leaders with their supporters shattered the unity, divided the kingdom, and launched Israel on the road to destruction. Solomon's death in 922 B.C. after forty years of regal rule created confusion. Unrest, especially among the northern tribes, fed talk of rebellion. A change of administration in Egypt turned the friendship cemented by Solomon's Egyptian queen into enmity. Jeroboam, not a descendant of David but a work foreman from the north, a dissident,

This gold-leaf figurine, found at Gezer, dates from the sixteenth century B.C. and is probably a representation of the Canaanite goddess Astarte.

DISCIPLE

gained asylum in Egypt even before Solomon died.

When Jeroboam returned from Egypt, he gathered his friends from the ten northern tribes and pled their case before the new young king. They asked Rehoboam to lessen the conscription, lower the taxes, share the prosperity. Whom did Rehoboam consult? Not God. The silence of Rehoboam is in stark contrast to the fervent prayers of his grandfather and father. The wise old sages might have saved him, for they knew the tribal feelings and understood the constant necessity to consult the Lord. Rehoboam, however, followed the advice of the young and arrogant Judean nobles, who like himself knew only the luxury of the palace and the isolation of the capital. He spurned the request from Jeroboam: "My father made your yoke heavy, but I will add to it; my father disciplined you with whips, but I will discipline you with scorpions" (2 Chronicles 10:14).

With angry words that rejected the Judean king, the kingdom, Jerusalem, and the Temple, the people answered,

"What share do we have in David?
We have no inheritance in the son of Jesse.
Each of you to your tents, O Israel" (10:16).

To the Chronicler, "to your tents" meant a return to tribal thinking; a rejection of covenant; a rebellion against God's Davidic kingdom, the Temple, sacrifices, spiritual unity.

Jeroboam's Israel

Jeroboam formed a kingdom of his own. That meant his own capital, his own army, his own places of worship—Bethel and Dan. Faithful stragglers, including priests and Levites, slipped down to Jerusalem to remain loyal to the Temple. Thus the Northern Kingdom (Israel) was established, in tension with Judah, built on a crumbling foundation of mixed loyalties and division.

Why didn't war break out between Judah and Israel? Because the prophets intervened, saying, in effect, the damage was done, God had divided them, and bloodshed between kindred was unnecessary. When the prophet Ahijah tore his clothing into twelve parts, it was done: God's mixture of punishment and mercy was in effect (1 Kings 11:30). The prophet Shemaiah stopped the war in its tracks: "Thus says the LORD: You shall not go up or fight against your kindred. Let everyone return home, for this thing is from me" (2 Chronicles 11:4). The division from God? Yes, as divine retribution for greed, arrogance, rebellion, faithlessness.

Now our historian sweeps through more than three hundred years of the Davidic kingdom, Judah. He ignores Israel except as it affects Judah, for it is considered apostate, doomed for destruction. The promise made to David that his kingdom would last forever if the kings and the people would be faithful now rests on the shoulders of Judah alone. Only Davidic (Judean) kings are tracked.

DETERIORATION

Kings Good and Bad

The first in the series of kings was Abijah, son of Rehoboam. He trusted the Lord, spurned the idols of the north, rejoiced with the priests of Aaron in the Temple, and in this way was successful in his conflict with Jeroboam. Then Asa "did what was good and right in the sight of the LORD his God" (2 Chronicles 14:2). How? He "took away the foreign altars"; he "commanded Judah to seek the LORD . . . and to keep the law and the commandment." He removed the high places, where worship mixed with Canaanite practices (14:3-5).

Encouraged by the pleas of Azariah the prophet, Asa destroyed idols in captured towns, repaired the altar in front of the Jerusalem Temple, and welcomed deserters from the northern tribes.

Then he stumbled. He sent money to Aram to ally against Israel. The prophet Hanani called his hand, "Because you relied on the king of Aram, and did not rely on the LORD your God, the army of the king of Aram has escaped you" (16:7). Asa put the prophet in stocks, became cruel to the people, found himself bogged down in constant warfare, got diseased feet, forgot to consult God, and died in the forty-first year of his reign, nevertheless honored by his people.

Do you see the theology of the Chronicler emerging? No longer is God showing up with miracles, special intrusions, unusual divine happenings. God is now seen working quietly behind the scenes, providentially rewarding the faithful, punishing the disobedient. Relentlessly, God acts within cause and effect upon the kings of Judah. The kings, of course, symbolize the whole people. They lead, but they also follow; they embody the spirit of the age, the attitudes of the governed. God's rewards and punishment, cause and effect, are at work within the community.

How do you see God working today through cause and effect?

Jehoshaphat "walked in the earlier ways of his father; . . . sought the God of his father and walked in his commandments. . . . Therefore the LORD established the kingdom in his hand" (17:3-5). His only sin? Allying with Israel against Ramoth-gilead. His salvation? Fasting and praying before fighting. His reward? An internally quiet realm, and he "was buried with his ancestors in the city of David" (21:1).

First-born son Jehoram murdered all his brothers, "walked in the way of the kings of Israel," married King Ahab of Israel's daughter, and "did what was evil in the sight of the LORD" (21:1-7). Jehoram died an agonizing death, with no honorific funeral fire, no burial with the kings, no regrets of the people (21:19-20).

DISCIPLE

God's mercy and intention to save the Davidic line is shown when Jehoshabeath, the half-sister of King Ahaziah saves the infant son of the king from an imperial bloodbath. This child, Joash (Jehoash), raised by the priests and Levites, did good things—tore down the house of baal, reinstituted the Temple tax levied by Moses to restore the Temple. Later he went bad, received wrong counsel, had a priest's son killed, forgot the kindnesses of the priests, lost a war against Aram. His own people killed him and refused to bury him in the tombs of the kings.

So it goes. Across the years the Davidic kingdom struggled to maintain its territory, its identity, its Temple worship. As long as they sought the Lord, God made them prosper (26:5). Uzziah, a great king, ruled fifty-two years, built a prosperous, unified Judah "until he became strong"—and proud (26:15-16). He arrogantly ignored Mosaic rules, entered the Temple, and offered incense on the altar, a task reserved for the priests. His forehead turned leprous. He was forced into isolation, died, and was buried in a separate field. Notice the high premium the historian places on worship; ritual integrity; honor for Temple, priests, and Levites.

Ahaz "did not do what was right in the sight of the LORD" (28:1). He cast images for the baals, offered child sacrifice, and engaged in fertility rites. Defeated by Aram and Israel alike, he turned in desperation to Assyria, frantically appealing to everyone except the Lord.

Hezekiah reopened and purified the Temple; sanctified the Levites; repented; instituted proper worship including music, psalms, and sacrifice (29:20-36). He sent couriers from Dan to Beersheba, inviting the people to come to Jerusalem to celebrate Passover. Many Israelites, however, scorned the invitation, laughed. Too many wars had been fought, too much hatred vented. But those who did come returned peaceably to their homes after Passover (31:1). The Chronicler uses Hezekiah's hospitality to show that the people of Israel everywhere can cross political barriers, attend the great festivals in the Temple, and restore spiritual unity. Hezekiah's reward— riches, years of peace, healing when he was sick, support by prophets and priests, survival when the Assyrians laid siege, burial in the tombs of David, honor at his death.

Except for a glimmer of hope during Josiah's reign, events spin downward. Manasseh offered child sacrifices, consulted wizards and mediums, brought foreign idols into the holy Temple. With some drama, the Assyrian commander put the king in manacles and took him to Babylon (33:11), a symbol of all Judah's being exiled later.

The reforms of Josiah gave hope to everyone. While the Temple was being repaired, a priest discovered the book of the law of Moses (part of Deuteronomy). When Josiah heard it read aloud, he tore his robes and wept. He prepared a great Passover—the biggest ever. But playing with politics, he got caught up in the war between emerging powers (Egypt, Neco;

Babylon, Nebuchadnezzar). Wounded in battle, he died in Jerusalem, and Judah's hopes died with him.

Jehoiakim, Jehoiachin, and Zedekiah fumbled in political and religious confusion. The sins of Judah and its kings had caught up with it. Babylon razed the city, burned Solomon's Temple, carried into exile most of those who escaped the sword. Only after some sixty years, with a gracious edict by the Persian king Cyrus II, would the remnant come home. The Chronicler has made his point. God will never abandon the covenant people, but the rewards and punishments are part and parcel of God's providential care.

Surely not everything that happens is cause and effect. When have you seen exceptions to this philosophy?

_____

_____

MARKS OF FAITHFUL COMMUNITY

A humble people who continually seek the counsel of God will be strong and will prosper.

What is your understanding of the relationship between humility and leadership?

_____

_____

Identify causes of deterioration in the community of faith.

_____

_____

What does the Chronicler call us to do about such deterioration?

_____

_____

Being faithful community, we freely choose to be bound together as the people of God.

THE RADICAL DISCIPLE

Recognizing the human tendency to self-seeking that so often undermines the desire to seek God, the radical disciple practices prayer and repentance as disciplines of faithfulness—not once but continually.

IF YOU WANT TO KNOW MORE

Keeping in mind what you have read about Solomon in Second Chronicles, read the account of Solomon in 1 Kings 4–11.

REBUILD

> "Thus says King Cyrus of Persia: The LORD, the God of heaven, has given me all the kingdoms of the earth, and he has charged me to build him a house at Jerusalem in Judah. Any of those among you who are of his people—may their God be with them!—are now permitted to go up to Jerusalem in Judah, and rebuild the house of the LORD, the God of Israel—he is the God who is in Jerusalem."
>
> —Ezra 1:2-3

4 To Build Again

OUR HUMAN CONDITION

Sometimes an opportunity comes along to take a bold action or an unpopular stand that requires total commitment, great risk, and uncertain outcome. We hesitate, then stay put. The obstacles are too great, the cost too heavy. We play it safe.

ASSIGNMENT

We begin with lamentations over a lost city and a lost heritage and then watch the renewal of hope in those who returned to restore the Temple and its worship, the city and its walls. Read for theological meaning rather than for historical detail.

Day 1   Lamentations 1–5 (lament over Jerusalem); Ezra 1–2 (Cyrus's edict, returned exiles)

Day 2   Ezra 3–6 (Temple foundation laid, opposition to rebuilding, Darius's decree); Haggai 1–2 (prophetic encouragement and warning); Ezra 7–10 (Ezra's mission, mixed marriages); Psalm 85 (prayer for restoration)

Day 3   Nehemiah 1:1–7:4 (Nehemiah's prayer, return to Jerusalem, rebuilding the wall)

Day 4   Nehemiah 7:5–10:39 (list of returned exiles, reading the Law, public confession and covenant)

Day 5   Nehemiah 11–13 (Jerusalem residents, dedication of the wall, Nehemiah's reform); Psalms 147; 149–150 (hymns of praise)

Day 6   Read and respond to "Fruit From the Tree of Life" and "Marks of Faithful Community."

Day 7   Rest

THE RADICAL DISCIPLE

Assuming the radical disciple is one who is at the direction of God in a way that is unusual, who is the radical disciple in this week's Scripture? If Cyrus, what is radical? If the returning exiles? If Ezra? If Nehemiah? If Darius or Artaxerxes? Consider the various persons and their actions. What about you? What unusual call is yours at the direction of God?

PSALM OF THE WEEK

As you pray Psalm 126 aloud daily, imagine creative ways to express its sense of joy—perhaps through dance, a drawing, or a banner. Find a hymnal with the song "Bringing In the Sheaves." Consider the words. What is the seed for sowing? the harvest reaped? the cause for rejoicing?

PRAYER

Pray daily before study:
"O God, be kind to Zion and help her; rebuild the walls of Jerusalem" (Psalm 51:18, TEV)

Prayer concerns for this week:

REBUILD

Day 1   Lamentations 1–5 (lament over Jerusalem); Ezra 1–2 (Cyrus's edict, returned exiles)

Day 2   Ezra 3–6 (Temple foundation laid, opposition to rebuilding, Darius's decree); Haggai 1–2 (prophetic encouragement and warning); Ezra 7–10 (Ezra's mission, mixed marriages); Psalm 85 (prayer for restoration)

Day 3   Nehemiah 1:1–7:4 (Nehemiah's prayer, return to Jerusalem, rebuilding the wall)

Day 4   Nehemiah 7:5–10:39 (list of returned exiles, reading the Law, public confession and covenant)

Day 5   Nehemiah 11–13 (Jerusalem residents, dedication of the wall, Nehemiah's reform); Psalms 147; 149–150 (hymns of praise)

Day 6   "Fruit From the Tree of Life" and "Marks of Faithful Community"

Stylized Tree of Life

DISCIPLE

FRUIT FROM THE TREE OF LIFE

The royal edict of Cyrus II that allowed exiles to go home closes Second Chronicles and opens Ezra. In reading Ezra and Nehemiah, don't count the Temple vessels or try to reconcile the number of people in each migration. Don't even worry whether the king is Artaxerxes I or II. The history is disjointed; lists and genealogies have been assembled; documents have been spliced. The historian has gathered material together to help us understand a much bigger matter. If you spend time tracking the history, you may miss the message. Instead of studying the list of returned exiles, ask why it is included. A whole people has been broken and scattered; now they have an opportunity to become a people again. With superhuman effort, total commitment, purity of motive, and with God's help they can reclaim their identity, regain their religious community, restore the covenant. From time to time, a religious community or a city or a nation must come up from the ashes, must struggle to rebuild. The purpose of the books of Ezra and Nehemiah is to say it can be done, and it doesn't take forever if the leadership is dedicated to the cause, if the people are committed, if it is the plan and purpose of God.

The Persian royal edict is a powerful hinge on which the history of Israel swings. Genesis through Second Kings tells of creation, promise, exodus, land, monarchy, glory, dissension, disaster, and exile—from daybreak to destruction. Now the people of Israel search for a future. God made a promise through Jeremiah to the exiles: "to give you a future with hope" (Jeremiah 29:11). Will it be fulfilled? Can Israel start over?

God's Anointed

The edict was a miracle, a bolt out of the blue—an act of God. The Persians reversed public policy. Whereas the Assyrians demolished cities and mixed the races, whereas the Babylonians tore down temples and transported captives, Cyrus of Persia established satrapies divided into districts, maintained a powerful military force, and exacted heavy taxes. But he honored local traditions and saw no need to ravage temples or uproot people. The prophet Isaiah called Assyria the "rod" of God's anger but named Cyrus as God's "anointed."

"Thus says the LORD . . .

'He is my shepherd,
  and he shall carry out all my purpose'"
    (Isaiah 44:24, 28).

In earlier times, nations in war believed it was one army's god against another army's god. But Cyrus had a larger frame of reference. For him human events seemed mysteriously in the hands of a mighty divinity, and he had been chosen to rule (Ezra 1:2).

So the edict was signed and sealed. The exiles, scattered

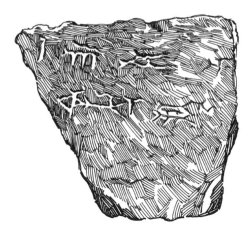

This fragment of a stone vase from the time of the Persian Empire (fifth to fourth century B.C.), found at Sepphoris, shows two lines of cuneiform writing that read "Artaxerxes, King" in Elamite and Babylonian.

throughout the Persian Empire, could go home. But the people of the ten northern tribes had been living in exile for nearly two centuries. They had homes, families, jobs. They were a minority people, often oppressed; but they had a place. Besides, they were not offered political freedom, only freedom to build the Temple. Jerusalem and the surrounding villages of Judah had never been their home. They had not given allegiance to the Temple since the time of Solomon. Imagine yourself, after many generations, uprooting your family, walking hundreds of miles, carrying meager possessions, facing land others were now farming. Likely, you would rather send gifts, goodwill, and prayers. You would let others go.

But the more recent exiles, those from the tribes of Judah and Benjamin who had been transported to Babylon only fifty years before, felt the tug of home. They remembered Zion (Psalm 137:1-6). In their mind's eye they pictured the city, the stone buildings of Jerusalem, the Temple, and the Temple Mount. A few old-timers actually recalled making pilgrimage to the Temple for the yearly festivals. Priests and Levites dreamed of fulfilling their destiny—blowing the ram's horn, singing the psalms, and offering the sacrifices. These exiles longing for Jerusalem believed God would "make straight in the desert a highway" (Isaiah 40:3). The Judean Jews, the people of the Temple, would be the heartbeat of the new Judaism. These scholars and priests would shape the future beliefs and practices of the Jews.

Four Returns of Exiles

The exiles came back at four different times, over a period of more than a century. The first group traveled under the direction of Sheshbazzar. They cleaned up rubble and in the month of Tishri (the seventh month, September/October), they built an altar and offered sacrifices. No doubt, they recalled that on that very spot David had offered his sacrifice and later Solomon had placed the ark of the covenant in the newly-built Temple in the seventh month. For the first time in years they celebrated Sukkoth, the Feast of Booths. In the second year they laid the foundation for the Temple, but then political opposition closed them down. The foundation lay with no building, a symbol of despair.

A few years later Zerubbabel and Jeshua led a second return of exiles. With encouragement of the prophets Haggai and Zechariah, Zerubbabel, a descendant of David, and Jeshua, the high priest, went to work to rebuild the Temple. The new king, Darius (521–485 B.C.), issued a decree to his officials in the Persian province to let the work go forward and, furthermore, to pay for the work and the daily sacrifices from the royal treasury. With help from exiles abroad (Haggai 2:6-9) and with assistance from King Darius, who wanted them to pray for him, they finished the task in a few short years (515 B.C.). The old-timers wept because the new Tem-

This golden bowl, made by a Persian goldsmith between 522 and 404 B.C., is inscribed in Persian cuneiform with the name Darius.

ple was not as ornate as the one they remembered. The young people rejoiced; they had built it with God's help.

The returning groups faced serious opposition, both external and internal. External forces, the "people of the land," plagued them from the start. These people were a mixture of ethnic and religious backgrounds, dating back to the Assyrian policy of blurring populations in order to lessen local pride and rebellion. Imported peoples had intermarried with Jewish farmers and workers. In the eyes of the returning Judean Jews, they were outsiders, religiously suspect, polluting the faith. If the people of the land helped build the Temple, they would help perform the worship, creating an atmosphere ceremonially unclean. Had not Moses insisted, "You are a people holy [set apart] to the LORD your God" (Deuteronomy 14:2)? Idolatry issuing in immorality, the Judean exiles believed, was precisely what had caused Jerusalem's downfall.

Internal problems were equally frustrating. Some returned exiles were indifferent, so busy trying to build homes and make a living they gave no thought to town or Temple. Haggai chastised, "Is it a time for you yourselves to live in your paneled houses, while this house lies in ruins? . . . Go up to the hills and bring wood and build the house, so that I may take pleasure in it and be honored, says the LORD" (Haggai 1:4, 8). Then the economy took a nasty turn—no rain, no crops, inflation. Some people argued that the time was not right. Haggai insisted rather that the hard times were caused by their delays.

Ezra's Heart for the Law

The next group of exiles from Babylon came about half a century later, led by a scholarly priest named Ezra. His credentials were impeccable: He traced his ancestry back to Aaron, the chief priest and brother of Moses. "He was a scribe skilled in the law of Moses" (Ezra 7:6). His purpose was clear—to head up a religious community that would know and keep the religious law, jot and tittle, "for Ezra had set his heart to study the law of the LORD, and to do it, and to teach the statutes and ordinances in Israel" (7:10).

Ezra selected members of the most devout families, heavily loaded with priests. When he learned he had no Levites, he recruited several to fill this religious void (8:15-20). Then he proclaimed a fast to pray for safe travel. Armed only with prayer and a letter from King Artaxerxes, he began the journey. Even though they were carrying treasure for the Temple, he did not ask for a military escort. He told the king that God was with them and would protect them (8:21-23). Upon arrival, Ezra, man of integrity, conducted a complete accounting of gold, silver, and vessels (8:33-34). He concluded the trip with the offering of sacrifices (8:35) and carefully delivered his credentials to local authorities (8:36).

Almost immediately, a report came to Ezra that some of the

men had taken foreign wives. Ezra pulled out his hair, tore his clothes, fasted, and prayed. Spiritually the community was in crisis. If they polluted their practices, they were doomed. Introduction of pagan gods and practices by foreign wives had contributed to Judah's destruction and exile in the first place. Had they not been punished enough for idolatry?

Earlier layers of law had not forbidden such marriages, only pagan worship. But Solomon and subsequent kings allowed their foreign wives to worship the idols of their traditions. Assimilation of pagan idolatries brought down the wrath of God and the prophets. Earlier, in preparing the people of Israel for their new land, Moses had warned them not to intermarry with the Canaanite people because of their idols, their sacred poles, their pagan altars (Deuteronomy 7:1–6). The Law did not require divorce or demand that Jewish fathers send their children away—but that was Ezra's interpretation. If they lost their religion, they lost everything. Exclusiveness became the order of the day.

In a cold, heavy rain, Ezra called on the assembled people to confess. A few men took exception to his demand to send wives and children back to their own people. But Ezra and the majority prevailed. Feeling the need to reaffirm the "set-apartness" of Israel, the requirement to be the "holy seed"—and without a divorce law to cover the situation—a covenant was made. Over the next three months one hundred and ten families separated out wives and children to be returned to their families.

Nehemiah's Vision of a Rebuilt Wall

Two hundred miles east of Babylon, in his winter palace in Susa, King Artaxerxes had a trusted steward named Nehemiah who was heartsick. Nehemiah had learned from his brother Hanani that Jerusalem's wall was in ruins. Robbers roamed the city; traders and foreigners desecrated the sabbath; the surrounding area was economically depressed. The Temple was unprotected, the people disheartened.

Nehemiah had uncommon access to the king. He selected, tasted, and served all the king's wine to guard against the king's being poisoned. The trust level between the two men was unusually high. When the king noticed his tears, Nehemiah was ready with a respectful request—to rebuild the city of his ancestral tombs. The king granted the request for a leave of absence, permission to restore order according to Jewish religious rules and Persian imperial law, and authorization to rebuild the wall. Soon after, he named Nehemiah governor of Judah. Accompanied by military escort, Nehemiah took other Judeans and traveled from today's Iran, through Syria to Jerusalem. This group of exiles was the fourth to return to Judah.

Like Ezra, he rested only three days. Then, secretly at night, he inspected the ancient wall and found fallen, broken

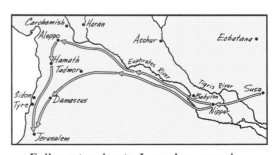

Exiles returning to Jerusalem came in four waves at different times and probably used two different routes. The northern route from Susa followed the Euphrates River from Babylon to Aleppo, then turned south to Jerusalem. The southern route through less settled areas was shorter but more dangerous.

DISCIPLE

stone and burned-out wooden gates. Nehemiah was able to challenge a fractured, frustrated group of people to extraordinary effort. He did it with prayer, by working day and night (he and his men slept with their clothes on), by refusing to line his own pockets (he gained no lands, rejected the governor's expense account), and by avoiding arrogance (he called the community together for consultation).

As a leader, Nehemiah kept the holy vision before the people: "Come, let us rebuild the wall of Jerusalem, so that we may no longer suffer disgrace" (Nehemiah 2:17). He urged them to give of themselves wholeheartedly, and he assigned a certain portion of the wall to each guild or family. The opposition, which other leaders had experienced, now intensified because the wall was tangible; it carried political and economic realism. Political enemies surrounded Nehemiah and his people—Sanballat of Samaria to the north, Tobiah and the Ammonites to the east, Gesham and the Arabs to the south and southeast. Ashdod and the ancient Philistines were to the west. Sanballat tried intimidation: "Will they sacrifice? (4:2). Tobiah tried to demoralize: "Any fox going up on it would break it down" (4:3). Nehemiah inspires us today with his reply to an invitation that was a trick: "I am doing a great work and I cannot come down" (6:3). Some insiders like Shemaiah were bribed to say, "They're coming to kill you. Let's go hide in the Temple!" Nehemiah responded, "Would a man like me go into the temple to save his life? I will not go in!" (6:11).

In the midst of construction, a crisis erupted. The wealthy were squeezing the life out of the workers. Farmers and workers had to borrow money to pay for food, for seed, and the heavy Persian land taxes. The farmers were building the wall, neglecting their family chores from July to early September, and it was a dry year. The wealthy Judean nobles foreclosed on their loans. They forced grown children into debt servitude, sold them as debt slaves to foreigners, and took possession of the farmers' land.

Nehemiah was furious. He called the community together, rich and poor alike. He chastised the wealthy for breaking Jewish law. Jews were forbidden to charge interest to other Jews (Deuteronomy 23:20). They were forbidden to force kindred to be slaves. Nehemiah said, "We have bought back our Jewish kindred who had been sold to other nations; but now you are selling your own kin, who must then be bought back by us!" (Nehemiah 5:8). The rich had shattered the covenant that put a safety net under the poor (Leviticus 25). Nehemiah reminded everyone that he was refusing to use the governor's expense account, that he gave loans without interest plus gifts of food to the workers, that he was feeding 150 people a day at his table, at his own expense. He shamed the nobles into silence. They agreed to return lands and people, restore collected interest, and help sustain the community. Without bloodshed or rebellion, the crisis was averted, and the work continued.

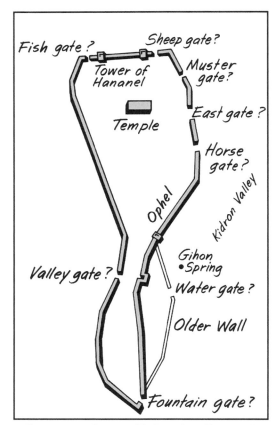

Jerusalem after the Exile, when Ezra and Nehemiah rebuilt the city, was much smaller than before the Exile. The city walls were much higher up on the eastern slope above the Kidron Valley. Much of the city that remained was in ruins.

Nehemiah finished the wall in fifty-two frantic days. The taunts of Sanballat and the jabs of Tobiah were silenced. On his second tour of duty, Nehemiah threw out Tobiah, who had settled into a room in the Temple area, stopped merchants who were breaking the sabbath, and reaffirmed the tithe to support the priests and Levites.

Ezra had set the theological tone; Nehemiah set the political structure. Jerusalem and the Temple would outlast the Persian and Greek empires and would sustain and encourage Jews throughout the world. Ezra and Nehemiah had prevailed.

The tension between exclusiveness and inclusiveness plagues all religious communities. Identify strengths and weaknesses of each perspective.

MARKS OF FAITHFUL COMMUNITY

God opens up new opportunities. God inspires people to work together with renewed strength to achieve great things.

Describe a time you experienced divine power helping you and your group accomplish something important.

Being faithful community, we stand ready to hear rather than not hear, ready to do rather than not do in order to respond to God's call and direction.

What great work needs to be done in your community for which the time seems right?

In what causes are you willing to link arms with others? to take a risk in the face of opposition?

How do you deal with your own doubts or doubts of others when your efforts to respond to God's direction seem blocked?

IF YOU WANT TO KNOW MORE

Learn what you can about Persian administration of the "province Beyond the River," including Judah. Consult Bible dictionaries, commentaries, encyclopedia, and the internet.

PREVAIL

"If you keep silence at such a time as this, relief and deliverance will rise for the Jews from another quarter, but you and your father's family will perish. Who knows? Perhaps you have come to royal dignity for just such a time as this."

—Esther 4:14

5 For Such a Time As This

OUR HUMAN CONDITION

Being different can bring trouble, can even be dangerous. Better to keep what we believe to ourselves. Certainly don't want to offend anyone by what we say or do. Being serious about beliefs seems to rub people the wrong way. We want to get along with others, especially people in power. Better lie low.

ASSIGNMENT

Esther is read in the Jewish community each year at the Feast of Purim. We will read both the Hebrew version and the Greek version. You will need a Bible with the Apocrypha for the Greek.

The designation Additions A–F appears in the NRSV. Other Bibles may use only numbers for indicating chapters and additions in the Greek version of Esther in the Apocrypha.

Day 1 Esther 1–3 (Queen Vashti, Mordecai and Esther, Esther becomes queen, Haman's plot); Exodus 17:8–16 (Israel defeats Amalekites)

Day 2 Esther 4–6 (Esther plans to help her people, Mordecai honored); 1 Samuel 15 (Saul's war with the Amalekites)

Day 3 Esther 7–10 (Esther's feast, Haman hanged, Mordecai promoted, edict revoked, enemies of the Jews destroyed, Purim)

Day 4 Esther (Greek Version, Apocrypha)—Introduction; 11–12 (Addition A); 1–3; 13 (Addition B); 3–4; 13 (Addition C)

Day 5 Esther (Greek Version, Apocrypha)—14 (Addition C); 15 (Addition D); 5–8; 16 (Addition E); 8:13–10:3; 10:4–11:1 (Addition F)

Day 6 Read and respond to "Fruit From the Tree of Life" and "Marks of Faithful Community."

Day 7 Rest

PSALM OF THE WEEK

Keep Esther's people in mind as you pray Psalm 83 aloud daily. While the psalmist names nations and people threatening Israel in his day, call to mind the many forms of persecution Jews have faced down through history. Pray daily for Israel and its neighbors now that they may achieve a peace beneficial to all.

PRAYER

Pray daily before study:
"Save us by your might; answer our prayer,
    so that the people you love may be rescued"
    (Psalm 60:5, TEV).

Prayer concerns for this week:

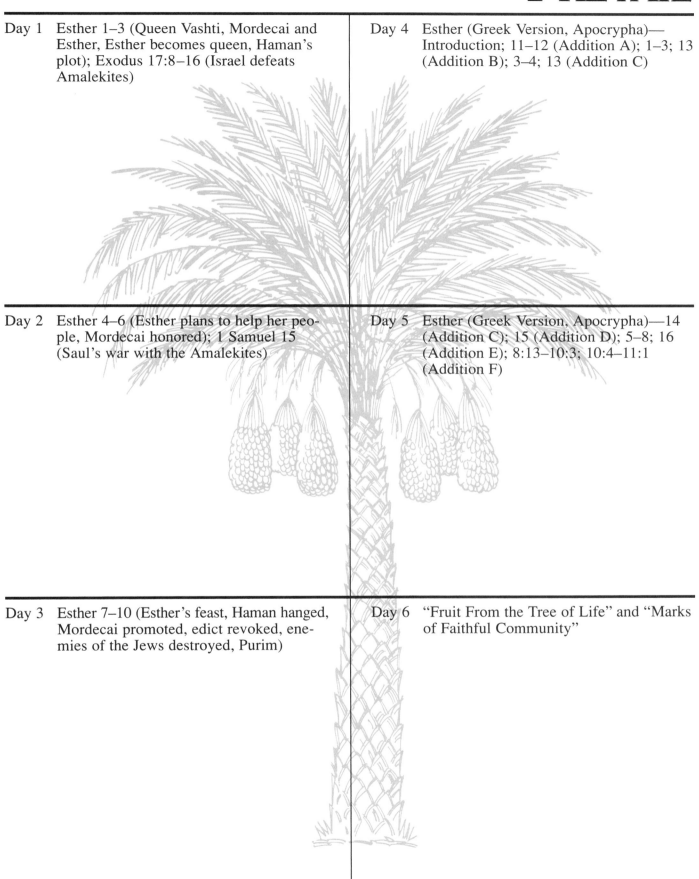

Day 1 Esther 1–3 (Queen Vashti, Mordecai and Esther, Esther becomes queen, Haman's plot); Exodus 17:8–16 (Israel defeats Amalekites)

Day 4 Esther (Greek Version, Apocrypha)—Introduction; 11–12 (Addition A); 1–3; 13 (Addition B); 3–4; 13 (Addition C)

Day 2 Esther 4–6 (Esther plans to help her people, Mordecai honored); 1 Samuel 15 (Saul's war with the Amalekites)

Day 5 Esther (Greek Version, Apocrypha)—14 (Addition C); 15 (Addition D); 5–8; 16 (Addition E); 8:13–10:3; 10:4–11:1 (Addition F)

Day 3 Esther 7–10 (Esther's feast, Haman hanged, Mordecai promoted, edict revoked, enemies of the Jews destroyed, Purim)

Day 6 "Fruit From the Tree of Life" and "Marks of Faithful Community"

Date Palm Tree

DISCIPLE

FRUIT FROM THE TREE OF LIFE

Jews read Esther to remember—to remember and to celebrate that they are still alive, surviving a history of persecutions and pogroms. The author of the book has placed the story in Persian history, but the message is for all times. Much of Jewish history, including our own century, has been characterized by attitudes expressed in these words: "There is a certain people scattered and separated among the peoples . . . of your kingdom; their laws are different from those of every other people, and they do not keep the king's laws, so that it is not appropriate for the king to tolerate them" (Esther 3:8).

Jews in Exile

Mordecai and Esther were Jews of the Diaspora. Mordecai, a Benjaminite Jew from Israel's smallest tribe, was a minor official in the Persian king's court. He had a young cousin, an orphan named Esther, whom he helped to raise. Her Hebrew name was Hadassah, meaning "myrtle"; her Persian name was Esther, meaning "star."

Haman was a descendant of the Amalekites (the Agagites), the first and fierce enemy of the Jews. Mere mention of the words *Agagite* and *Amalekite* struck chords of anger and fear. Was this ancient enmity the reason Mordecai refused to bow down before Haman? Haman's rage seems so disproportionate, so out of control. He planned genocide because of one man's affront. Was his paranoid reaction tied to the memory of a long-standing hostility?

The power person is King Ahasuerus, who opens the story with an outlandish banquet that lasts 180 days. How can a banquet—even an imperial Persian banquet—last six months? Then he threw a second party that lasted seven days. He pulled out all the stops. This dinner party portrayed power on parade, pomposity in extreme—couches of gold, patios of mother of pearl and colored gems, wine in golden goblets flowing without restraint.

When all the men are drunk, really drunk, the king calls for Queen Vashti to come in and show off her beauty. Was she to wear only her crown? We're not sure, but she refuses. The King of Persia cannot control his own wife. The powerful leaders in charge of the great empire are a bunch of intoxicated buffoons. We giggle as we remember the proverb,

"Pride goes before destruction,
and a haughty spirit before a fall" (Proverbs 16:18).

In the eyes of the world pomp and circumstance look like might and glory, but in the eyes of God they are froth on the water. King Ahasuerus can't seem to make a decision without assembling his advisers. When he issues an edict, he's tangled up in it. The hyperbole continues. Preparations for a Miss Persia contest go on for a year. Haman plans to wipe out an entire race because one man would not show respect. Gigantic gallows are built seventy-five feet high. And in a reversal

In this stone relief from a stairway in the banquet hall of the Persepolis palace of Xerxes, built about 465 B.C., crown prince Xerxes (Ahasuerus in the book of Esther) stands behind the throne of his father Darius I.

of a plot, seventy-five thousand enemies of the Jews are killed in a day.

The subplot of men versus women is intriguing. King Ahasuerus deposes Queen Vashti, but she is the one who shows strength of character. The king didn't know what to do, had to call a meeting. The edict that each man should be master of his own household makes us laugh. Haman's wife Zeresh tells him how high to build the gallows. He goes to her for advice every time he's in trouble. In the end it is a woman, Esther, the king's wife, who takes over the decision-making, saves her people, and establishes the Purim festival.

The Power of the Story

Some Jewish and Christian scholars have questioned the inclusion of the book of Esther in the Bible. The Hebrew text never mentions God's name. People fast but do not pray. No one celebrates sabbath, pays attention to dietary laws, goes to synagogue, or honors Torah. By contrast, the book contains much that offends the sensitive religious conscience—wild drunken orgies, men parading women as beauty objects, a bed test to choose a queen, schemes of raw ambition, hangings, anger culminating in slaughter. Across the centuries, some people have said Esther has no religious content, no pious thought. Yet God has given us the Bible. Jewish and Christian councils have given us Esther. Why?

The Bible does not back off the human condition. The Bible puts a mirror before our eyes, revealing arrogance and atrocities, greed and abuse of power, eruption of ancient animosities, use and misuse of sex, rage and revenge. Not a day passes but that Esther is reenacted somewhere in our world.

When the hammers were banging—building gigantic gallows for Mordecai—when Esther fasted for three days afraid to enter the court of her husband, when the edict for genocide was set in concrete, when ruthless human power seemed poised to destroy the Jews, God seemed to be hiding, absent.

Mordecai puts steel in our backbones when he challenges his adopted daughter, "Who knows? Perhaps you have come to royal dignity for just such a time as this" (Esther 4:14). Our resolve is shored up when Queen Esther says, "I will go to the king, though it is against the law; and if I perish, I perish" (4:16).

But wait. God's silence can mean mystery, not absence. God's name is not evoked, but God is not dead. Was it by chance Mordecai heard about the assassination plot of the eunuchs (2:19-23)? Was it merely chance Esther was chosen the fairest of the land? Hear the hint of God when Mordecai speaks: "If you keep silence at such a time as this, relief and deliverance will rise for the Jews from another quarter" (4:14). The Name is not used, but the Presence is felt. Even the discussion between Haman and his wife Zeresh reflects God's activity. She says, "If Mordecai, before whom your downfall has begun, is of the Jewish people, you will not pre-

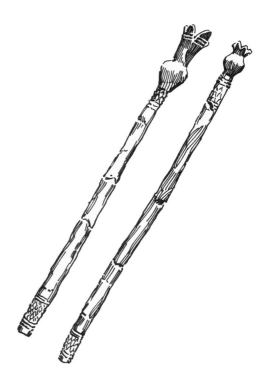

These two ivory scepters with carved pomegranate heads were found in a temple in Lachish and date from the thirteenth century B.C. In the ancient Near East a scepter was a symbol of a ruler's power and authority, a refined version of a stick or club used as a weapon. Extending his golden scepter to Esther, the king showed his favor, or welcome; in touching it, she acknowledged his favor without fear of his power (Esther 5:2).

DISCIPLE

vail against him, but will surely fall before him" (6:13). The tables have turned.

Why is the massacre in the story? Without justifying the cruelty, we can acknowledge the feelings of revenge, particularly when a people's own survival is threatened. Anger can well up in an oppressed people. Esther, like the Psalms, opens up the human heart with its full range of emotions. That is why, when we read Esther, it is good for us to laugh, laugh at the fools we make of ourselves—when we strut like peacocks, when we lord it over others, when we envy or begrudge others their differences, when our best laid plans meet reversal.

The Two Texts—Hebrew and Greek

Two texts of Esther have come down to us—the Hebrew text (Masoretic) and the Greek translation of the Hebrew text (Septuagint). The two texts are similar except the Greek translation of Esther includes six additional chapters (Additions A–F). Those Additions appear in what we call the Apocrypha. The Additions enhance the drama of the story and stress that Jewish piety must not compromise with the culture. As to which account carries more power—the subtle or the explicit, the Hebrew or the Greek text—the reader must decide.

Purim

Jews read the book of Esther on the Feast of Purim. Purim means the day appointed by the *pur*. The *pur*, or "lot," usually marked stones, was thrown to help the Persians and the Jews make decisions. Haman, angry at Mordecai, cast the lot (*purim*, plural) to determine the most propitious day for destruction of the Jews. The lot fell on the thirteenth day of the twelfth month, Adar (February / March). Later when the king allowed Mordecai and Esther to issue a countermand, the Jews were permitted to defend themselves on the day set for their annihilation.

Purim celebrates survival, deliverance from persecution. Purim is not grounded in the law of Moses as are Passover, the Feast of Booths, and other festivals. But mandated by the book of Esther, Purim stands as a kind of freedom celebration emerging from Jewish history and tradition. Remembering the victory of the thirteenth day of Adar, Purim takes place on the fourteenth and sometimes extends into the fifteenth. Esther's fast is observed on the thirteenth. That evening, as the Jewish day begins, the handwritten scroll, the *Megillah*, carefully folded like Esther's letter, is opened and read. Next morning Esther is read again along with Exodus 17:8-16. All ages celebrate with costumes and merriment. When Haman's name is read, infants shake their rattles, children hiss and boo, adults stomp their feet, drowning out the dreaded name. Purim parties are victory celebrations with feasting and drinking, singing and dancing.

Additions. In the Hebrew text, prayer is not mentioned; but in the Additions, Mordecai prays long and hard, recalling the great deeds of God in the past (13:8, Addition C). In the Additions, Esther not only fasts; she strips off her queenly garments, washes off her perfume, puts on sackcloth and ashes, and prays to the Lord God of Israel (14:1-3, Addition C). Doubting that the reader will observe God's providence, the Additions name the Name. *God* or *Lord* is referred to over fifty times.

In Mordecai's dream in the Additions, the whole world is in crisis. The human plot is expanded into a vast universal battle; good and evil seem locked in combat. So the struggle is not just between Haman and Mordecai, but between cosmic forces.

In the Additions, Esther tells God, "I hate the splendor of the wicked and abhor the bed of the uncircumcised" (14:15, Addition C). She despises the crown "like a filthy rag" (14:16, Addition C) and avoids the food, conscious of dietary laws (14:17, Addition C).

The long letters of the king are written out in detail in the Additions. And sometimes the thirteenth of Adar is the day of the execution of enemies, sometimes the fourteenth day.

In modern Israel, Purim is observed with exuberance, recalling survival of the Jews from the pogroms of recent centuries as well as persecution in Persian times. The three-day celebration includes parades, contests for best costumes (Haman is ugly; Esther is beautiful), and puppet shows. People eat a three-cornered cookie shaped like Haman's hat and filled with poppy seeds. The basis for the cookie is a word play on Haman's name. *Ha* is Hebrew for *the*. The Yiddish word for poppy seed is *mon*. Hamon. Haman is a poppy seed, nothing at all.

At Purim, gifts of food are exchanged—at least two gifts between friends and at least one gift to the poor. The poverty-stricken Jew is not receiving charity but a gift from a friend within the religious community. After Purim the houses are cleaned, purification starts, and the people begin preparing for Passover. Esther, a woman, is honored at Purim for saving the Jews in Persia. Some weeks later at Passover, Moses, a man, is honored in the more somber festival that remembers Jewish freedom from Egypt. The words used at the Passover Seder are appropriate for both festivals: "Not one only [Pharaoh] has risen up against us, but in every generation some have arisen against us to annihilate us, but the Most Holy, blessed be He, always delivered us out of their hands."

Why do Jews need Esther? Why do Christians need Esther?

MARKS OF FAITHFUL COMMUNITY

For Christians, some religious and ethical issues are bedrock. We take a stand when these issues jeopardize our faith, commitment, and religious community.

What issues are bedrock?

How can we show respect to people with different religious practices without compromising our own beliefs?

In what ways do your religious practices put you out of step with your culture? with your neighbors? with your family?

THE RADICAL DISCIPLE

The radical disciple confronts in self and others attitudes and language that stereotype any group and cause or allow persecution to continue.

IF YOU WANT TO KNOW MORE

You might enjoy locating a recipe for *hamantaschen* (the three-cornered cookie with poppy-seed filling) and making cookies to share with family or friends while telling the story of Esther. Consult cookbooks or the internet.

NOTES, REFLECTIONS, AND QUESTIONS

Being faithful community, we act in God's name when God seems silent. We stand up to persecution on God's behalf—whatever the form, wherever it occurs.

RESCUE

"I make a decree, that in all my royal dominion people should
tremble and fear before the God of Daniel:
For he is the living God,
    enduring forever.
His kingdom shall never be destroyed,
    and his dominion has no end.
He delivers and rescues,
    he works signs and wonders in heaven and on earth."

—Daniel 6:26-27

6 The Approaching Kingdom

OUR HUMAN CONDITION

Because we assume our times and systems are
forever, we make the necessary tradeoffs to fit in.
Whether we recognize it or not, we all tend to conform—in small ways, every day.

ASSIGNMENT

Daniel is remembered history, prophecy, and
apocalypse designed to give encouragement to persecuted people. Assigned reading in the Apocrypha
includes First and Second Maccabees, which provide historical information related to events referred
to in Daniel, and Second Esdras, an example of
apocalyptic literature.

Day 1   Daniel 1–3 (Daniel and his friends, Nebu-
        chadnezzar's dream, the fiery furnace);
        Leviticus 11 (clean and unclean animals);
        17:10-12 (life is in the blood)
Day 2   Daniel 4–6 (Nebuchadnezzar's second
        dream, handwriting on the wall, the lions'
        den); Psalm 55 (prayer for deliverance)
Day 3   Daniel 7–12 (Daniel's visions, prayer for
        the people, end time)
Day 4   2 Maccabees 5–6 (Antiochus IV's persecu-
        tion of Jews); 1 Maccabees 1–4 (introduc-
        tion of Greek culture and religion, desecra-
        tion of Temple, Jewish revolt, rededication
        of Temple)
Day 5   2 Esdras 3:1–5:20 (Ezra in Babylon, vision,
        God's ways incomprehensible, questions
        about coming age)

Day 6   Read and respond to "Fruit From the Tree of
        Life" and "Marks of Faithful Community."
Day 7   Rest

THE RADICAL DISCIPLE

The radical disciple actively resists faith-denying
elements in the culture. List the values most important to you, the principles that align you with God's
kingdom. During the coming week, try to spot dis-
crepancies between your values and your behavior.

PSALM OF THE WEEK

Let Psalm 9 guide you in praying for the nations
of the world. As you pray the psalm aloud, let the
verses suggest to you needs of particular nations.
Keep a balance in your view of nations as you pray
for judgment, mercy, justice.

PRAYER

Pray daily before study:
    "LORD, I have come to you for protection;
        never let me be defeated!
    Because you are righteous, help me and
        rescue me.
        Listen to me and save me!
    Be my secure shelter
        and a strong fortress to protect me;
        you are my refuge and defense" (Psalm
        71:1-3, TEV)

Prayer concerns for this week:

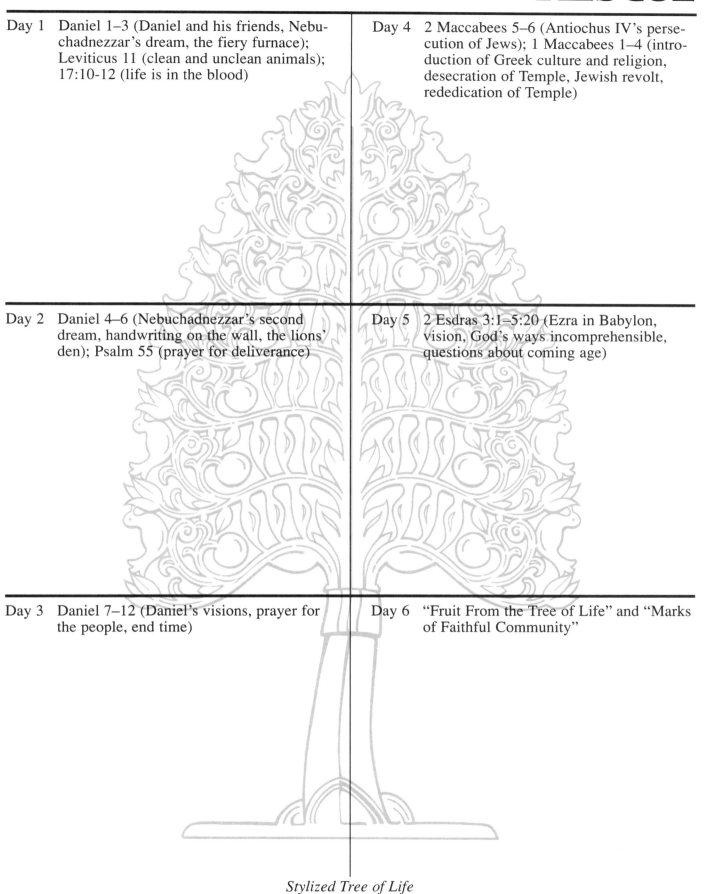

Day 1 Daniel 1–3 (Daniel and his friends, Nebuchadnezzar's dream, the fiery furnace);
Leviticus 11 (clean and unclean animals);
17:10-12 (life is in the blood)

Day 4 2 Maccabees 5–6 (Antiochus IV's persecution of Jews); 1 Maccabees 1–4 (introduction of Greek culture and religion,
desecration of Temple, Jewish revolt,
rededication of Temple)

Day 2 Daniel 4–6 (Nebuchadnezzar's second
dream, handwriting on the wall, the lions'
den); Psalm 55 (prayer for deliverance)

Day 5 2 Esdras 3:1–5:20 (Ezra in Babylon,
vision, God's ways incomprehensible,
questions about coming age)

Day 3 Daniel 7–12 (Daniel's visions, prayer for
the people, end time)

Day 6 "Fruit From the Tree of Life" and "Marks
of Faithful Community"

Stylized Tree of Life

Disciple

FRUIT FROM THE TREE OF LIFE

Three Israelite exiles speak the language of resistance when they stand boldly before the king of Babylon and say, "If our God whom we serve is able to deliver us from the furnace of blazing fire and out of your hand, O king, let him deliver us. But if not, be it known to you, O king, that we will not serve your gods and we will not worship the golden statue that you have set up" (Daniel 3:17-18).

Power and Persecution

The book of Daniel—its stories, dreams, visions—springs from a people, once proud and independent, now stripped of their pride, their possessions, their plot of ground. Torn from their homeland, separated from family and friends, deprived of their traditions, forced to speak a strange language, expected to worship different gods, they faced economic and political uncertainty. Such folk romanticize their stories, revise history, use bizarre imagery in order to survive.

The issue is power—who has it and who doesn't. The king has eyes and ears everywhere. Any hint of disobedience is dangerous. The context is fear—what will happen if you do not eat the assigned food, kneel before the statue, obey the latest decree?

In Daniel the symbols of tyranny are strong—lavish banquets, sacred vessels stolen from the Jerusalem Temple and filled with wine, life-and-death bans carelessly written and sealed, a golden statue ninety feet high. The oppressed are powerless, for they are under the control of others, their names changed, their identity taken away, their personhood diminished.

Daniel, Hananiah, Mishael, and Azariah must have been awed by the splendor of Babylon with its magnificent palaces and world-renowned hanging gardens. Uprooted from home and family by the Babylonian siege of Jerusalem, they found themselves in a strange kind of exile. Young, foreign-born, captive, yet because of their noble birth, their wisdom and intelligence, their winsome appearance, they were selected to be trained for royal service.

New language, new surroundings, new Babylonian names—Belteshazzar, Shadrach, Meshach, and Abednego. New food, strange and non-Israelite. "The king assigned them a daily portion of the royal rations of food and wine" (Daniel 1:5). To the oppressed, food—rich extravagant food—is always a symbol of power. The young men were being seduced into the dominant culture. For centuries their families had observed the dietary laws of their tradition. Grounded in Mosaic law, the food laws are a means of being holy, "set apart" (Leviticus 11:45); and they transform an act of nourishment into a celebration of the spirit.

Now what were these young men in a foreign culture to do? There was no middle ground. All fruits and vegetables were allowed. Water was OK. The boys bargained for their identity, for their religious commitment. They did not "defile" themselves (Daniel 1:8). The palace master was nervous, perceiving an act of resistance (1:10). God blessed their discipline by making them healthy and strong, even wise and knowledgeable (1:17).

Daniel, like devout Jews across the centuries, prayed three times a day—in the morning, in the afternoon, and at night. Undaunted by the king's ban, Daniel opened the windows of his highly visible roof apartment so all the world could see his nonviolent resistance (6:10). Daniel prayed toward Jerusalem's Temple where sacrifices had been offered for centuries and where prayers for all Israel still were being said. His regular prayer ritual made him an easy target for those who sought to destroy him. Why is it that religious practices, even unobtrusive acts such as prayer, seem to make other people uncomfortable?

Strengthened by his prayers, Daniel was not overly impressed by the pomposity of the court. He had the clear-eyed insight to spot the mental illness of the king brought on by the king's pride and self-indulgence (4:19-33). Daniel perceived an empire about to collapse (5:24-30). Did his simple diet of vegetables and water, combined with his disciplined prayer life, give him unusual spiritual perception?

Daniel's three friends—Shadrach, Meshach, and Abednego—were caught refusing to bow down before Nebuchadnezzar's golden statue. For the young men, the commandments were clear: "You shall not make for yourself an idol, whether in the form of anything that is in heaven above, or that is on the earth beneath, or that is in the water under the earth. You shall not bow down to them or worship them; for I the LORD your God am a jealous God" (Deuteronomy 5:8-9).

Jews and Christians alike have been strengthened by the defiant words of the three men thrown into the fire. They were steadfast in their loyalty to God. How would you describe today's idols? When and how are we tempted to bow down to them?

The three men were untouched by the flames of the furnace. God was with them. And to the amazement of the king, God rescued Daniel from the lions' den. These stories have held out hope for the persecuted of all ages.

In a secular society, there is pressure to conform. How do you experience this pressure?

Ancient rabbis asked the question, Can you stoop down to tie the strings on your sandals as you walk by the idol? No was their concerted answer.

DISCIPLE

The Book of Daniel

Scholars argue about Daniel, who wrote it and when. The difference of opinion comes partly because Daniel is a secret book written during persecution. Like the Revelation of John, it was meant to be obscure. "Daniel, keep the words secret and the book sealed until the time of the end" (Daniel 12:4).

The text is a mixture of Aramaic and Hebrew. Names of government officials are not always clear, dates not always verifiable. We know from secular history that Nebuchadnezzar destroyed Jerusalem in 587/586 B.C. and took Judeans into exile. A similar deportation had happened ten years earlier. Tradition remembers a righteous man named Daniel, referred to by the prophet Ezekiel (Ezekiel 14:14, 20). One of the Babylonian kings did suffer from mental illness, was absent for several years, and was restored by a Jewish diviner. The Babylonian Empire did come crashing down, crumbling from within. No sword was drawn and no blood was shed when Cyrus of Persia rode in. Extravagant oriental banquets, often orgies, were signs of opulence and wealth. The handwriting could well have been "on the wall."

The questions for scholars increase when we begin to read Daniel 7. The book of Daniel becomes "apocalyptic," that is, a revelation envisioning end times. Daniel sees the kingdoms of this world becoming the kingdom of the Lord. When we read John's Revelation, we will see many allusions to Daniel and the prophets.

Some scholars think the book was written by Daniel around 530 B.C. after Cyrus the Persian captured Babylon (see NIV, for example). This view understands Daniel as prophesying the great Babylonian, Median-Persian, Greek, and Roman kingdoms, culminating in the eternal kingdom ruled by God alone as king. Other authorities think the book of Daniel was written during the unbearable persecution and martyrdom under Antiochus IV in 167–164 B.C. when the Temple was desecrated and Jewish practices forbidden (see NRSV, for example). This view has the writer reaching back to draw on the faithfulness of the Daniel of the six stories to inspire the Jews to be loyal even unto death. The four human kingdoms then in retrospect might be Babylonia, Media, Persia, and Greece, with the little horn representing the Seleucid period of Antiochus IV. This perspective also culminates in God's victorious rule.

Beyond the debate, what is clear is that Daniel, written by a Jew under foreign domination, gives powerful encouragement to loyalty and faith during political, social, and religious persecution. Read Daniel not so much as history but as faith nourishment. Whether we understand the human kingdoms as if the writer were looking forward or backward, they represent times filled with resistance to oppression. We need the vision of God's ultimate victory now, and as long as the kingdoms of this world endure.

Found in 1877 on the banks of the Oxus River in Afghanistan, this golden armlet (bracelet) from fifth-century B.C. Persia is solid gold and originally had semiprecious stones and colored glass filling the spaces in the bodies of the winged monsters. It is an example of the riches of the Persian Empire.

The Vision

Leaving Daniel 1–6 and entering Daniel 7–12 is like walking from one room into another. The reader can feel the transition. In the first half of the book, people confront one another face to face. Even power plays, acts of arrogance, brave resistance, and miraculous escapes occur in human settings. Dreams are discussed, verified, and soon lived out.

But Daniel's dream (7:1) takes us into the mysterious, the apocalyptic. The struggle becomes cosmic: Heavenly hosts join forces with the "holy ones" to wage war against evil empires. The imagery of resistance was subtle in Daniel 1–6, as if we were thinking only about a few brave souls standing up for their beliefs. In Daniel 7–12 the imagery is veiled differently with pictures of strange beasts representing mighty kingdoms. Out of the sea (chaos and evil) come terrifying beasts—a lion with eagles' wings, standing up like a human being (Babylon); a bear with three tusks in its mouth (Media); a leopard with four heads and four wings (Persia); a dragon-like beast with iron teeth and ten horns (the Greek Empire under Alexander the Great); and finally, a little horn with eyes like human eyes and a mouth "speaking arrogantly" (Antiochus IV).

Antiochus IV

A second dream has different figures. A ram with two horns must be the Medes and the Persians, yoked and irresistible under Cyrus. A goat with one horn must be Alexander, conquering the western world by the time he was thirty. After Alexander's death, his generals struggled, finally splitting the empire into four parts. Our vision focuses on two—the Ptolemies in Egypt and the Seleucids in Asia Minor and Mesopotamia. Daniel 11 tells of constant warfare between the two empires, complicated by peace talks full of lies, treaties sealed by marriages that failed, and the uncontrolled ambition of competing rulers. Palestine was ravaged by both sides. The struggle climaxed with the rise of Antiochus IV, the "little horn" (7:8; 8:9). The story of his oppression goes like this: In 175 B.C. Antiochus IV seized Seleucid rule, arrogantly taking the name *Epiphanes,* which means "the manifest god." (In Rome, they nicknamed him *Epimanes,* the madman.) He is known as one of history's cruelest tyrants. His armies marched eastward successfully and then westward, winning a major battle against the Egyptians. Aristocratic families in Jerusalem jockeyed for position, bribing and buying the office of high priest, giving support first to one country, then to another. That's why, in the vision of the great cosmic conflict, the angel refers to "the lawless among your own people" (11:14).

Antiochus Epiphanes marched again to Egypt only to find, this time, that the "ships of Kittim" (Rome) (11:30) had arrived. Suddenly he was surrounded by Roman legions allied

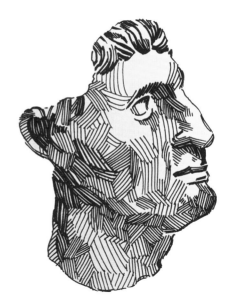

Mask of Antiochus IV, called Epiphanes, whose desecration of the Jerusalem Temple and restriction of religious practices set off the Maccabean revolt in 167 B.C. He is the "contemptible person" of Daniel 11:21.

DISCIPLE

with Egypt, so he turned and headed home, humiliated and angry. In Jerusalem, factions had been feuding. Some thought him dead, so they abandoned their self-serving loyalties. Others were ready to rise up in armed revolt (the Maccabees), while a group of religious zealots (the Hasidim, the "pious ones") saw the whole matter as violation of Torah. Antiochus, needing a victory as he marched homeward, took out his wrath on the Jews, slaughtering pigs and priests together on the Temple altar, tearing the altar down, extinguishing the eternal flame, and erecting pagan altars in the Temple. He burned all copies of Torah he could find, outlawed the holy festivals, forbade circumcision on penalty of death. He built a military garrison next to the Temple, increased already oppressive taxes, and executed thousands of Jews. "His heart shall be set against the holy covenant" (11:28).

Until the Time of the End

But wait. A consultation is taking place in the courts of heaven. The Ancient One is ascending the throne. The angels are astir. If you think the fire was hot in Nebuchadnezzar's furnace, you should feel the flames around the throne of God. Antiochus thinks he has soldiers? The Almighty has thousands of thousands, ten thousand times ten thousand (Daniel 7:9-10). Israel's protector angel, Michael, is at work; so is the angel Gabriel.

God is angered by Antiochus's arrogance. The Almighty—who had rescued Daniel from the lions' den, who had turned a king into a drooling beast, who had collapsed mighty Babylon overnight—will wage a cosmic war against the beasts and their earthly allies.

Michael and all his angels, linked with the "holy ones" and "the wise," will battle the beast. They will receive "a little help" (11:34) from rebels like the Maccabees; but they do not need it, for God will win the mighty struggle. The battle will be fierce: "Some of the wise shall fall, so that they may be refined, purified, and cleansed, until the time of the end, for there is still an interval until the time appointed" (11:35).

But how long? How long will the "time of anguish" last (12:1)? When will deliverance come?

Daniel fasted, flung himself on the ground, and prayed until he was exhausted (Daniel 9:3-19). Gabriel brought the answer—an answer that had been formed even as the prayer began. Seventy weeks of years (70 times 7 = 490 years) shall pass after the destruction of the Temple by Babylon (9:24). The days of Antiochus, who thinks he is the manifest god, are numbered. A year, two years, and a half year (12:7) and "he shall come to his end, with no one to help him" (11:45).

The expression, "a time, two times, and half a time" is triply mysterious. It is cryptic, hidden from the persecutors. It is brief, indicating the quick end of Antiochus IV. But it is veiled, to show the soon but undated coming of God's final

NOTES, REFLECTIONS, AND QUESTIONS

The Hasmoneans were a Jewish priestly family who led a revolt against the religious oppression of Antiochus Epiphanes, who tried to force Greek culture and worship on the Jews by replacing the high priest and outlawing all Jewish religious practices under penalty of death. An old Hasmonean priest named Mattathias and his sons led a rebellion that came to be known as the Maccabean Revolt, because the oldest son, Judas, was called "the Maccabee," probably meaning "the hammer." Judas and his followers took over the Temple in 164 B.C., cleansed its altar, and rededicated it. This event is commemorated in the Feast of Dedication (Hanukkah). Daniel 11:31-35 refers to Antiochus's desecration of the Temple and the Maccabean resistance to his control.

deliverance. (Antiochus died in Persia or Babylon in 164/163 B.C., about three and a half years after his desecration of the Temple.)

What should we do in the "interval until the time appointed"? We are to hold fast, with the "wise" and the "holy ones." "Happy are those who persevere" (12:12). Some will die. The Bible knows and we know not all oppressed people are rescued from the fiery furnaces or from the dens of lions. But deliverance will come to all who are faithful—and not from human hands but from the hand of God. For the first time in the Old Testament, a clear note of resurrection is sounded: "Your people shall be delivered, everyone who is found written in the book. Many of those who sleep in the dust of the earth shall awake, some to everlasting life, and some to shame and everlasting contempt. Those who are wise shall shine like the brightness of the sky" (12:1-3).

Do not lose hope. Hold fast. Final days are at hand. Shrouded in mystery, end time, God's full and final victory is coming soon. You may be a martyr, but you will be saved. Persevere! Daniel is instructed to seal the book "until the time of the end" (12:4). "But you, go your way, and rest; you shall rise for your reward at the end of the days" (12:13).

MARKS OF FAITHFUL COMMUNITY

God is in control of history. Evil forces will not prevail. God's kingdom is coming soon. So we believe. So we pray, "Your kingdom come."

What elements in our culture oppose or deny faith and its practice?

_____

_____

What are examples of passive resistance to faith-denying elements in our culture? example of active resistance?

_____

_____

When you look at our culture from the perspective of the coming Kingdom, what do you see?

_____

_____

IF YOU WANT TO KNOW MORE

Do some research on the impact of the spread of Greek culture under Alexander the Great on Judaism and later on Christianity.

Being faithful community, we actively resist faith-denying elements in our culture, whatever the cost.

WISDOM

"The fear of the LORD is the beginning of knowledge;
fools despise wisdom and instruction."

—Proverbs 1:7

7 The Beginning of Knowledge

OUR HUMAN CONDITION

We don't like being told what to do, how to live. We resent the notion that anyone knows more about how we should act than we do. The old sayings probably aren't true anyway. We sure don't want to be bossed around, much less be disciplined by anyone else. We're not worried about consequences; we'll beat them.

ASSIGNMENT

Read "Fruit From the Tree of Life" before reading assigned Scripture. It provides context and information for reading the wisdom of Proverbs. Think of wisdom as a being, even a woman, who knows truth.

Day 1 Read "Fruit From the Tree of Life."
Day 2 Proverbs 1–3 (awe and reverence toward God, value of wisdom)
Day 3 Proverbs 4–6 (parental instruction and warnings)
Day 4 Proverbs 7–9 (warning against adultery, the call of wisdom, wisdom at Creation, folly's invitation)
Day 5 Proverbs 10–12 (wise sayings, rewards of righteousness, dangers of wickedness)
Day 6 Proverbs 13–15 (rewards of wisdom, consequences of folly, danger of anger). Read and respond to "Marks of Faithful Community."
Day 7 Rest

PSALM OF THE WEEK

In Psalm 1, the righteous are compared to trees and the wicked to chaff. As you read Psalm 1 aloud on Days 1–4, think about what other images might replace *trees* and *chaff* and still carry the psalm's message. Make note of characteristics of trees and chaff. On Days 5–6, rewrite the psalm, replacing *trees* and *chaff* with other images.

PRAYER

Pray daily before study:
"My sins, O God, are not hidden from you;
    you know how foolish I have been.
Don't let me bring shame on those who trust
    in you,
    Sovereign LORD Almighty!
Don't let me bring disgrace to those
    who worship you" (Psalm 69:5-6, TEV).

Prayer concerns for this week:

WISDOM

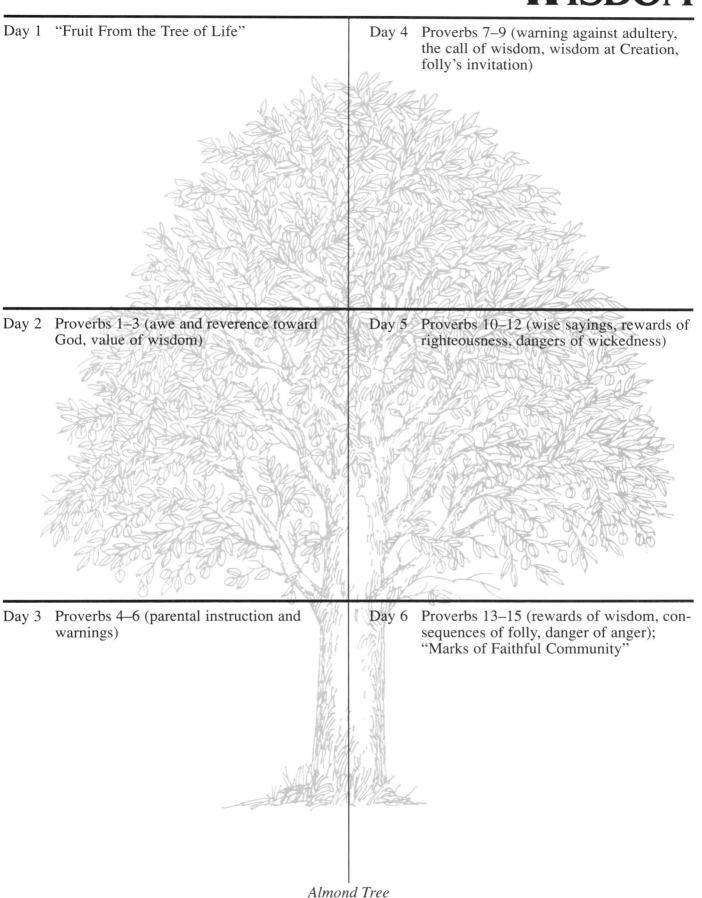

Day 1 "Fruit From the Tree of Life"

Day 2 Proverbs 1–3 (awe and reverence toward God, value of wisdom)

Day 3 Proverbs 4–6 (parental instruction and warnings)

Day 4 Proverbs 7–9 (warning against adultery, the call of wisdom, wisdom at Creation, folly's invitation)

Day 5 Proverbs 10–12 (wise sayings, rewards of righteousness, dangers of wickedness)

Day 6 Proverbs 13–15 (rewards of wisdom, consequences of folly, danger of anger); "Marks of Faithful Community"

Almond Tree

DISCIPLE

FRUIT FROM THE TREE OF LIFE

We walk out of the Temple and into the streets. In Proverbs, we leave behind the priests and the rituals, the altar and the sacrifices. Worship is not forgotten, but our focus now is on day-to-day living.

We also lay the Scriptures aside. Torah is not forgotten. Torah is at the heart of wisdom, but now our textbook is not the written page but the human situation. Parents will guide us; experience will be our teacher. We will learn through observation and reason. Now we watch teenagers slip out of their bedroom windows at midnight; we hear of robbers breaking into stores; we listen to parents pleading with their children. We will take notice of our neighbor sleeping with his best friend's wife. We will listen to witnesses testifying in court. Our classroom is the world; our textbook is everyday life. We will discuss practical matters, and we will ask, Where will wisdom be found?

Origins of Wisdom

Within the cluster of books (as grouped in the Hebrew Bible) called the Writings, we have the books of wisdom—Proverbs, Job, Ecclesiastes. Solomon prayed for wisdom and gained the reputation of unrivaled wisdom. Around his persona swirled talk of wisdom, wise sayings, tales that came to be legend. Thus the volumes of wisdom literature are heavily honorific, intended to receive reflected glory from the wise King Solomon and to give honor to his name. Forever now, when we think of Moses, we think of law; when we think of David, we think of psalms; when we think of Solomon, we think of wisdom.

The book of Proverbs seems to flow from two sources—the teachings of parents and the writings of sages. In an oral culture, where few people could read or write, traditions and truths were passed down by word of mouth through story, poem, witty saying, or pithy proverb. Across the centuries, mothers and fathers, grandparents, elders in the tribe taught the children, using all the memory devices they could muster. From ancient Egypt and Mesopotamia came similar sayings that must have been grounded in the wisdom of the home.

Yet the material in Proverbs is so cleverly crafted, truth or opinions so aptly worded, that scholarly, sophisticated hands and heads must also have been at work. Even before Solomon, sages were an organized part of a king's court. Apparently, teachers were under royal sponsorship to instruct the young, especially the bright young men of the court. Sages must have taken earthy proverbs common to the home, sharpened their style, grouped them, and placed them in theological settings.

Gender Specific

The book of Proverbs shakes our modern sensibilities because it is so gender-specific. Clearly, the setting is a patriarchal society where fathers and mothers are trying to teach their adolescent sons how to live in the real world. The gender issue is pronounced in sexual imagery and male and female characterizations. Evil "men" speak perversely; wicked "women" entice sexually. Wisdom is personified as a gracious woman whose ways lead to life. Folly is personified as a wicked woman whose ways lead to death. Women are portrayed generally in terms of their relationships to men. Men find wisdom and a good wife in almost the same breath.

How can we go behind this gender delineation, this ancient patriarchal culture to get at the human condition, the eternal truths, guidance for our own culture? We must first acknowledge the power of specifics. Generalities tend to lose the power of directness and conviction. We can talk about art, but we are not moved until we see a particular painting. So let us read the sharp specifics, the concrete imagery. Let us try to get inside this culture where the family was crucial for survival, and let us learn all we can from it.

Different Bible translations illustrate the situation. In the original text, mother and father give instruction to "my son" (Proverbs 1:8). The evil or wicked are evil or wicked "men" (2:12). The Jewish Scriptures (*Tanakh*) and the New International Version use this literal or traditional translation. Such translations keep the sharpness, the specific, the concrete imagery, but maintain the strong gender associations. The New Revised Standard Version replaces "my son" with "my child" and renders "evil men" "the way of evil," seeking to make the meaning more inclusive.

If we use the specific, we must explore the gender metaphor and relate the concrete truths to men *and* women, appreciating the vivid, particular picture but looking for the human application. If we modify the text, softening the gender references, we lose some of the concrete visualization that helps drive the point home; but we open or broaden the point to address both women and men.

One creative approach is to read Proverbs both ways to gain maximum access to its truths. Get downright specific— boys joining gangs, women luring men into a brothel. Then quickly acknowledge that daughters as well as sons must be taught wisdom, that women as well as men can lie, that both men and women can be sexually promiscuous, that all human beings can be wise or foolish. The conflict is not between male and female; it is between wisdom and folly.

Parental Instruction

We begin simply enough:
> "Hear, my child, your father's instruction,
>   and do not reject your mother's teaching"
>   (Proverbs 1:8).

Most children have heard their father offer instructions on the right way to do something. Did you not receive some words

DISCIPLE

of advice from Mom? Mother and father even draw on earlier generations.

"When I was a son with my father,
    tender, and my mother's favorite,
he taught me, and said to me,
'Let your heart hold fast my words;
    keep my commandments, and live.
Get wisdom; get insight: do not forget, nor turn away
    from the words of my mouth'" (4:3-5).

Mother and father remember the past and have lived long enough, and have seen enough of life, to know the consequences of various decisions.

Picture Mother with some gray in her hair, pulling the curtain aside, noticing a young man, a friend of her son, walking down the street only to be stopped by a young married woman out in the yard. Her husband is out of town. Mother watches the two go into the house and not come out. She is sad. She knows. She tries to tell her son (7:6-27). But will he listen?

Father and mother know the fire that burns in a young man's loins. They know the hunger for affection in a young woman's heart. They have been there. But they have watched a bird walk helplessly up to the grain in the trap, never to come out again. They have seen marriage after marriage broken by adultery. Oh, if only they could warn, could teach so that the young would know and understand.

Wisdom

Parents know children will not always listen. They know teenagers think they have all the answers. So mother and father point to something beyond themselves—truth, a reality bigger than they are. In Proverbs, truth is more than a set of principles; truth is knowledge, experience. Wisdom is the way things really are. In Proverbs, the right way to live is not merely a group of parental instructions, not simply some helpful guidelines from the religious community. Wisdom touches every atom of the universe. It reflects reality in heaven and on earth and sea. It contains the character of God in the stuff of existence.

"The LORD by wisdom founded the earth;
    by understanding he established the heavens;
by his knowledge the deeps broke open" (Proverbs 3:19-20).

But Proverbs 1–9 makes Creation more vivid, more personal. The wisdom God used in Creation becomes personified. Wisdom is a person. A woman. Wisdom was with God in the beginning, before God created the heavens and the earth.

"The LORD created me at the beginning of his work,
    the first of his acts of long ago. . . .
I was beside him, like a master worker;
and I was daily his delight,
    rejoicing before him always,

rejoicing in his inhabited world
and delighting in the human race" (8:22, 30-31).

Wisdom Personified

Wisdom, like mother and father, wishes to instruct us in the ways of life. She is not God, but she lives so close to the Creator she knows God's thoughts, and she wants to convey those thoughts to us. Wisdom is at home with God. But she is also at home in the world; she "tents" with us. Wisdom knows how human beings feel and think and act. She knows what makes for good human relationships. Wisdom can help us live in tune with the rhythms of the universe.

Does wisdom search for us, or do we search for wisdom? Both. She calls,

"On the heights, beside the way,
at the crossroads she takes her stand;
beside the gates in front of the town,
at the entrance of the portals she cries out"
(Proverbs 8:2-3).

She stands where everyone travels, at the intersection where people pass, at the "gates" where judgment is rendered, decisions made. She does not work hidden but in broad daylight. Her words are the straight truth, the words of life:

"All the words of my mouth are righteous;
there is nothing twisted or crooked in them" (8:8).

On the other hand, we are to seek wisdom,

"seek it like silver,
and search for it as for hidden treasures" (2:4).

By seeking wisdom, we are seeking God and God's way to live. God reaches to us, but our hearts need to respond in trust and obedience, for "the fear of the LORD is the beginning of knowledge" (1:7).

Folly

Amid human reality, a second voice calls continually—beckoning, wooing, pleading. Folly uses strong sexual allurements. Her lips drip honey; her mouth "is slicker than olive oil." But she is more than sex. Her sexuality is a metaphor for folly; her "openings" are not only an invitation to her body but an invitation to evil in general. Her path, her house, are ways that lead to destruction. "Her feet go down to death" (Proverbs 5:5).

So we read folly on two levels: direct warnings about promiscuous sex, prostitution, and adultery, but also as a symbolic entrance into foolishness, whether that be lust for wealth, reckless lending of money, laziness, or bloodthirsty violence. The "door" of her house represents the threshold, the point of entry and the point of no return:

"Keep your way far from her,
and do not go near the door of her house" (5:8).

Folly does not laugh at her conquests. She seems content

DISCIPLE

with her prey. But wisdom ironically laughs when we discover our plight. When we spit into wind, and get wet, she laughs because we are so surprised. She has warned us. So we are to choose the one we will embrace, the path we intend to walk.

Consequences

Choices have consequences. In Proverbs, life is a path that, if chosen wisely, leads to health, family, prosperity, long life. If, on the other hand, the chosen path is folly, it leads to confusion, disarray, broken relationships, financial ruin, death. While it is possible for God to intervene, to bless or punish from the outside, most results come from within. The thought leads to action; action has consequences. Why? Because that's how God made the world. The wise person knows when and how to act accordingly. We will love wisdom or folly.

To heed and embrace wisdom means walking a path that leads to life. Look at the promised results:
• You will maintain the family farm, the inherited property. You will "abide in the land" (Proverbs 2:21).
• If you give the Lord the first fruits of your produce, "then your barns will be filled with plenty" (3:9-10).
• Your feet "will not stumble" (3:23).
• When "you sit down, you will not be afraid; / when you lie down, your sleep will be sweet" (3:24).
• You will enjoy health; you will have "healing for your flesh / and a refreshment for your body" (3:8).

The result will be a good and happy and long life, for wisdom followed will give you "length of days and years of life" (3:2). You will even die wealthy, for
> "Long life is in her right hand;
> in her left hand are riches and honor" (3:16).

You will be able to leave something to your children and their children (13:22). You will bless a city—even a nation—with your righteousness, and it will be exalted (11:10-11). When you die, your memory will be a blessing (10:7). Why? "The fruit of the righteous is a tree of life" (11:30).

If you listen to Folly, or follow your own desires, spurning the instructions of parents and wisdom, you will walk a different path. You will be "robbed of sleep" (4:16). You will drink the "wine of violence" (4:17). You will be walking in darkness. You will stumble along, but you won't understand what you are stumbling over (4:19). Instead of walking with the wise you will walk with fools, and you will suffer "harm" (13:20). Honor will be stripped from you, and you will be ruined in the public eye (5:14). You will even lose years of your life (5:8-9).

Listening to folly, or being "wise in your own eyes "(3:7), you will be slow to rise in the morning, resulting in your poverty. Lying, cheating, bearing false witness, you will fall into disrepute.

Of particular danger is the falling under the spell of a

Almond Tree

"strange" or "loose" woman. She seems sweet at first, but soon she becomes "bitter as wormwood" (5:4).

MARKS OF FAITHFUL COMMUNITY

Wisdom helps us discern God's ways. We seek to live a righteous and productive life, not for reward but to live in harmony with God's creation.

When we think about choices and consequences, we consider where each choice will take us. What stands in the way of our considering the final destination when choosing between two paths?

What wisdom did you hear early in life and later have confirmed by experience?

Identify one or two proverbs that have been helpful to you and one or two that were harmful or did not fit your situation.

THE RADICAL DISCIPLE

The radical disciple, open to wisdom's guidance and correction, practices both discernment and discipline: *Discernment* in choosing the right path to wisdom and deciding which teachings apply in a given situation. *Discipline* in staying on the path and in making decisions informed by wisdom along the way.

IF YOU WANT TO KNOW MORE

Get acquainted with The Wisdom of Solomon in the Apocrypha. Read the introduction and scan the subject headings at the top of the pages. Select and read a few passages to get the flavor of the book.

Give a friend or relative a gift of wisdom. Select some proverbs from Proverbs 1–15 appropriate for the recipient (child; teenager; young, middle, or older adult). Put the wisdom in your own words and arrange it attractively on a page or in a small booklet. Add more proverbs from next week's Scripture.

NOTES, REFLECTIONS, AND QUESTIONS

Being faithful community, we listen to wisdom and try to incorporate those insights into daily behavior.

INSTRUCTION

"Whoever heeds instruction is on the path to life."

—Proverbs 10:17

8 The Path to Life

OUR HUMAN CONDITION

We're not sure which of today's voices to listen to. We have trouble sorting the false from the true. Actually, unless this so-called wisdom can fit on a T-shirt or a bumper sticker, we're not interested. We want what's current, even temporary, not necessarily wisdom.

ASSIGNMENT

Read "Fruit From the Tree of Life" before reading assigned Scripture to understand the wide range of subject matter. As you read daily Scripture, follow the instruction to choose a theme and find proverbs to fit the theme, and to look for proverbs that relate to each of the Ten Commandments.

Day 1   Read "Fruit From the Tree of Life."
Day 2   Proverbs 16–18 (perils of pride, dangers of strife, relationships)
Day 3   Proverbs 19–21 (virtue of integrity, rewards of justice)
Day 4   Proverbs 22–24 (sayings of the wise; dangers of drunkenness, gluttony; weakness and laziness)
Day 5   Proverbs 25–27 (wise sayings, the nature of folly, virtue tested)
Day 6   Proverbs 28–31 (penalties of fear, need for wisdom, four types of sinners, a capable wife). Read and respond to "Marks of Faithful Community."
Day 7   Rest

PSALM OF THE WEEK

Each day choose a path and pray Psalm 25 aloud as you walk it. Or if you have access to a labyrinth (a circle design used for meditative walking), pray the psalm as you walk the labyrinth.

PRAYER

Pray daily before study:
"I praise you, O LORD. . . .
I delight in following your commands
    more than in having great wealth.
I study your instructions;
    I examine your teachings.
I take pleasure in your laws;
    your commands I will not forget" (Psalm 119:12, 14-16, TEV).

Prayer concerns for this week:

Day 1   "Fruit From the Tree of Life"

Day 2   Proverbs 16–18 (perils of pride, dangers of strife, relationships)

Day 3   Proverbs 19–21 (virtue of integrity, rewards of justice)

Day 4   Proverbs 22–24 (sayings of the wise; dangers of drunkenness, gluttony; weakness and laziness)

Day 5   Proverbs 25–27 (wise sayings, the nature of folly, virtue tested)

Day 6   Proverbs 28–31 (penalties of fear, need for wisdom, four types of sinners, a capable wife); "Marks of Faithful Community"

Stylized Tree of Life

DISCIPLE

FRUIT FROM THE TREE OF LIFE

The problem with reading Proverbs is that the sayings roll in upon us with blinding speed. They come at us, dozens after dozens, blending, blurring, abandoning their individual identity, losing their punch. We readers encounter a torrent of proverbs, all seemingly unconnected and without context.

Since proverbs need to be understood in a life-setting in order to ring true, how can we study them effectively?

Form or Style

We can study the form of the sayings. Sometimes a proverb takes the form of *parallelism*, two lines saying the same thing:
"Honest balances and scales are the LORD's;
all the weights in the bag are his work" (Proverbs 16:11).
Sometimes the *word order is reversed*, giving a sense of rhythm and balance, as
"those whose paths are crooked,
and who are devious in their ways" (2:15).
To be more dramatic, on occasion the lines are stated in *opposites* or direct contrasts, as in 10:12:
"Hatred stirs up strife,
but love covers all offenses."
Then there is the *number and number plus one* poetic style, meaning "not only this but also that."
"There are six things that the LORD hates,
seven that are an abomination to him" (6:16).
Sometimes we see *proverb pairs* in which the second proverb qualifies or counters the first.
"A friend loves at all times . . .
[but] it is senseless to give a pledge,
to become surety for a neighbor" (17:17-18).
Many sayings are *admonitions*.
"A soft answer turns away wrath,
but a harsh word stirs up anger" (15:1).
Others are simply *observations:*
"'Bad, bad,' says the buyer,
then goes away and boasts" (20:14).
Literary allusions, metaphors, and earthy figures of speech grab our attention: "Like vinegar to the teeth" (10:26) or "Like a gold ring in a pig's snout" (11:22).
Interesting *body language* reveals inner thoughts:
"Haughty eyes, a lying tongue,
and hands that shed innocent blood, . . .
feet that hurry to run to evil" (6:17-18).
Repetition is not accidental. Ideas are driven home by being repeated. Good teachers know how to reinforce the lesson.

Subject Matter

Choose a theme. Then pick out appropriate sayings that address that theme. The process becomes intriguing as we study the theme from diverse viewpoints, like examining a diamond from various angles. As an example, let's consider proverbs about poverty and wealth. We'll use the *Good News Bible: Today's English Version* for freshness in translation.

Sloth, laziness, indifference will lead to poverty. The fields of a lazy person are "full of thorn bushes and overgrown with weeds. . . . Fold your hands and rest awhile, but while you are asleep, poverty will attack you like an armed robber" (Proverbs 24:30-34, TEV). The self-indulgent become poor also. Stuffing yourself with food, drinking lots of wine will reduce you to poverty. "If all you do is eat and sleep, you will soon be wearing rags" (23:21, TEV).

Better to get up and go to work. Be continually diligent with your labors. If you don't, you'll run out of money. "Look after your sheep and cattle as carefully as you can, because wealth is not permanent" (27:23-24, TEV) or "riches do not last forever" (27:24).

Proverbs observes that the poor are often disliked, shunned by neighbors (14:20). Such attitudes are not recommended, just recognized. Some poverty comes from folly, but not all. Proverbs does not forget the widow and the orphan, where fate seems to have caused destitution. Much of wealth is hard work, but not all. God and fate sometimes intervene.

Getting rich seems to be a good thing in Proverbs, unless you get rich by dishonesty (10:2), by lying (21:6), or by charging high rates of interest (28:8).

Riches are nice, but they won't help you on Judgment Day. And if you lie and steal, your riches will end up in the hands of the righteous (13:22). Besides, there are things more important than money: "It is better—much better—to have wisdom and knowledge than gold and silver" (16:16, TEV).

Neither poverty nor riches are romanticized. Poverty may cause you to steal (6:30). Riches may make you proud and self-indulgent (28:11). Goodness is deeper than wealth. It is better to be honest, even if you are poor (19:1), than to be rich and dishonest (28:6).

Those wanting to be rich can fall into all sorts of foolish traps. They can focus on gold instead of wisdom; they can wear themselves out trying to get rich (23:4). They can become stingy (23:6), forget the poor, trust in their riches (11:28). Better to be wise. Better to be happy. If anger or hatred or dishonesty characterizes your life, of what good is money? "Better to eat vegetables with people you love than to eat the finest meat where there is hate" (15:17, TEV).

About the worst thing the rich can do is to forget the poor. "If you want to be happy, be kind to the poor; it is a sin to despise anyone" (14:21). Why? Because "the rich and the poor have this in common: the LORD made them both" (22:2).

Generosity is blessed by God. Not only do wise or righteous persons not cheat the widow by moving the boundary stones on her farm, not lie or cheat the orphan; they open their pocketbooks. "Be generous and share your food with the

DISCIPLE

poor. You will be blessed for it" (22:9, TEV). Someday the situation may be reversed: "If you refuse to listen to the cry of the poor, your own cry for help will not be heard" (21:13, TEV).

Above all, regardless of circumstances—but especially fitting for the wealthy—do not allow yourself to become arrogant, puffed up, self-righteous, for
> "Pride goes before destruction,
> and a haughty spirit before a fall" (16:18).

Now try some themes yourself.

The Ten Commandments

How have Jews and Christians explained the wisdom that helped God create the universe and teaches humanity how to live? Christians have understood wisdom to be the *Logos* or *Word* of God, incarnate in Jesus Christ. We will study this concept in John.

Jewish scholars have understood wisdom to mean teaching or instruction as embodied in Torah. The Torah, or Pentateuch—the first five books of Scripture—came to be wisdom made available, revealed to human beings by the gracious work of God. Thus, historically, as Jewish people of faith look for wisdom, "more precious than jewels" (Proverbs 3:15), they read Torah. The center of Torah is the Ten Commandments (Deuteronomy 5:6-21), the basic tenets of life upon which all other law or teaching is based.

Search Proverbs 1–31 from this perspective: Read each commandment, and look for proverbs that dramatize it, spell it out, enlarge upon it, or graphically weave it into life. You may not find much material on God's name or sabbath, for as we have said, in Proverbs we leave the Temple and the religious legislation and look at the everyday world. But Proverbs illustrates the other commandments profusely. As you read, look for proverbs that relate in some way to the commandments. The commandments are printed in the column to the right. Jot down references and a few key words to remind you of the connections you see. Look for meaning you may have missed before.

The Capable Wife

Who in the world can find a "capable wife" like the woman in Proverbs? She not only gets up early; she does the work of ten. Actually, she is an "ideal," a model of perfection. Proverbs 31:10-31 is an acrostic poem; each verse begins with a letter of the Hebrew alphabet in sequence. So our poem is a carefully crafted description of a woman embodying all the virtues of wisdom. In a patriarchal society, she is a role model for young wives and mothers, not a portrait of the woman next door.

Let us try to unravel her perfect character to observe the threads of Torah, the yarn of wisdom of which she is made. She, like wisdom, is "more precious than jewels" (Proverbs

THE TEN COMMANDMENTS
Deuteronomy 5:6-21, TEV

- "I am the LORD your God. . . . Worship no god but me" (Deuteronomy 5:6-7, TEV).

- "Do not make for yourselves images of anything in heaven or on earth or in the water under the earth. Do not bow down to any idol or worship it, for I am the LORD your God and I tolerate no rivals" (5:8-9, TEV).

- "Do not use my name for evil purposes" (5:11, TEV).

- "Observe the Sabbath and keep it holy, as I, the LORD your God, have commanded you. You have six days in which to do your work, but the seventh day is a day of rest dedicated to me" (5:12-13, TEV).

- "Respect your father and your mother, as I, the LORD your God, command you, so that all may go well with you" (5:16, TEV).

- "Do not commit murder" (5:17, TEV).

- "Do not commit adultery" (5:18, TEV).

- "Do not steal" (5:19, TEV).

- "Do not accuse anyone falsely" (5:20, TEV).

- "Do not desire another man's wife; do not desire his house, his land, . . . or anything else that he owns" (5:21, TEV).

After studying Proverbs from the perspective of the Ten Commandments, why, in your view, are the Ten Commandments the wisdom or path that leads to life?

3:13-15; 31:10). She is faithful to her husband; he has complete trust in her (31:11). Their family will prosper, their home gain in worldly possessions. Why? She will work hard, rising while it is yet night (31:15). She exhibits great home-making and strong organizational skills. She is a smart buyer in the marketplace. Her business judgment is striking; she does not fit a simple domestic stereotype. She exercises her talents; she "considers a field and buys it," and she uses the earnings from her sewing and spinning (31:24) to buy roots for a vineyard that will last for years (31:16). Surely she must be thinking of her children and her children's children. She must never sleep. Like many a mother of small children, "her lamp does not go out at night" (31:18).

What does it mean, "she laughs at the time to come" (31:25)? Maybe she trusts her husband as he trusts her. She has confidence in her family and friends. Though she has possessions, she could go on even if the possessions were swept away, for she knows they are not the basis for life. She trusts in God. She has her priorities straight.

One suspects she offers first fruits to God, because she does not forget the poor. Not all women have strong faithful husbands; some have been cut down by war; some by accident and disease; some by flood, earthquake, or famine. Some husbands have fallen into folly, breaking the marriage bond, becoming alcoholics or drug addicts. Wisdom, this worthy woman, doesn't ask us to sort out the reasons some people are strong, some are weak, some are fortunate, some experience calamity. "She opens her hand to the poor," drawing the blessing of the Lord (31:20).

Like the ant gathering its winter food in summer (6:6-8), she is prepared when the snow flies (31:21). Therefore she can help others.

Honor is a strange thing. How does a husband honor his wife?

_____

How does a wife honor her husband?

_____

How do we honor other people so they succeed and we in turn feel clothed in "strength and dignity"?

_____

"Capable wife" knows how to guide children. Experts on child behavior say children learn from and emulate best what their parents love to do. Making a child do something the parent hates is seldom successful. If this model woman whistles while her hands fly carding, spinning, and weaving wool into cloth, and if she teaches wisdom to her children as she goes, she may very well have youngsters rise up and call her

DISCIPLE

blessed. She does not spare discipline, but "the teaching of kindness is on her tongue" (31:26).

Somehow, through faithfulness and diligence, this woman in Proverbs has found wisdom, the instruction for living the happy and productive life that comes from God. She has learned how God put the universe together, and she tries to live in harmony with those rhythms. In her heart of hearts, she "fears the LORD" (31:30), for she knows "The fear of the LORD is the beginning of wisdom" (9:10).

Another Point of View

Who is Agur (Proverbs 30:1)? Nobody knows. Agur is not a typical Hebrew name; he is a stranger. His comments are like the clashing of cymbals in an otherwise peaceful, pastoral symphony. Proverbs lays life out in a straight line: Work hard; obey your parents; save your money, but don't be stingy; give first fruits to the Lord; tell the truth; speak carefully and softly; love and honor your spouse; respect authority; instruct and discipline your children; be generous to the poor. You will enjoy a happy and healthy life. Your barns will be full; your children will bless you; you will live to be old. When you die, people will come to your funeral and remember you with gratitude.

The message of Proverbs has much truth, and we long to lay hold of it. But something inside us says, "That's not the whole story." The formula of Proverbs is too simple; life is more complex than that. So with some relief to us, the unknown Agur hints at the mysterious, points to the reality that we don't know all the answers, not even all the questions.

Agur's chapter is a perfect bridge to the book of Ecclesiastes and to Job. The old Teacher in Ecclesiastes will raise questions about the proverbs. Job lived the recommended life but came to ruin. Agur hints at forthcoming questions.

Can we know the mind of God? We do have some wisdom revealed to us. As the prophet Isaiah reminds us, God's word comes down like rain from heaven and does not return empty. It will accomplish God's purpose (Isaiah 55:10-11). Yes, the Scriptures do prove true (Proverbs 30:5-6). But, says Agur, I am only able to comprehend this much: I don't want to be a liar, and I don't want too little or too much, lest I steal through poverty or boast through riches (30:7-9). So much of life is mysterious.

I see strange things: people who curse their parents, people who think they are "pure," arrogant people—"how high their eyelids lift," people whose words cut like knives and they eat up the poor (30:11-14). Hard work is good, possessions are pleasant, but a person ought to be able to go to sleep at night without grasping for more (30:15-16).

Who can understand the way an eagle soars, a snake slithers, a ship sails, or how a man and a woman make love? These realities are beautiful but mysterious.

Scripture scrolls, wound on wooden rollers, are held together with a cloth binder and stored in a container called a holy ark. Rollers, simple on the bottom where they are held, often have highly carved or decorated tops. Each roller is called a "tree of life" because Torah "is a tree of life to those who lay hold of her" (Proverbs 3:18).

Usually the world is solid, built on a secure foundation. We like it that way. But sometimes the world starts shaking: A fool eats too much; there is a loveless marriage; or underlings upstage their bosses (30:21-23).

The gap between God and humans is immense. Human knowledge is so limited. We can study the tiny atom or the vast universe, we can study the ants and the stars, but we don't know how or why they do what they do (30:24-31). If you exalt yourself, you may be humbled. You may even raise your blood pressure (30:32-33).

Thank God for this detour into humility. We'll struggle with the dialogue between wisdom and mystery for the rest of our lives.

MARKS OF FAITHFUL COMMUNITY

Good choices lead to life, even if the payoff is delayed. We trust God's wisdom, for God is the giver of life and joy.

When does the path to life seem particularly difficult for you?

_____

_____

What proverbs have high priority for you?

_____

_____

What proverbs are most challenging for you? most threatening? Why?

_____

_____

Being faithful community, we trust God's wisdom, not the world's wisdom, in making our choices.

THE RADICAL DISCIPLE

The radical disciple goes beyond "being good" for reward to living rightly regardless of reward. What are you doing that requires passion, vision, hard work, proverbial wisdom, sacrificial love?

IF YOU WANT TO KNOW MORE

Read many wonderful proverbs, some with a new twist, in Sirach 1–9 in the Apocrypha. Sirach is sometimes called "Ecclesiasticus." Notice the personification of wisdom in Chapter 1.

Choose proverbs from Proverbs 16–31 to add to your gift of wisdom suggested in Lesson 7.

FUTILE

> "'Meaningless! Meaningless!'
> says the Teacher.
> 'Utterly meaningless!
> Everything is meaningless.'"
>
> —Ecclesiastes 1:2, NIV

9 Destined to Die

OUR HUMAN CONDITION

We live as if tomorrow were a sure thing. We accumulate. The next new experience, the next new possession—we gather them around us to distract us from the fact that nothing lasts. That we're going to die.

ASSIGNMENT

We will read Ecclesiastes twice: this week from the perspective of futility, next week from the perspective of joy.

As you read, shake your head at accepted truisms. Look for mystery, vain things, incongruities, ambivalence, irony, chance, punctured pride, injustice, tragedy, and death. Look at life as it really is. Consider your own death.

Day 1 Ecclesiastes 1–2 (futility of wisdom and pleasure)

Day 2 Ecclesiastes 3–4 (a time for everything, value of a friend, impermanence of fame)

Day 3 Ecclesiastes 5–7 (injustice and hopelessness, wisdom and folly)

Day 4 Ecclesiastes 8–9 (God's mysterious ways)

Day 5 Ecclesiastes 10–12 (vulnerability of wisdom, diligence, zest for life, youth and old age)

Day 6 Read and respond to "Fruit From the Tree of Life" and "Marks of Faithful Community."

Day 7 Rest

PSALM OF THE WEEK

In Psalm 39 the psalmist puts into words what we often have thought: Life goes by too quickly. As you read the psalm aloud daily, talk back, raise questions, speak your mind—either aloud or with paper and pen.

PRAYER

Pray daily before study:
"Hear my prayer, O God;
    don't turn away from my plea!
Listen to me and answer me;
    I am worn out by my worries" (Psalm 55:1-2, TEV).

Prayer concerns for this week:

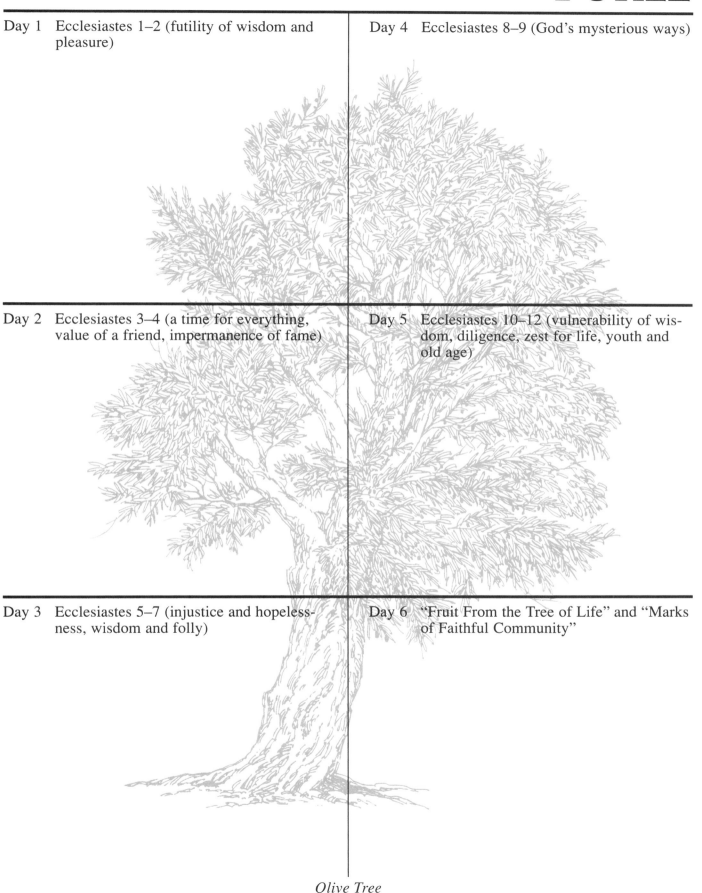

Day 1 Ecclesiastes 1–2 (futility of wisdom and pleasure)

Day 4 Ecclesiastes 8–9 (God's mysterious ways)

Day 2 Ecclesiastes 3–4 (a time for everything, value of a friend, impermanence of fame)

Day 5 Ecclesiastes 10–12 (vulnerability of wisdom, diligence, zest for life, youth and old age)

Day 3 Ecclesiastes 5–7 (injustice and hopelessness, wisdom and folly)

Day 6 "Fruit From the Tree of Life" and "Marks of Faithful Community"

Olive Tree

DISCIPLE

FRUIT FROM THE TREE OF LIFE

The book of Ecclesiastes was written during the post-exilic period, perhaps around 300 B.C., at a time of relative stability, a time when national and religious passion was expressed in routine Temple worship. The dynamic theology surrounding the return to Jerusalem had now become a settled orthodoxy, guided by the wisdom sages.

The Teacher was a thoughtful man, not country bred like David but city bred like Solomon. He had known the intensity of scholarship, the complexity of planning and administration, the effort to gain wealth, the joy and pain of writing books. He was a scholar and a poet. Word pictures swirled through his mind and into his language. He reasoned in concete rather than abstract imagery. When he wrote of death, he pictured a pulley wheel broken on the old family cistern (Ecclesiastes 12:6). As an old man, he remembered episodes from the past. He was able to say those words so exasperating to youth, "I've been down that road!"

Some scholars think he was a bachelor. He writes about a tragic love affair, a time when his heart was vulnerable. But the woman jilted him, broke his heart, and left him disillusioned (7:26). Whenever he mentions children, he refers to the children of others, usually in terms of inheritance. He urges men to be faithful to their wives—as if he were an onlooker—and admonishes them to enjoy their marriage.

Now, picture this gray-haired Teacher sitting, looking over Jerusalem as the sun begins to sink behind the wall. The cataracts in his eyes blur his vision so the sights of the city, especially at dusk, are softened. His hearing misses the high tones so the evening sounds are not so sharp. His hips and knees feel the ache of arthritis; he shifts his position from time to time. His thoughts reach out to merchants closing their shops, to housewives cooking the evening meal, to children running home from their games. He glances at the Temple where the priests have been offering the sacrifices. He looks across to the school where he and his fellow teachers have spent their lives explaining Torah to the upper-class youth in Jerusalem, preparing them for careers in business, government, and Temple service. He undoubtedly taught his students the message he penned in his book. He wanted his book of wisdom to help others avoid the foolishness he had experienced and observed.

I've Tried It Myself

He begins his teaching thinking about the study of wisdom. "I devoted myself to study and to explore by wisdom all that is done under heaven. What a heavy burden God has laid on men! I have seen all the things that are done under the sun; all of them are meaningless" (Ecclesiastes 1:13-14, NIV).

> "What do people gain from all the toil
> at which they toil under the sun?" (1:3).

He questions the assumption that the righteous are rewarded by health, wealth, and happiness in this life and sinners punished by illness, poverty, and early death. What about random events, accidents beyond human intervention or control?

Thoughts of fate or chance nearly drive him crazy. He has been taught that God rules, God is just, the righteous prosper. The Chronicler taught that the kings who trusted God caused Judah to have peace, and kings who followed their own devices led Judah into destruction and exile. A plus B equals C.

His observations are "under the sun," for he thinks only in the framework of this world. He uses the word *all* because everything that happens is within the Creator's design and control. No exceptions, or so it seems. So when bad things happen to good people, or when good things happen to bad people, where is God? Where is justice? This mysterious world is neither predictable nor comprehensible. Death is everywhere. Just as surely as the sun rises and sets, every man, woman, child, and every beast of the field will die. The grave is the destiny of all. Much thinking and planning is chasing the wind.

The Teacher becomes personal, saying in effect, I've studied hard to figure out life, trying to understand how to live a good life. The more I learned, the less I knew. The more I studied, the more headaches I got. "The wiser you are, the more worries you have" (1:18, TEV). Trying to understand it all is absurd. The mystery is deep, too deep for the human mind. No use trying to heap up wisdom and joy (2:26) or trying to predict the future (10:14).

I was taught

"The teaching of the wise is a fountain of life,
   so that one may avoid the snares of death" (Proverbs 13:14).

But I discovered that just as the fool dies, so will I. What good is my wisdom? I know it is better to have eyes in our head than to walk like a fool in darkness (Ecclesiastes 2:13-14), but in the end what have we gained by trying to understand God's ways and the way life works? It's like trying to grab hold of the wind (2:17). I even thought maybe I'd leave my wisdom to somebody else, somebody younger perhaps, but "who knows whether they will be wise or foolish?" (2:19). What do people get for all their anxious study? "All their days are full of pain, and their work is a vexation; even at night their minds do not rest" (2:23). Those who want to store up wisdom are wasting their time.

I've Tested Pleasure

Finding the effort to store up wisdom futile, the Teacher decided to test pleasure as the way to the good life (Ecclesiastes 2:1). So he experimented to see if sensual pleasure would make him happy. With deliberate strategy he delighted his eyes with fishponds and garden pools. He massaged his

"What has been is what will be,
   and what has been done is what will be done;
   there is nothing new under the sun" (Ecclesiastes 1:9).
This limestone sundial, only two inches square, may have been a part of Herod's Temple. It was found in debris from the destruction of the Temple in A.D. 70.

DISCIPLE

ego by building beautiful buildings. He sought to satisfy his ears with the sound of music. He went to banquets and bars to find out what pleasure is all about. People were laughing, playing music, getting drunk. He stayed up all night, hired choristers to sing for him, "had all the women a man could want" (2:8, TEV). None of it made him happy. His experiences left him hollow, dissatisfied.

For his experience to have the greatest impact, he pretended for a moment to be the king (1:12–2:11). The rabbis explain this literary device by saying that if a nobody claimed he had tasted all of life's "good things," no one would believe him, for surely he hadn't eaten all the gourmet food, drunk all the expensive wines, sat beside all the lavish gardens, listened to all the orchestras, slept with all the sexy women. But we might listen to someone who had tried them all and come up empty. If anyone ever did, it was Solomon! Like a king, "I did not deny myself any pleasure" (2:10, TEV). Then "I realized that it didn't mean a thing. It was like chasing the wind—of no use at all" (2:11, TEV). I achieved no lasting value, and I did not become a happy man.

I've Noticed Other Vanities

I've noticed some grievous injustices "under the sun," he said. I've seen parents work hard, long into the night, saving money for their children, only to lose it all in a bad investment (Ecclesiastes 5:13-14). I know we are taught "the hand of the diligent makes rich" (Proverbs 10:4), but he insists, I've seen people lose everything through no fault of their own. Even worse, he says, I've seen them worry themselves sick and live the rest of their lives in bitterness.

I've noticed that some good people have lots of trouble and some wicked people seem to have all the luck (Ecclesiastes 7:15). That's a far cry from "The righteous will never be removed, / but the wicked will not remain in the land" (Proverbs 10:30). Sometimes the wicked are not apprehended, not convicted when they're caught, not punished when they're convicted. I know the tradition says, "The wicked will not go unpunished" (11:21). But with my own eyes, he says, I've seen people who lie, take bribes, and oppress the poor, then go to the Temple, offer sacrifices, say their prayers, and prolong their lives. When they finally die, they have a fancy funeral. The city even builds a monument or names a street for them (Ecclesiastes 8:10). Who says "The name of the wicked will rot" (Proverbs 10:7)? I even observed a city that was saved by a poor, wise man; but did he get a reward? No. In fact they forgot his name (Ecclesiastes 9:13-15). Who says "The memory of the righteous is a blessing" (Proverbs 10:7)?

I'm not saying we should be evil, or foolish. I'm saying things aren't always fair. Sometimes "there are righteous people who are treated according to the conduct of the wicked, and there are wicked people who are treated according to the conduct of the righteous" (Ecclesiastes 8:14). The race is not always to the swift; "time and chance" happen to everybody. Nobody knows when calamity will hit (9:11-12). People who try to make sense of what is happening are wasting their time (8:17).

What makes life so frustrating is that God has put thoughts in our minds—thoughts such as eternity. But what can we truly know? Some people think there is a time beyond the grave, but what do they know? Does God have a plan? Maybe. But if so, only God knows it. We don't even know what's going to happen tomorrow. People who babble on about the future are fools who don't even know the way to town (10:15).

So the Teacher has looked at life and has done a reality check. Not believing in life beyond the grave (or rather, not knowing anything about it), he limits his discourse to this world, to everything "under the sun." No Egyptian or Greek immortality of the soul for him. No hint of resurrection as in Daniel's vision for this philosopher. All he knows is that good living does not always receive full and complete reward in this world. He doesn't know exactly what God is doing, but the systems of reward and punishment in this world aren't always neat. Life is seldom fair. And as far as the Teacher can tell, death ends it all, for the rich and the poor, the wise and the foolish.

I've Asked Serious Questions

The Teacher continues. Then I asked, Who will inherit all this? I thought of people who worked hard all their lives, left their estate to their children who squandered it all in a few months. I thought how much time people spend to make sure someone doesn't steal their money. In fact, they can't sleep at night worrying about protecting all their property. Then I went to the funeral of a rich friend and saw his body dead and cold, just like a common worker, just like a beast of the field, and I thought, "It is useless, and it isn't right! You work and worry your way through life, and what do you have to show for it?" (Ecclesiastes 2:21-22, TEV). "It is like chasing the wind" (2:26, TEV). The saddest thing is to see some people who have everything the proverbs promise and they still aren't happy. If you gave some people a hundred healthy children and let them live two thousand years, they wouldn't enjoy it (6:1-6). Futile!

Don't be surprised if you see the poor oppressed (5:8). You know the proverb, "The LORD does not let the righteous go hungry" (Proverbs 10:3). Nonsense! I've watched wicked gluttons gorge on food they have stolen from the poor. I've seen hardworking farmers forced off their land, turned into sharecroppers and slaves. "I saw all the oppressions that are practiced under the sun. Look, the tears of the oppressed—with no one to comfort them!" (Ecclesiastes 4:1). The dead

DISCIPLE

are better off than some of the oppressed people; in fact, babies are better off unborn (4:2-3). Walk and talk carefully when you are dealing with the powerful. Some of them are fools. I've seen fools riding white stallions, wise men walking barefoot in the dust (10:7).

I thought about trying to change things, but the crookedness in this world will never be straightened out, not in the world I observe (1:15; 7:13). Things never change—rearrange or reorganize sometimes but never change. Cruelty and oppression recur. We think we see something new, but it has been before. The rivers keep swirling to the sea, but the sea never fills up. The powerful use their power to keep control, to look after themselves. Do you think the rich listen to the poor or that the powerful pay attention to the weak? Not at all. All they think about is wondering what their superiors think of them (5:8). The sun comes up in the east, goes down in the west, but it doesn't make any gains. We'll never get rid of injustice. It's a striving after wind.

Working for the Wrong Reasons

The most foolish thing of all, "I amassed silver and gold for myself" (Ecclesiastes 2:4-8, NIV). I was working for all the wrong reasons. It was futile, meaningless. I've watched other people work too hard just to make money. I'm not saying we shouldn't work. If we don't fix the roof, it will fall in; if we don't work, we won't eat (10:18-19). But if we work to get ahead of our neighbor, or get rich so we won't have to worry, or get famous so they'll build a monument in our memory, or leave an inheritance so our children will be grateful, forget it. Nothing is so futile as trying to amass wealth. The rich can't sleep at night; they can't digest the rich food (5:12). They toss in their beds, still envious of their neighbor (4:4). Vanity of vanities, all effort to hoard things is vanity. Considering the day when "the golden bowl is broken, and the pitcher is broken at the fountain . . . and the dust returns to the earth as it was" (12:6-7), we must ask, Of what use is our chasing after wind?

When have you experienced something that made you acutely aware of your mortality?

_____

_____

The natural rhythms of life (1:1-11) seem monotonous, offering nothing new. Explain why you agree or disagree.

_____

_____

MARKS OF FAITHFUL COMMUNITY

We accept life's mystery in whatever form—hardship or pain, routine or newness. Instead of elbowing our way, we try to make a contribution or perform an act of love. We are not afraid to die.

What doubts, fears, or other concerns keep you (or have kept you) from accepting death as part of life?

_____

_____

In a world of shopping malls, unlimited information networks, and continual entertainment, finding meaning is hard. What feelings of futility are you experiencing?

_____

_____

We travel light. What gathering or grasping behavior, what attachment to possessions are you trying to eliminate?

_____

_____

How do you see the time of your days—as friend or enemy? What might/do you do to see and receive time as friend?

_____

_____

THE RADICAL DISCIPLE

Enter into the spirit of the Teacher and identify those things over which you have no control. Relax in faith. Seek contentment rather than excess. Listen more than you speak. Find meaning in giving rather than getting. Let go the need to have final answers. Trust God.

IF YOU WANT TO KNOW MORE

Consider time. Reflect on how you think about and experience the passage of time at your present stage of life—young, middle, or older adult—and how you perceived and experienced the passage of time at earlier stages of life. Write a paragraph or two describing the differences you became aware of in your perception of the passage of time.

NOTES, REFLECTIONS, AND QUESTIONS

Being faithful community, we accept life's mystery in all of its forms, and we accept death as a part of life.

ENJOY

"This is what I have seen to be good: it is fitting to eat and drink and find enjoyment in all the toil with which one toils under the sun the few days of the life God gives us; for this is our lot."

—Ecclesiastes 5:18

10 Life Is a Gift

OUR HUMAN CONDITION

Only five more days till the weekend. Only eleven more months till vacation. Only twenty more years till retirement. We're preparing. One of these days we'll be able to enjoy life.

ASSIGNMENT

As we discovered last week, many people see only futility, even despair, in Ecclesiastes. Now, look for the good things in life. Look for the joys, modest though they may be.

Day 1   Ecclesiastes 1–2 (eat, drink, and enjoy your work)
Day 2   Ecclesiastes 3–4 (rhythm, dependability, and order in life and in the universe, good friends make life easier)
Day 3   Ecclesiastes 5–7 (keep your vows, enjoy possessions as a momentary gift, accept mystery and incongruity)
Day 4   Ecclesiastes 8–9 (all people and all deeds are in God's hands, death is inevitable, do your tasks with joy, enjoy life)
Day 5   Ecclesiastes 10–12 (be generous, sow generously, trust God, live now)
Day 6   Read and respond to "Fruit From the Tree of Life" and "Marks of Faithful Community."
Day 7   Rest

THE RADICAL DISCIPLE

Start the day with a prayer of thanksgiving. During the day, avoid complaining; express thanks to others. Reflect satisfaction in work done, help given and received. Be a friend. End the day with a prayer of gratitude and trust. Know that each day is a gift.

PSALM OF THE WEEK

Pray Psalm 90 aloud daily. Each day choose a verse or a line and meditate on it all day. Write it on a sticky note and put it where you will see it. Memorize 90:17 and pray it as you begin work each day.

PRAYER

Pray daily before study:
"What a rich harvest your goodness provides!
  Wherever you go there is plenty.
The pastures are filled with flocks;
  the hillsides are full of joy.
The fields are covered with sheep;
  the valleys are full of wheat.
Everything shouts and sings for joy" (Psalm 65:11-13, TEV).

Prayer concerns for this week:

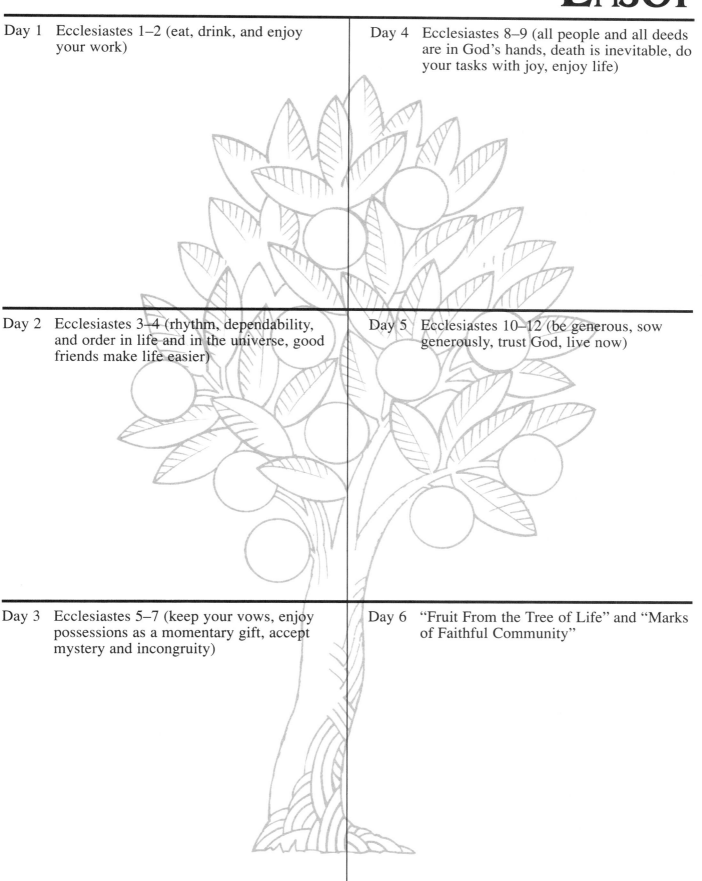

Day 1   Ecclesiastes 1–2 (eat, drink, and enjoy your work)

Day 4   Ecclesiastes 8–9 (all people and all deeds are in God's hands, death is inevitable, do your tasks with joy, enjoy life)

Day 2   Ecclesiastes 3–4 (rhythm, dependability, and order in life and in the universe, good friends make life easier)

Day 5   Ecclesiastes 10–12 (be generous, sow generously, trust God, live now)

Day 3   Ecclesiastes 5–7 (keep your vows, enjoy possessions as a momentary gift, accept mystery and incongruity)

Day 6   "Fruit From the Tree of Life" and "Marks of Faithful Community"

Stylized Tree of Life

DISCIPLE

FRUIT FROM THE TREE OF LIFE

Given that our philosopher limits his perspective to this world, only to the things he can observe "under the sun," how does he recommend we live our lives? Granted, we all go to the grave; what should we do about it? Because time and chance play havoc with our neat religious platitudes and because no one knows what will happen tomorrow, what ought we to do today?

The Teacher does not recommend we end our lives. Once or twice, after he has wracked his brain, trying to make sense of life, he has gone into his "blue period," when he fairly shouts, "I hated life!" (Ecclesiastes 2:17). But even then he goes on living, thinking, struggling. Just because we look death squarely in the eye doesn't mean we have to rush toward it or hurry it along. Just because life is like a breath doesn't mean it is not worth breathing. The Hebrew word *hebel* is translated as "vapor," "meaningless," "futile," "useless," "vanity," and refers to the absurd effort of gathering and heaping (2:26) and of trying to understand life. But just because we can't understand life doesn't mean we can't enjoy it—at least some of it. Just because we don't know what tomorrow will bring doesn't mean we should not get some satisfaction out of today.

Wisdom

Take wisdom, for example. No sense in staying up all night worrying about the universe, no sense in thinking that if you read or write ten more books it will all become clear. "When I applied my mind to know wisdom, and to see the business that is done on earth, how one's eyes see sleep neither day nor night, then I saw all the work of God, that no one can find out what is happening under the sun. However much they may toil in seeking, they will not find it out; even though those who are wise claim to know, they cannot find it out" (Ecclesiastes 8:16-17). Certainly there is no point in thinking you can pass all your wisdom on to your children (2:18-19). Who knows whether they will listen, and besides, they will want to find out for themselves. Just as the rivers run to the sea and don't fill it up (1:7), so you can't store up wisdom.

Yet wisdom has value. It is better to be wise than foolish (7:25). The poor wise man, forgotten though he was, did save the city (9:14-15). "Fools talk on and on" (10:14); their laughter is "like the crackling of thorns under a pot" (7:6). Wisdom can make you smile (8:1). "Wisdom helps one to succeed": Sharpen your ax before you cut down a tree (10:10).

But "do not act too wise" or pretend you are very good (7:16). You may destroy yourself. Everybody misses the mark sometimes (7:20). People may delight in bringing you down. Fear God, be a little humble, and don't forget God is in control (7:18). "One bungler" can destroy a lot of good work, can unravel all your so-called wisdom (9:18).

Once you come to grips with the brevity of life, you will be wiser than most. Obey the laws of God (12:1). Listen to the instructions, even though you don't know whether your obedience will pay off. Talk softly and not too much. Be respectful; you will at least avoid noisy, silly chatter (9:17; 10:12-14). Be wise, even though your wisdom will go down to the grave with you (2:16). At least, "the wise have eyes in their head, / but fools walk in darkness" (2:14).

Go to the Temple, but don't make bold vows (5:4). Who knows whether you can keep them. The Teacher would have agreed with the counsel of Jesus: "Let your word be 'Yes, Yes' or 'No, No'" (Matthew 5:37). And again, "When you are praying, do hot heap up empty phrases as the Gentiles do; for they think that they will be heard because of their many words" (6:7). The Teacher thinks God is not impressed by a lot of pretentious piety. The Teacher's God does not need a lot of advice on how to run the world. If Proverbs and Ecclesiastes were a two-volume set, they would be embraced by these bookends: "The fear of the LORD is the beginning of knowledge" (Proverbs 1:7) at the beginning and "Fear God, and keep his commandments" (Ecclesiastes 12:13) at the end. As for wickedness, never does the Teacher recommend it. He would agree wholeheartedly we should resist the enticements of folly. Not all the wicked are punished; not all the righteous are rewarded. But it is still foolish to lie, to cheat, to bribe, to steal, to bear false witness. Who knows the judgments of God? Besides that, what have you gained (2:13; 7:25)?

Work

The Teacher saves his strongest words for the foolishness of trying to get ahead, trying to lay up wealth for the future. He's not opposed to considering "the ant" (Proverbs 6:6). It's better to work than to be idle. But the Teacher scorns its misuse. The word *toil* is used fifty-five times in the Old Testament, twenty-two of these times as a noun in Ecclesiastes. God sent Adam and Eve from the garden (Genesis 3:22-24), leaving them to earn their bread by the sweat of their brow. Tough as that is, humankind makes it worse. Our appetites are never satisfied. The sea keeps receiving more water; our bellies ask for food (Ecclesiastes 1:7; 6:7). Toiling miserably and anxiously day after day to accumulate wealth is useless, futile. Wealth cannot be relied on to endure, he writes; we can't take it with us when we die (5:13-16), and we can't control it after we're gone (2:18-21). Trying to make a name for ourselves is silly, he says. No one remembers us after we're gone (2:16).

But work is necessary—toilsome though it is. Work also can provide some satisfaction. There is "a time to plant, and a time to pluck up what is planted" (3:2), "a time to tear, and a time to sew" (3:7). Work is part of the rhythm of life. If "all toil and all skill in work come from one person's envy of

DISCIPLE

another" (4:4), that indeed is vanity. Competition may drive the economic engine, but it is a "chasing after wind." If we can participate in nature's suitable rhythms, ah, that is the secret of life.

Notice how often the Teacher reminds us "there is nothing better than that all should enjoy their work" (3:22). "This is what I have seen to be good: it is fitting to eat and drink and find enjoyment in all the toil with which one toils under the sun the few days of the life God gives us" (5:18). The Teacher remembers the tired pleasure of washing up after a hard day's work, sitting down to a simple supper with family or friends, laughing a bit. He remembers how good the food tasted because he was hungry. "Go, eat your bread with enjoyment, and drink your wine with a merry heart; for God has long ago approved what you do" (9:7). That's as good as it gets, and that's all there is.

Even a good night's sleep is pleasant. "Sweet is the sleep of laborers, whether they eat little or much; but the surfeit of the rich will not let them sleep" (5:12). The Teacher ridicules princes who feast until the morning hours; better they should eat a simple evening meal, like a laborer, to keep their strength up for noble governing (10:16-17). A glass of wine with a meal is a joy, but drunkenness is folly (9:7). Obviously our Teacher is no hedonist.

"Let your clothes always be freshly washed" (9:8, *Tanakh*). Don't be drab or downcast. Wash your face; comb your hair; put on a little perfume. Why be sad? Seize the day! "Be cheerful" (9:7, TEV). In his admonitions, the Teacher was in harmony with Jesus' teachings that would come later. "Do not worry about tomorrow, for tomorrow will bring worries of its own. Today's trouble is enough for today" (Matthew 6:34).

Prudence

Call it unsolicited counsel if you will, but the Teacher can't help giving some practical advice: Because time and chance come to everyone, because no one knows which way the wind of fortune will blow tomorrow, better diversify your investments. Who knows which will succeed and which will fail (Ecclesiastes 11:2)? When the season comes to plow, then plow; to plant, then plant (3:2). If you wait until the sun and the wind are just right, you'll never plow or plant (11:4).

"Cast your bread upon the waters,
　　for after many days you will find it again" (11:1, NIV).

Some interpreters take this phrase as commercial advice—expand your investments, and one of these days you will make a profit. But other interpreters of Jewish and Christian tradition believe the Teacher is recommending a generous spirit. The Teacher knows he cannot save the world, yet he always encourages us to keep God's commands. No teaching of Torah is more significant than aiding the widow and the orphan. So happy, prudent people do not grasp or clench their fists tightly; but like the capable wife in Proverbs, they open their hand to the poor and reach out to the needy (Proverbs 31:20). The Teacher guards against greed and honors God. Who knows "what disaster may happen" (Ecclesiastes 11:2) and when you will need the generosity of others (10:14)?

Love

Intimacy, friendship, marital love—these draw the Teacher's gentle affirmation. "Two are better than one" (Ecclesiastes 4:9). Friends can work more effectively and enjoyably, even though tomorrow may never come. If one stumbles, the other can offer aid. Two sleeping in the same bed can stay warm. If three friends stand together, they will not likely be overpowered (4:10-12).

What should a married man do with his brief, meaningless life? Not make the bar scene, not fall into sexual escapades, but "enjoy life with the wife whom you love, all the days of your vain life that are given you under the sun" (9:9). Marital love, sexual togetherness is affirmed as one of the temporal blessings. Enjoy your marriage. Make love. The hour is soon coming when "desire fails" (12:5). Let young people enjoy their youth, have their dreams, fall in love, throw themselves into their interests and skills. They aren't going to be young very long. "But know that for all these things God will bring you into judgment" (11:9-10).

Death

Some interpreters consider the Teacher's description of the slow decline of the human body morbid. Does he want us to be preoccupied with death? No. We're to face death, eyes straight ahead, shoulders square—even in our youth. Read Ecclesiastes 12:1-8 aloud: Start strong; go more slowly and softly; end in a whisper. If we live long enough, the day will come when our "grinders" won't chew, our eyes dim, scarcely discerning the stars at night or the sun by day. Our ears will fail to hear birds chirping or music playing. We will fear falling, our hair may turn white, and we will slowly place one foot before the other, perhaps with a walker.

That's why we need to go to some funerals. "It is better to go to the house of mourning /than to go to the house of feasting; /for this is the end of everyone, /and the living will lay it to heart" (7:2). This advice is not meant to be morbid, but to help us evaluate life, think about our few days. Our prayer then becomes, "So teach us to number our days, that we may apply our hearts unto wisdom" (Psalm 90:12, KJV). The young are urged to "Remember your creator in the days of your youth" (Ecclesiastes 12:1), not just to be respectful of God but to get a grasp on the brevity and the preciousness of life.

Aging is not tragedy. Death is not defeat. Growing old is like the sun going down in the west. God's appropriate rhythms are at work. Sunsets, like sunrises, can be glorious.

DISCIPLE

There is "a time to be born, and a time to die" (3:2). "He has made everything suitable [even 'beautiful,' NIV] for its time" (3:11). We can enjoy and celebrate life. Don't try to make sense of it. "God has done this, so that all should stand in awe before him" (3:14). "A generation goes, and a generation comes" (1:4). But the Teacher is convinced that once we have made our peace with death, we can enjoy life!

What Is Good?

Life is God's greatest gift—all life—the good and the bad, the long and the short, the past and the hint of eternity and the seeming finality of the grave. We must not waste time and energy chasing after wind, because to only a few people is given the capacity to enjoy life (Ecclesiastes 5:19). That's it! The good gift of God is the freedom to enjoy the daily gifts, the simple gifts. For many people, life is toil and trouble; but some blessed folk enjoy a sunrise (11:7), find pleasure in a day's work, open their hand to the poor, have a few friends, feel good after a shower, enjoy a meal, love their spouse, and smile when the young people are excited about life. "Even those who live many years should rejoice in them all" (11:8). That's why the end is better than the beginning (7:8). The beginning is possibility; the end is completion. And a successful completion is no small thing. Spending one's life rejoicing is a suitable and beautiful part of the rhythm of life, like the sun rising and going down.

Festival of Sukkoth

Judaism has The Five Scrolls (*Megilloth*), one for each of the major festivals. Why is Ecclesiastes read at Sukkoth, the Feast of Booths? Because Sukkoth celebrates the bleak days in the wilderness when God's providential care was all Israel had. God provided manna and water—enough for each day, nothing left over. And the people were expected to rejoice. The people couldn't get ahead of their neighbors, couldn't hoard, couldn't "heap" (Ecclesiastes 2:26). Just a simple trust, living one day at a time. When the people grumbled, God was unhappy because they were making themselves miserable. Sukkoth reminds us we should rejoice in the day and be grateful we have enough.

The poetry of Ecclesiastes is magnificent. It has inspired authors, poets, preachers, songwriters, and speechmakers across the centuries. Read aloud 1:2-11; 3:1-8, 11; and 12:1-8. Then jot down phrases familiar to you, that you've heard or read.

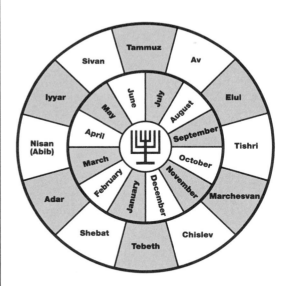

Feasts, or festivals, mark high points in the Jewish calendar. The diagram above shows the Hebrew months and their equivalents in our calendar. The list below identifies each festival and the date it takes place in the Jewish year.

Passover (Pesach) • 14 Nisan (Abib)
Feast of Unleavened Bread 15–21 Nisan (Abib)
Feast of Weeks (Shavuoth) • 6 Sivan
Feast of Booths (Sukkoth) • 15–20 Tishri
Feast of Dedication (Hanukkah) • 25 Chislev
Purim • 14/15 Adar

The natural rhythms of life (1:2-11) can provide a kind of peaceful security, offering a framework in which to enjoy life.

What framework for enjoying life do these verses offer you?

_____

_____

While knowing Jesus Christ and believing in life after death, what advice of the Teacher continues important for you to follow?

_____

What advice, if any, do you reject?

_____

What advice from the Teacher can help you reconsider the ways you spend your time?

_____

_____

MARKS OF FAITHFUL COMMUNITY

We enjoy today. Our work is a service to the Lord and others. It is even an act of praise. We take time to enjoy family and friends. We are grateful to God for daily providence. We thank God just for life.

When was the last time you sat down to a meal with family? invited friends for a meal? Was there laughter?

_____

How do you find joy in living each day?

_____

_____

Where do you find joy in your work? Or what keeps you from finding joy in your work?

_____

_____

Describe how joy and peace from God feel to you.

_____

_____

IF YOU WANT TO KNOW MORE

Look up Matthew 5–7 and list times Jesus echoes the insights of the Teacher.

NOTES, REFLECTIONS, AND QUESTIONS

Being faithful community, we receive life as a gift, live it now, enjoy it, and thank God for it.

CALAMITY

"The LORD said to Satan, 'Have you considered my servant Job? There is no one like him on the earth, a blameless and upright man who fears God and turns away from evil. He still persists in his integrity, although you incited me against him, to destroy him for no reason.'"

—Job 2:3

11 A Just Complaint

OUR HUMAN CONDITION

We want clearly defined rules of cause and effect. If we live a good life, work hard, eat right, exercise, save our money, obey the rules, we surely deserve health and prosperity. We pretend that life as it is meant to be doesn't include anything bad, that life should work so we avoid suffering and pain.

ASSIGNMENT

Job puts tension into wisdom literature. Job's three friends try to defend the narrow tradition that all suffering is caused by sin. Pretend you are standing nearby. Listen in on the argument.

Day 1   Job 1–3 (prologue, attack on Job, Job curses the day of his birth)
Day 2   Job 4–8 (first speech of Eliphaz, Job replies, first speech of Bildad)
Day 3   Job 9–14 (Job replies, first speech of Zophar, Job replies)
Day 4   Job 15–17 (second speech of Eliphaz, Job replies)
Day 5   Job 18–21 (second speech of Bildad, Job replies, second speech of Zophar, Job replies)
Day 6   Read and respond to "Fruit From the Tree of Life" and "Marks of Faithful Community."
Day 7   Rest

PSALM OF THE WEEK

Recognizing that basic injustices do exist, pray Psalm 17 aloud daily for yourself and also on behalf of others. Recall your own experiences of injustice, your sense of things being unfair. Each day think of someone who needs deliverance of some kind, who needs justice. Plead that person's cause as you pray the psalm aloud.

PRAYER

Pray daily before study:
"How much longer will you forget me, LORD? Forever?
How much longer will you hide yourself from me?
How long must I endure trouble?
How long will sorrow fill my heart day and night?
How long will my enemies triumph over me?" (Psalm 13:1-2, TEV).

Prayer concerns for this week:

Day 1   Job 1–3 (prologue, attack on Job, Job curses the day of his birth)

Day 4   Job 15–17 (second speech of Eliphaz, Job replies)

Day 2   Job 4–8 (first speech of Eliphaz, Job replies, first speech of Bildad)

Day 5   Job 18–21 (second speech of Bildad, Job replies, second speech of Zophar, Job replies)

Day 3   Job 9–14 (Job replies, first speech of Zophar, Job replies)

Day 6   "Fruit From the Tree of Life" and "Marks of Faithful Community"

Fig Tree

DISCIPLE

FRUIT FROM THE TREE OF LIFE

Now enter the book of Job. We discover not a patient Job, as praised by Jewish and Christian piety, but a frustrated, questioning, impatient Job who wants answers to ultimate questions of life and death, good and evil, sin and suffering. Patient, no. Persistent, yes.

The style and form of the book add to its complexity. The prose beginning and ending sound so simple, like a lovely story that begins "once upon a time" and ends with "they lived happily ever after." Did our sophisticated author take an ancient story of a righteous man named Job, who suffered and got over it, and thrust a sharp, anguished debate into the middle of it? Is this story an attempt to enlarge upon the meaning of the first commandment to love God only? Or is the mixture of pious tradition and jarring dispute intended to cause us to think, to question deeply, to agonize with one another?

The Story

The story assures us Job was *blameless* and *upright,* a righteous man who *feared God* and *turned away from evil* (Job 1:1), a good man, a man of faith and integrity. This fourfold expression signifies completion. So when Job protests he has obeyed Torah, he tells the truth (23:11-12). God has said so.

The name *Job* is not Hebrew. The land of Uz may be Edom, southeast of Israel. But none of that matters. Job is every nationality, every religion, every race. Job is every person who has suffered tragedy.

Job was wealthy in the ways a man of wisdom should be wealthy, with plenty of sons and daughters to carry on the family name and traditions. Everything was perfect, even the numbers—seven sons, three daughters, ten children. The numbers seven, three, and ten all symbolize completeness, the ideal family. The sheep and camels were in perfect ratio; oxen and donkeys were in balance. Job's family and property were complete. Job has been blessed by God.

The word *Satan* is better translated the *Accuser* or the *Adversary,* meaning the one in God's realm who raises questions, argues with God. The Accuser usually votes no.

The Accuser's task is interesting. He roams the earth looking for upright people who do not expect a reward for being good. But when God brags on Job's integrity, the Accuser, true to his nature, shifts the ground. God asks if the Accuser has considered Job, and the Accuser responds, "Does Job fear God for nothing?" He intends to prove people love God because they think it will pay off. God, the Accuser, and life itself now put Job to the test. Will Job be able to say,

> "Though the fig tree does not blossom,
>   and no fruit is on the vines; . . .
> though the flock is cut off from the fold,
>   and there is no herd in the stalls,
> yet I will rejoice in the LORD" (Habakkuk 3:17-18)?

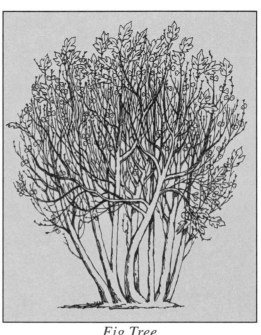

Fig Tree

Is Job perfect on the outside but secretly flawed underneath? The Accuser asks God to "stretch out your hand now, and touch all that he has" (Job 1:11). God does not, but allows the Accuser to do it. God allows the suffering to occur.

Sometimes tragedies happen in bunches—first the animals and servants, then the family. All gone. Job tore his robe in mourning, shaved his head, but was able to say, "The LORD gave, and the LORD has taken away; blessed be the name of the LORD" (1:21).

A second test—sores. From the bottom of his feet to the top of his head. Job went into shock. He sat among the ashes for seven days and seven nights as if numb. His three friends sat with him, silent as a tomb.

Job's Lament

Job cursed not God but the day he was born. He wished his birthday could be stricken from the calendar: "Let the day perish in which I was born" (Job 3:3). He even bemoaned the night of his conception. He asks why daylight (life) is given to people who cannot see "the way,"—the way of goodness the proverbs and psalms talk about (3:23).

Job's lament is like a raging mountain stream after a cloudburst. His friends do well to let him shout. The very thing he feared—calamity—has come to him. Why? The fundamental beliefs upon which Job built his life—faithfulness and obedience to God; practice of righteous ways that brought him health, happiness, family, and prosperity—have now been called into question. The world is no longer a trustworthy place. Job gives suffering a voice. His cry is a demand, born in helplessness, to know what went wrong. In what kind of a world do we live; in what kind of God do we trust?

Eliphaz Speaks

Job's friends, after the silence of love, now want to be of further help. Eliphaz speaks first. He says Job has always given encouragement to others. Can he not now be comforted by those same words? Others have had trouble; "now it has come to you, and you are impatient" (Job 4:5). This friend speaks the religious wisdom that has held the world together for Job and him: "The fear of the LORD is the beginning of wisdom" (Proverbs 9:10). Is that not our "confidence"? Our steadfast "integrity" is our hope (Job 4:6).

But Eliphaz has some private doubts. In Eliphaz's vision no one is "pure"; no one can claim to be completely righteous before God; even the angels aren't perfect (4:18). Eliphaz is trying to make the reward-punishment thing work. Job somehow must have earned his fate. Eliphaz is afraid of Job's words, apprehensive because the ambiguity threatens his philosophy of life. Now, the best thing to do is put trust in God.

Eliphaz gives another religious suggestion, always popular: God is disciplining you, as a loving parent would disci-

Structure of the Book of Job

Prologue	1–2
Debate Between Job and Three Friends (3–27)	
First Cycle	3–14
Job's Lament	3
Eliphaz	4–5
Job	6–7
Bildad	8
Job	9–10
Zophar	11
Job	12–14
Second Cycle	15–21
Eliphaz	15
Job	16–17
Bildad	18
Job	19
Zophar	20
Job	21
Third Cycle	22–27
Eliphaz	22
Job	23–24
Bildad	25
Job	26
Zophar	(none)
Job	27
Poem on Wisdom	28
Job Speaks	29–31
Elihu Speaks	32–37
God Speaks to Job	38–41
Job Responds to God	42:1-6
Epilogue	42:7-17

pline a child. You'll learn from this experience. Job cringes as he thinks of his children and hears the words, "Happy is the one whom God reproves" (5:17). Job hears Eliphaz's words of wisdom as reproof. Job will be forthright to the end; "I will not lie to your face" (6:28). God has laid him low. He wants to know why.

Job ignores his friends and complains directly to God. He pleads, "Let me alone" (7:16) long enough for me to swallow my spit. Job wonders why he has been targeted (7:20). If he has done something wrong, why doesn't God just forgive him and let him be? Or let him die and be beyond God's power.

He twists Psalm 139:8, "If I make my bed in Sheol, you are there." Even if Job dies, God seems to be the kind of God who would search him out and bring him more trouble: "You will seek me, but I shall not be" (Job 7:21). He mocks Psalm 8:4: "What are human beings that you are mindful of them?" Job pleads to God to forget him for a while. He pictures God as his enemy, not his friend. Unlike his friends who speak philosophically, Job speaks out of firsthand experience.

Bildad Speaks

Bildad is bound by tradition even more tightly than Eliphaz. Job has said, "teach me," so Bildad launches into a philosophical explanation. "Does God pervert justice?" (Job 8:3). Surely God must be treating Job justly, for God is *just* and *righteous*. "Righteousness and justice are the foundation of his throne" (Psalm 97:2). Job and his friends are trapped in the idea that sin causes suffering.

Bildad touches a tender spot. Job's children must have sinned, and Job is suffering because of their sins. Israel struggled across the centuries with the idea that a person could suffer because of the sins of others. But both Ezekiel (18) and Jeremiah (31:29-30) insist people must bear responsibility for their own actions. Yet the consequences of one person's sins often do fall on another. Bildad focuses on the sins of the children. He doesn't know the sins; he simply reasons back from the consequences. If God is just and righteous, someone is to blame.

Bildad knows the wicked forget God and wither like papyrus without water. But there is hope for Job. Not my ideas, says Bildad, for we "know nothing." But the wisdom of "bygone generations" teaches us recovery is possible. Bildad says Job must repent, then approach God in true faith and humility and become morally pure and upright. God will then restore Job's blessings.

Job wants to argue, not with his friends but with God. But how can a person argue with God? Job uses praise language to complain. God "moves mountains," "shakes the earth," "stretches out the heavens" (Job 9:5-8, NIV). "How then can I dispute with him?" (9:14, NIV). If the struggle is a matter of strength, Job has no chance. He is overmatched.

Then a tiny thought emerges in Job's mind—a ridiculous thought, an unthinkable thought. What if I faced God in a trial, where both of us were on trial? But who would issue the summons (9:19)? No way exists, "that we should come to trial together. / There is no umpire between us" (9:32-33).

Legal metaphors abound in Scripture, but God is usually the judge.

"The LORD rises to argue his case;
    he stands to judge the peoples" (Isaiah 3:13).
Occasionally God will act as an attorney, arguing for the people against their enemies: "The LORD of hosts is his name. He will surely plead their cause" (Jeremiah 50:34). But Job has the audacity to suggest putting God on trial!

Of course, the trial will be perilous, fraught with danger. Job likely will be crushed by such an opponent. But Job's greater fear is that God will twist him, make him say things he doesn't mean, cause him to lie on the witness stand. The worst thing that could happen would be for Job to lie, to lose his integrity, to have words come out of his mouth that deny his innocence. To lose his integrity would dissolve his very self (Job 9:20-21).

Bildad said, if Job would get his heart right, God would fill Job's mouth with laughter (8:21). Job reverses the expression and claims God is laughing at him instead (9:23, TEV). The very One who crafted him, as a potter would craft a vessel (Jeremiah 18:6), is the one who breaks him (Job 10:8-9).

Job's ability to imagine a trial gives him new strength. His backbone stiffens; his self-confidence increases. No longer does he curse his birthday or desire to die. Now, as he imagines a confrontation, he pleads,

"Let me alone, that I may find a little comfort
    before I go, never to return,
        to the land of gloom and deep darkness" (10:20-21).

Zophar Speaks

Job's third friend, Zophar, doesn't mince words. He listens to Job's brilliant speeches and accuses Job of many foolish words. From his perspective, Zophar sees Job's challenge to God as blasphemous, as treating God with contempt (Job 11:3). Zophar, too, wishes God would speak, but speak to reprimand Job's disrespect.

Zophar bluntly names Job as the villain. God's superior wisdom discerns sins Job cannot see. In Zophar's eyes, Job's bitter complaints against religious tradition only add to his sin. Zophar believes Job must get right with God. He thinks God already has tempered punishment with mercy: "Know then that God exacts of you less than your guilt deserves" (11:6). God knows every sin. If Job is to set his heart right, he must put iniquity away and reorder his life, and thereby be able to lift his face to God (11:13-15). Then his past trauma no longer would have power over him.

DISCIPLE

What is wrong with pious platitudes? Job says they taste like ashes in the mouth. Job now calls his friends "worthless physicians." Their words have not brought healing.

> "I desire to speak to the Almighty
>   and to argue my case with God" (13:3, NIV).

When Job asks rhetorically, "If mortals die, will they live again?" (14:14), the implied answer is no. Therefore Job needs God to act quickly (13:22). A tree can be chopped down and will sprout again; but when people die, they will not awake to gain justice (14:7-12).

Second Cycle of Speeches

The second cycle of speeches begins with Job 15. The tension heightens with accusations of "useless words," "speeches that have no value" (15:3, NIV). Eliphaz believes Job's sin comes now from his mouth (15:5-6). Eliphaz claims tradition (gray hair) is on his side. How can anyone claim to be righteous? Job proves he is a sinner by his "defiance" (15:25).

Job insists God rushes on him like a warrior, yet Job has done no violence. God has attacked him violently. It isn't fair. A just court of law would make amends.

When Bildad says he and his friends are "counted as cattle," he means Job has dismissed the herd mentality of their pious platitudes. The friends are stuck in the traditional mindset, and Job is breaking out of it. Everyone knows "the lamp of the wicked goes out" (Proverbs 13:9; Job 18:5), but Job knows that proverb doesn't fit him. By refuting tradition, he experiences a new kind of suffering—alienation.

This alienation expresses itself in broken fellowship (Job 19). Now the community isolates him. Relatives distance themselves; friends disappear; the religious community has cut him off. Even his wife leaves him alone. He pleads, "Have pity on me, O you my friends" (19:21), but they turn a deaf ear.

Job is about to die, and he fears his cause will be forgotten. If only someone would write down his complaint on a scroll—no, stronger, with an iron pen and lead; no, more permanent, engraved on a rock forever. The confusing words "in my flesh I shall see God" may mean "in my flesh I must see God" before it is too late (19:26). Somewhere a "Redeemer" or vindicator must exist. But where?

Intuitively Zophar senses that Job's suffering, if innocent, undermines morality as he understands it. When Job attacks the presumption that suffering is a consequence of sin, Zophar feels threatened. But Job will not let up. He enlarges on his own suffering to insist that the wicked often prosper and gain honor (21:7). The old teacher in Ecclesiastes said injustice happens sometimes. Job exaggerates and makes it a standard procedure. Job is not content merely to separate sin from suffering. Now he argues that in his experience, sin itself is not punished. If you don't believe me, ask "those who travel the roads" (21:29). Is Job not right, at least in part?

So Job not only disputes the cause-and-effect relationship between sin and suffering; he undermines the claim of Psalm 1 that the wicked "are like chaff that the wind drives away." What do you think?

_____

_____

Perhaps even more than justice, Job wants God, wants a relationship with God that is honest, open, caring.

MARKS OF FAITHFUL COMMUNITY

Some things nobody can fix. Some questions nobody can answer. Job's friends were most helpful when they sat quietly. They were least helpful when they responded with conventional answers.

Why do you choose to live a righteous life, knowing no one is immune to calamity in life?

_____

_____

What understandings of God and our relationship to God make us secure enough to confront God when tragedy strikes?

_____

_____

Describe an experience when you provided or received the ministry of silent presence.

_____

_____

Being faithful community, we recognize the need to ask why when we experience suffering and injustice, and are assured of God's presence even when answers do not come.

THE RADICAL DISCIPLE

We prefer the cycle of *we believe, God blesses, we give thanks*. But tragedy comes. The radical disciple resists the urge to give pat answers. But more, the radical disciple goes to those who have lost their money, had their house burn down, or lost a family member to death and offers help and love in the name of Jesus. Most of all, the radical disciple practices the ministry of presence.

IF YOU WANT TO KNOW MORE

The term *Satan* appears several times early in Job. Use a Bible dictionary and a Bible concordance to trace the development of the concept of Satan and use of the term in the Old Testament, intertestamental, and New Testament literature.

MYSTERY

"Where were you when I laid the foundation of the earth?
Tell me, if you have understanding.
Who determined its measurements—surely you know!"

—Job 38:4-5

12 On God's Terms

OUR HUMAN CONDITION

We struggle to know how we fit into the scheme of things. We want to know why things happen the way they do. We think if we can learn how life works, we can control the outcome. We are uncomfortable with mystery.

ASSIGNMENT

Review Job 1–21 to track the debate between Job and his friends. Page headings and biblical annotations provide quick information. Read God's two speeches (Job 38–41) carefully, paying attention to the picture language God uses. Look for what satisfies Job in God's speeches. Notice what is involved in Job's restoration.

Day 1 Job 22–24 (third speech of Eliphaz, Job's complaint in reply)
Day 2 Job 25–28 (third speech of Bildad, Job's reply; wisdom found only in God)
Day 3 Job 29–31 (Job's final defense)
Day 4 Job 32–37 (four speeches of Elihu)
Day 5 Job 38–42 (first speech of God, Job's reply, second speech of God, Job's reply, epilogue)
Day 6 Read and respond to "Fruit From the Tree of Life" and "Marks of Faithful Community."
Day 7 Rest

PSALM OF THE WEEK

We are trying to live in the psalms. Pray Psalm 102 aloud daily and reflect on what it means to live in a psalm, parts of which may not connect with your experience at the moment. Be aware of whether the words strike you differently each day.

PRAYER

Pray daily before study:
"Your righteousness, God, reaches the skies.
You have done great things;
there is no one like you.
You have sent troubles and suffering on me,
but you will restore my strength" (Psalm 71:19-20, TEV).

Prayer concerns for this week:

Day 1   Job 22–24 (third speech of Eliphaz, Job's complaint in reply)

Day 4   Job 32–37 (four speeches of Elihu)

Day 2   Job 25–28 (third speech of Bildad, Job's reply; wisdom found only in God)

Day 5   Job 38–42 (first speech of God, Job's reply, second speech of God, Job's reply, epilogue)

Day 3   Job 29–31 (Job's final defense)

Day 6   "Fruit From the Tree of Life" and "Marks of Faithful Community"

Stylized Tree of Life

DISCIPLE

FRUIT FROM THE TREE OF LIFE

Until the third cycle of speeches, no one has accused Job directly of having a wicked heart. His children must have sinned, or Job has committed secret sins known only to God, or he has been too loud or too mocking, or he must have sinned inadvertently. These thoughts have passed through the lips of Job's friends. None specifically called him wicked.

But Eliphaz is so surprised by Job's devastating attack on the justice of retribution that Eliphaz declares Job an outright sinner. Believing God uses suffering as punishment for sin and God does not punish piety, Eliphaz insists Job is a wicked person. Wickedness would entail foreclosing on a family, stripping the poor, refusing water to the thirsty, seizing land, exploiting widows and orphans. Eliphaz says Job must have done all these things.

Job's only hope, declares his friend, is repentance. Receive religious instruction, return to God, remove all iniquity, search for wisdom instead of gold, pray, and fulfill vows. Then he will escape destruction. Eliphaz believes repentance of a sinner can remove apparent contradictions and resolve the problem of Job.

Job Wants to Make His Case to God

Job is more than willing to go to God. "Oh, that I knew where I might find him" (Job 23:3). But Job will not go hat in hand. "I would lay my case before him" (23:4). Job's mouth would be full of arguments. Job even suspects God would acquit him if God would ever let his case get on the docket (23:7). But where is God?

"If I go forward, he is not there;
    or backward, I cannot perceive him" (23:8).

Job insists he has "kept his way." As the wisdom writers pleaded, Job has put one foot in front of the other in the Lord's way. Even more, "I have treasured in my bosom the words of his mouth" (23:12).

Once again he protests that the wicked prosper. They remove the stones that mark boundaries, steal sheep, take a widow's only ox as pledge so she cannot farm, push poor people off the road. Powerful people design business procedures, tax structures, and land policies that oppress the poor. When sick people cry out for medical attention, when children beg for food, the wicked ignore them and God does not hear their prayer (24:12). Job ends this speech seeming to plead with God to bring down the wicked. Surely their prosperity must not go on. Looking at all the evil and suffering in the world, Job brings a powerful indictment against God's justice.

God knows Job is righteous. Job knows he is innocent. Everyone else, except Satan, the Accuser, who is not yet sure, is convinced Job is a fool, a blasphemer, a wicked man. Job insists, "until I die . . . I hold fast my righteousness" (27:5-6).

Job 28 jars us. The poem seems like an intrusion from the book of Proverbs, as if someone were trying to tone down Job's radical remarks. Yet the poem, "Where shall wisdom be found?" heightens the sense of mystery; it makes murky both the piety of the friends and the rebel cry of Job. Questions have been raised that have no answers!

"The fear of the LORD" may be "the beginning of wisdom" (Proverbs 9:10), but "mortals do not know the way to it" (Job 28:13). We can't buy it. It is hidden from all living things. Even death doesn't understand. Only God knows the way to the place of wisdom.

In Job 28 we have been given a short rest on the rocky road of spiritual struggle. Some mysteries no one but God can understand. The poem does not attempt to explain anything. It leads us into faith where we cannot see or know but only trust. Read Job 28 aloud and be grateful.

Job's Final Defense

Job's climactic speeches in Job 29–31 show strength and vitality. Gone now are the expressions of rage, the clamoring "why," the longing for death.

Now Job is strong enough to remember the good times "when I was in my prime," when his children were around him, when people stood up as he walked into a room, "when the friendship of God was upon my tent" (29:4).

In candor, without boasting, Job recalls those times when he fed the hungry, helped the poor, "caused the widow's heart to sing for joy" (29:13). He had stood up against evil. People listened to him. He gave them solid advice. He gave comfort to mourners. And Job received the people's respect. His sense of worth came from his family, his aid to the marginalized, his influence in the community.

In Job's lament (30–31) we observe a prominent man, now a part of the marginalized, once a rich man, now made poor. Against his sensibilities, he is now one of the wretched. Earlier he gave them alms, tried to help their children. Now he is one with the people who have no power, no prestige. No one asks his advice. People he looked down on in the past now taunt him and make fun of him.

Job's body hurts much of the time. He used to be so healthy, took long strides. He has learned not everyone helps the needy. Many turn away from them—and from him. Job has found it is easier to be wealthy and help the poor than it is to be poor, easier to be healthy and help the sick than to be sick, easier to have family and friends and speak to the lonely than to be lonely. Job has joined the human race.

God Speaks

God spoke out of the whirlwind. Job wanted a direct confrontation, a trial. He got God's answer, straightforward, but on God's terms. God is now asking the questions. "Who is

DISCIPLE

this" who talks about the universe when he doesn't know the first thing about it? Stand up straight; tuck in your shirt. God is going to ask Job questions that will take his mind where it has never gone before.

"Where were you when I laid the foundation
of the earth?
Tell me, if you have understanding" (Job 38:4).

Job and his friends had alluded to God's creation, but God dramatically enlarges the scene. When I built the universe, says God, the way Solomon built the Temple—footings, foundation, cornerstone—where were you? Why did I build the universe that way? Surely you know. And when all "the morning stars sang together," the way the Levites sang psalms in the Temple, where were you? Who orchestrated the music (38:7)? Surely you know. When I birthed the sea, opening the womb of creation, and wrapped it in swaddling clothes like a newborn baby, and put up barriers for the sea, as a parent would protect a toddler, where were you?

God probes the mysteries. Who gives orders for the sun to come up every morning? Who shakes out the wicked of society as a housekeeper daily shakes the bedbugs from a blanket (38:13)? Do you know why the hot desert winds come scorching out of the east? Do you know why sweet rain falls in the wastelands even though no one lives there (38:26)? Where did the human mind and its capacity to think come from? Creation is continual, fresh every morning.

God points to an orderly universe; but it is a big universe, full of mystery, full of variety, greater than the human mind can comprehend. Job has never seen the architectural plans, but he should not think the universe is out of control. Wisdom, the wisdom who rejoiced with the Almighty when the first words of Creation were spoken (Proverbs 8:22-31), has helped guide the entire constructive process.

After pointing to the seas and the stars, God talks about the animals. God does not speak of sheep or camels but of wild, ferocious, untamed animals such as lions and vultures, mountain goats and deer, the wild ass and the wild ox, the strange ostrich and the war horse. Does Job understand why an ostrich lays its eggs on the ground, why an eagle eats bloody prey? Undefined mystery.

Job and his friends want rain to fall on their cropland. They don't care if rain falls on the wastelands. Job and his friends know the exact number of days their heifers carry their calves, but they don't know or care about the length of gestation for a mountain goat or deer. God has created "wild" in the world—snakes and lizards and eagles and thunderstorms and hurricanes. Why? God doesn't say. Job doesn't know.

Why does God, after picturing the order of Orion, point to the disorder of desolate lands and strange animals? Because there is some randomness in the world, some things that are wild, untamed, unpredictable.

Job and his friends see the wild things, the desolate places as outside God's care. But God has the whole world in his hands. God embraces those dehumanized and marginalized people Job and his friends thought sinners.

Why is the first speech of God not enough? Job has been reduced to silence, his anger tempered. Confronted by the majesty of God's infinite wisdom, Job is silent, not able, as God demands, to speak up. Job still doesn't get it.

God Speaks Again

So God tries again, this time using two strange mythological creatures to illustrate—Behemoth, a gigantic hippopotamus-like creature that, in the minds of ancient peoples, lived on land, and Leviathan, the monstrous crocodile or dragonlike creature people thought lived in the sea. Both are so powerful no person, army, government, or society can subdue them. They represent the aspects of life that don't fit the pattern. They represent chaos; the element of danger; the possibility of accident, natural disaster, disease—on land and sea.

In some religions such symbols of chaos are God's eternal enemies. But in the book of Job they are part of creation—not enemies but uncontrollable forces. Can Job put a fishhook in Leviathan's mouth? No! No more than he can keep an enemy tribe from stealing his donkeys, lightning from killing his sheep, a whirlwind from destroying his oldest son's home during a family celebration.

Behemoth and Leviathan are not satanic, but they are dangerous. They do not specifically punish sinners, but they do wreak havoc. Why did God create elements of chaos and confusion? God doesn't say.

Face to Face

Job finally catches on. First of all, his plea for the presence of God is fulfilled because God has come to him. Job receives God, not in sinfulness but in vulnerable humanness, the way the wasteland receives rain or a baby ostrich emerges from the egg. Formerly Job had *heard*—hearsay, tradition, Scripture, the teachings of the sages—but now he has *seen*. He has encountered God directly, face to face. God has answered not by removing the mysteries but by being present to Job. Job's painful prayer has been answered: God has come to him.

Yet, God does even more. He commends Job for his persistence, his integrity, his unwillingness to confess sins he hasn't committed, and his refusal to curse God or deny God's reality. Job loved God for God's own Being, not for benefits. Satan, the Accuser, lost his challenge. God challenges Job's desire to understand the mysteries of the universe—the whys of good and evil, suffering and happiness, life and death. But the friends, says God, were wrong about their neat reward-and-punishment rules. Rewards and punishments exist, but so do cancer cells and typhoons. The tightly structured, unbending tradition—that all suffering springs from sin, that all

DISCIPLE

blessings are reward for righteousness—was shaken, torn apart. Job understands chaos is part of God's creation.

Pray for your friends, God says to Job. Job is humbled, not as a sinner converted to faith but as a believer who has joined the human race, known pain, experienced the love of God. Heretofore Job has railed against reality. Now he is ready, like lamenting Israel to come up from the ashes.

> "Let us test and examine our ways,
>   and return to the LORD.
> Let us lift up our hearts as well as our hands
>   to God in heaven" (Lamentations 3:40-41).

Job is ready to eat a meal with friends, ready to establish community again. He has walked through the valley of grief and has emerged whole.

Job was alone. Now his prayer for his friends opens the door to fellowship. God tells Eliphaz, Bildad, and Zophar to bring seven bulls and seven rams and offer a great sacrifice.

We can't go backward in life. We must go forward in faith, together. Notice the way Job's fortunes are restored. What family is left—brothers and sisters and others—come together in family solidarity once known with sons and daughters. Family and friends share the fellowship meal. The harsh words once spoken are forgotten, cleared away by sacred sacrifice, replaced by newfound fellowship. Everybody brings gifts—"a piece of money and a gold ring," enough to put Job and his wife back on their feet again.

Mystery Continues

Most readers are surprised by the happy ending. Just as the beginning prose seemed too perfect, the dialogue too tragic, so the conclusion seems too happy. God promised to restore the fortunes to Israel, but this is unbelievable—seven more sons and three more daughters, twice as many animals as before. And he lived "one hundred and forty years," not only to see his children's children—a wisdom blessing—but to see four generations.

What is happening here? Is the gloriously happy ending merely the back bookend, the conclusion of an ancient prose story into which the agonizing poetry of Job and his friends has been injected? Did we struggle with the mighty mysteries of evil, sin, and chaos for a while, and now can relax until the next crisis? Or does the ending, with its extravagant claims, provide hope for those of us immersed in tragedy, assuring us God will bring us out of the abyss the way God promised in the Psalms?

Or does the exaggerated ending cause us to be dissatisfied, bewildered, full of questions? Do we stop and say, Wait a minute—a daughter or son lost to a random act of violence isn't replaced? Whole villages shattered by storm or ravaged by war may never recover. Some tragedies end in triumph, but many do not.

Is it possible the writer uses the prose/poetry shift, the unsatisfying, illogical finish to set our minds in motion? Does the story cause us to continue the human struggle to make sense of life's mysteries?

MARKS OF FAITHFUL COMMUNITY

Life is beyond our control. So is God. Coming into the presence of God was all that mattered to Job. He was content to live with mystery. And to trust the God who created him.

How does the book of Job conflict with the book of Proverbs?

_____

_____

When the cause-and-effect world of Job and his friends collapsed, what did Job learn? What did the friends learn?

_____

_____

What are some examples of randomness or chaos in the universe? When we acknowledge the fact of randomness, what difference does that make in how we live our lives? in our understanding of God and of God's relationship to the world?

_____

_____

_____

What assumptions about life and about God cause us to persist in asking the question why?

_____

_____

THE RADICAL DISCIPLE

The radical disciple accepts life for what it is—a mixture of order *and* chaos, joy *and* despair, good *and* bad, reason *and* mystery—and lives trusting in God's purpose.

IF YOU WANT TO KNOW MORE

To pursue the questions in Job, you might enjoy reading Rabbi Harold S. Kushner's book *When Bad Things Happen to Good People* (Schocken Books, 1989).

NOTES, REFLECTIONS, AND QUESTIONS

Being faithful community, we approach God with a sense of awe, accepting God's sovereignty, acknowledging life's mystery, and rejoicing in our place in God's creation.

BELOVED

"Set me as a seal upon your heart, / as a seal upon your arm;
for love is strong as death, / passion fierce as the grave.
Its flashes are flashes of fire, / a raging flame.
Many waters cannot quench love, / neither can floods drown it.
If one offered for love / all the wealth of one's house,
it would be utterly scorned."

—Song of Solomon 8:6-7

13 Affairs of the Heart

OUR HUMAN CONDITION

We underestimate the need and desire for intimacy. We think of love as a feeling that just comes and goes. We romanticize love and treat sex as an all-consuming end in itself.

ASSIGNMENT

Feel the poetry. Laugh at the goats on the hill. Come to the garden. Let the perfume intoxicate your senses. Hum your favorite love songs. Allow your heart to throb with young love.

Day 1   Song of Solomon 1–2 (love songs of the woman and the man)
Day 2   Song of Solomon 3–4 (woman dreams of searching for her lover, wedding procession, man praises her beauty); Genesis 2:4-25 (creation of man and woman)
Day 3   Song of Solomon 5–6 (dream of love, a search, the woman's beauty); Proverbs 2–3 (search for wisdom, trust and honor God)
Day 4   Song of Solomon 7 (delight and desire); Proverbs 4–5 (wisdom's way, faithfulness in marriage)
Day 5   Song of Solomon 8 (lovers' vows, promise of fidelity); Ecclesiastes 9; 11 (enjoy your wife, rejoice while young)
Day 6   Read and respond to "Fruit From the Tree of Life" and "Marks of Faithful Community."
Day 7   Rest

PSALM OF THE WEEK

As you pray Psalm 84 aloud daily, reflect on the similarities in the feelings of joy and anticipation associated with being in the presence of God and being in the presence of the lover. Consider ways love grows—the more it is expressed to God, the more it is expressed to the lover.

PRAYER

Pray daily before study:
    "As I lie in bed, I remember you;
        all night long I think of you,
        because you have always been my help.
    In the shadow of your wings I sing for joy.
    I cling to you,
        and your hand keeps me safe" (Psalm 63:6-8, TEV).

Prayer concerns for this week:

BELOVED

Day 1 Song of Solomon 1–2 (love songs of the woman and the man)

Day 4 Song of Solomon 7 (delight and desire); Proverbs 4–5 (wisdom's way, faithfulness in marriage)

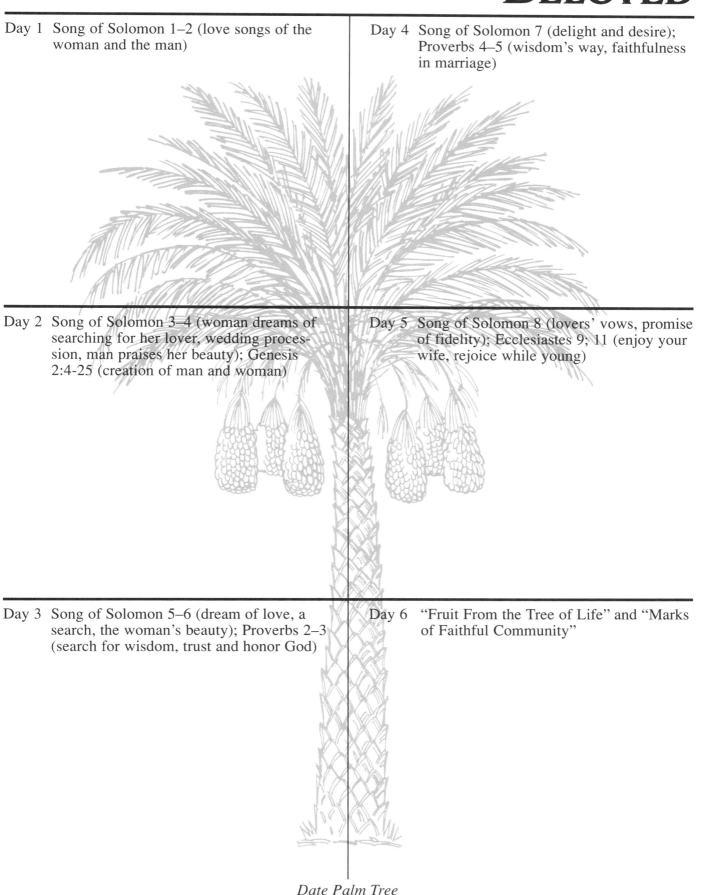

Day 2 Song of Solomon 3–4 (woman dreams of searching for her lover, wedding procession, man praises her beauty); Genesis 2:4-25 (creation of man and woman)

Day 5 Song of Solomon 8 (lovers' vows, promise of fidelity); Ecclesiastes 9; 11 (enjoy your wife, rejoice while young)

Day 3 Song of Solomon 5–6 (dream of love, a search, the woman's beauty); Proverbs 2–3 (search for wisdom, trust and honor God)

Day 6 "Fruit From the Tree of Life" and "Marks of Faithful Community"

Date Palm Tree

DISCIPLE

FRUIT FROM THE TREE OF LIFE

The Song of Solomon or Song of Songs barely made it into the Bible. No commandments, no covenant, no Moses, no Temple. No mention of God. The short book pulsates with love songs, love lyrics so earthy, so erotic as to make a prudish Pharisee or a puritanical Christian blush. The passionate poems throb with so much sensuality some religious leaders tried to keep the book out of the canon. Yet Rabbi Akiva, one of the most revered of the rabbis, at a critical moment in history called it a holy book, even the "holiest of the holy." Why?

Jewish teachers often allegorize the book to depict the passionate love of God for Israel. Early church leaders and Christian scholars and preachers have done the same, picturing Jesus Christ as the bridegroom, the church as the bride. Bernard of Clairvaux, monk and mystic, preached eighty-eight sermons from the first two chapters alone of Song of Songs—all on the love of God.

The book is one of the "Five Scrolls" of Judaism. Song of Songs is read at Passover, the spring festival when the early flowers follow the rains, when the turtledoves migrate through Israel, when the people remember the passionate God who rescued them from slavery.

"For now the winter is past. . . .
The flowers appear on the earth;
    the time of singing has come,
and the voice of the turtledove
    is heard in our land" (Song of Solomon 2:11-12).

The Song in Creation

Yet long before the allegories were inspired, a love deep within the poems themselves glorified the God of creation. These songs touch the elemental forces of creation. They lead us by the hand into the garden of Eden where Adam and Eve loved each other in innocent ecstasy. They revisit innocence. God said, "Let the earth put forth vegetation: plants yielding seed, and fruit trees of every kind" (Genesis 1:11). Our lovers are surrounded by the fragrance of apple trees in blossom (Song of Solomon 2:3), fig trees forming their first figs (2:13), grapevines blooming in the vineyard (2:13). Animals and birds of every description inhabit the garden of delight. Poetic gazelles leap over the hills (2:9); fawns feed among the lilies (4:5); the mare (1:9), the turtledove (2:12), even the lions and leopards (4:8) dwell in this idyllic garden. "God created . . . every living creature that moves . . . and every winged bird of every kind. And God saw that it was good" (Genesis 1:21). No tree of knowledge distracts the lovers; no serpent beguiles them; no shame hides them. As Adam found Eve to be "bone of my bones and flesh of my flesh" (2:23), so our lovers are mutual companions, lovers standing on equal footing.

"A river flows out of Eden to water the garden" (2:10). Our sun-tanned girl and her shepherd lad are invited to "drink: / drink deeply, O lovers!" (Song of Solomon 5:1, RSV).

She will be his garden. She is a walled-in garden now (4:12), but her heart says,

"Let my beloved come to his garden,
    and eat its choicest fruits" (4:16).

If God is love, if God created human beings able to love, if God created sexual beings able to touch and kiss and make love, then Song of Songs is a holy book.

Attributed to Solomon

Three books are attributed to Solomon—Ecclesiastes, Proverbs, and Song of Songs. How might they be seen together? The rabbis explain: Old folks speak of the vanity of things; the middle-aged utter practical proverbs; the young sing of love. But love is not limited to the young. Love is a father's teaching (Proverbs 4:1-4), the safety of a mother's chamber (Song of Solomon 3:4); love is the protective concern of older brothers (8:8); love is a couple's commitment stronger than the grave (8:6).

The tribute to Solomon, however, is honorary. Song of Songs is the only book of the Bible that speaks primarily from a woman's point of view—perhaps even written by a woman. Fifty-six of the verses are hers; and they share a mixture of longing and fear, ecstasy and disappointment, intimacy and loneliness. If Ecclesiastes speaks to our mind, Song of Songs speaks to our heart. Millions of love songs have been written, but this book is considered the superlative, the "song of songs." Solomon's name comes into the poems repeatedly. Perhaps his name helped get the book into the Bible. His name is linked with love of women; it is also linked with the magnificent Temple where Israel came to express love to God through worship and to receive assurance of God's love for Israel. But mostly, the bride-to-be sees herself as queen, as princess, and her shepherd lover as king. References to King Solomon help us know we are surrounded by feelings as precious as royal purple.

A Collection of Love Poems

The book is not a continuous flow, with a logical, advancing story line. The poems are a kaleidoscope of images and colors, a flower basket of pleasant smells, sweet sounds of birds, tastes of juicy sun-ripened fruit, the touch of gentle breezes and soft caresses—erotic images designed to make the heart beat faster. Its unity comes from repeated words, reenacted scenes, and the delicate moods of love and devotion.

The book is not easy to translate. Some words are found nowhere else in the Old Testament. Words are given new meanings, fresh twists. Some phrases are obscure, some allusions far-fetched. The romantic poetry often has double

DISCIPLE

meanings, deliberately teasing, hinting, coyly winking at us, like a woman's eyes behind a veil. If you read a dozen translations, for some texts you will enjoy a dozen pictures.

The book uses a maze of mixed subjects—*I, you, he, we*—partly because the songs rush along, stepping on one another's heels. One person speaks, then another. Sometimes the maiden whispers about her lover, then to her lover, even if he is absent. Or she calls him by a love name. We are reading poetry, uncertain whether we are listening to an experience shared, a dream recalled, or a fantasy explored.

Girl Becoming Woman

She is an adolescent—yesterday a girl, today a woman. Apparently she has no father; so her older brothers guide her, protect her, make her work alongside them. They think she is too young for romance. She is not developed enough, in their eyes, for home and family. Probably they plan to arrange a "suitable" marriage later with a wealthy man. No doubt they are saving silver for her dowry. They worry she is boy crazy; they fear she will run off with some neighbor lad. They have walled her in, awaiting their definition of her maturity. These big brothers do not want some stranger stealing her virginity, "entering her door" (Song of Solomon 8:9). But she knows who she is. She is bursting with vitality, ready to love, hungry to find intimacy and affection, eager to marry.

She is no city girl, protected from sweat and sun, no aristocrat's daughter sipping cold drinks beside a pool. Her skin is dark, black as burnt toast from working in the sun. With her brothers, from sunup to sundown, she works hard in the vineyard, digging around the roots, pruning the branches, gathering the heavy bunches of grapes. But her mind is on the shepherd boy across the way. She dreams of kissing him in some shaded glen, not toiling day in, day out. She has cared for the vineyards, but she worries, "I had no time to care for myself" (1:6, TEV).

She believes she is beautiful, yet she has self-doubts. Am I pretty enough? Are my girlfriends looking down on me (1:6)? She yearns for reassurance, especially from her lover. She fishes for compliments, suggesting that she is only a field flower among the thousands of spring blooms in the Sharon valley (2:1). She thrills with his exuberant response: She is like a lily amid a hillside of thorns (2:2).

We can hear them tease each other, this couple in love. The rhythms of courtship contain yes and no, here and gone, today or maybe tomorrow. She is playful: "If I had known where you were, I would have come to you and we could have been together, lying in the grass while the sheep rested." He teases back, "Why, you could just have followed the tracks of the sheep and you would have found me."

She cannot sleep at night, thinking about him, imagining his touch. Was that a sound at the window? Did he reach in

A simple shepherd's pipe was made of a single reed or of two reeds tied together.

through the latch? Though she can hardly breathe, she still can act shy. "I'll get my feet dirty walking across the floor," she giggles. "All I have on is my nightgown." But then silence. He's gone—if he was ever there. Did she dress, go out into the city streets at night, suffer the abuse of sentinels, searching for him? Or did she fantasize such a quest, frightened she had lost him even in her dreams? Night after night she can't get him out of her mind (5:2-8).

Oh, if only her lover were her brother, then she could hug him on the street, kiss him on the cheek, and no one would notice. She could even bring him into her mother's home, and no one would say anything (8:1-2). Though she is not free, she is bold within herself. Her sexuality, her charm, her beauty, her independence, though not yet cultivated, are ready to be expressed. She wants to break out, but it's scary. She hardly can go out like one who wanders in the night. If only she could set aside social conventions. Yet she knows love cannot be expressed until the appropriate time.

Our young maiden dreams of her wedding day. The chorus of girls, the daughters of Jerusalem (3:10), seems like a bridal party; and the marching soldiers could be attendants for the groom (3:7). The groom will be like Solomon riding in a chariot; she, like a princess, beside him. We can imagine they want the whole world to shout Psalm 45 for them:

"The princess is decked in her chamber with gold-woven robes;
in many-colored robes she is led to the king;
behind her the virgins, her companions, follow.
With joy and gladness they are led along
as they enter the palace of the king" (Psalm 45:13-15).

Yet their love is more precious than a king's court. Her lover would not trade her for all of Solomon's wives (Song of Solomon 6:8-9; 8:11–12).

Beauty's Function

In the ancient Hebrew mind, beauty was functional, not descriptive. His face was radiant and "ruddy"—healthy, robust—the same word used to describe young David when he was introduced to Samuel (1 Samuel 16:12). His legs were "alabaster columns" (Song of Solomon 5:15)—strong, muscular, straight. Our young man stands out in a crowd of young men, like an apple tree in full bloom amid a grove of ordinary trees (2:3). Her tresses tumble across her shoulders like a herd of coal-black goats moseying down Mount Gilead (4:1). Her teeth are perfectly matched, not crooked or irregular, but side by side like twin lambs, white as newly-shorn sheep. Her eyes, often the point of greatest beauty, were not descriptively dove gray, but gentle, cooing "tu-tu-tu" like mated turtledoves. They are lovebird eyes: "You have ravished my heart with a glance" (4:9). Her breasts are alive, like two gently moving fawns. She is as beautiful as a city set on a hill, a safe walled

DISCIPLE

city like Tirzah, the early capital of the Northern Kingdom, or like Jerusalem, city of David.

Was there a dance called "a dance before two armies"? Did she dance draped in gossamer veils (6:13)? We can understand the fertility image of wheat at her waist, but what about a nose "like a tower of Lebanon," a head "like Carmel"? He must mean self-confidence, strength, assurance—even majestic boldness. "My sister," "my bride," "brother," "my beloved," "my friend"—these are terms of endearment, meaning sweetheart or dearest one, not to be taken literally.

Equal in Love

Why are we so shocked at the romantic, erotic imagery? In daily life we see material many times more explicit on magazine racks or on television screens. Are we surprised that our biblical lover would want to climb the palm tree of her body and take hold of "its clusters," her breasts? Is it merely modesty, or have we allowed the pornography and obscenity of the world to drive us away from the innocence of creation, the beauty of romantic love, the sheer joy of falling in love?

Much sexuality, in the Bible and in life, involves power—manipulation, rape, political marriages, family prestige. Often the male has power over the female. But our lovers in Song of Songs seem unusually equal, unbridled by issues of power, willingly and equally sharing their love. Solomon rented out his vineyards, but she freely gives the one vineyard that is hers.

The repeated refrain "do not stir up or awaken love until it is ready" (Song of Solomon 2:7; 3:5; 8:4) seems to point to the "suitable time" in Ecclesiastes: "For everything there is . . . a time"—that time when will locks in with will. Then they will sleep under the same apple tree where his mother conceived him, the same bedroom where her parents made love. Marriage is no barrier to love, but the vehicle for its full expression. They have dreamed of being alone together to explore each other's souls and bodies. A love "like blazing fire, / like a mighty flame" (8:6, NIV) is God's gift to them, a part of God's mysterious creation. They pledge their lives to each other:

> "Set me as a seal upon your heart,
> as a seal upon your arm" (8:6).

But our young lovers have more than romance. They sense a growing, deepening love that surpasses passion. Their love, like the love of God, has an eternal quality. It will last at least as long as life itself,

> "for love is strong as death,
> passion fierce as the grave. . . .
> Many waters cannot quench love,
> neither can floods drown it" (8:6-7).

No wonder our Jewish and Christian predecessors saw in these poems the mighty love of God, a love that never will let us go.

If these love poems lead us to the God who loves us passionately, let it be so. The prophet Hosea, thinking of his own wife, let God cry out to Israel, "I will take you for my wife forever; I will take you for my wife in righteousness and in justice, in steadfast love, and in mercy. I will take you for my wife in faithfulness" (Hosea 2:19-20). God loves us even more than our young lovers adore each other.

MARKS OF FAITHFUL COMMUNITY

Love, like a flower, buds and blossoms at the appropriate time. But we know there is more. Intimacy. Intimacy—with the lover and with God—offers the possibility not only to love and to be loved but to know and to be known. The disciplines of character and commitment are designed by God to magnify, not minimize, the joys of sexual love. We can love with all our heart.

What can we do to reclaim the innocence and mystery of young love in a culture that values sex as a commodity?

Being faithful community, we express and respond to the need and desire for intimacy by imitating God's lavish self-giving to us.

How can the church affirm healthy love relationships without buying into society's notions of love and sexuality?

What causes people to be hesitant or fearful of intimacy, whether with God or with another person?

THE RADICAL DISCIPLE

Risking vulnerability in loving and being loved, in knowing and being known, the radical disciple practices lavish self-giving and joyfully receives the self-giving of another. How are you doing?

IF YOU WANT TO KNOW MORE

To add meaning to the many geographical images in Song of Songs, locate each place name using the maps in your Bible. Then read about each location in a Bible dictionary.

Hymnbook

"Praise the Lord!
How good it is to sing praises to our God;
for he is gracious, and a song of praise is fitting."

—Psalm 147:1

14 Songs of Faith

OUR HUMAN CONDITION

Pain, anger, sorrow, disappointment, loneliness—even joy, delight, and love—go unspoken, unexpressed. Wholeness and integrity are strangers. Where is release?

ASSIGNMENT

This week read the study manual before reading Scripture in order to be alert to both content and structure of the psalms. Power in Psalms lies in the words and in the ways the words are put together. Notice the different kinds of psalms. Try to match your mood to the psalms—victory, defeat, joy, sorrow, praise.

Day 1   Read "Fruit From the Tree of Life."
Day 2   *Book I*—Psalms 1 (wisdom psalm); 2 (royal psalm); 22 (individual lament); 23 (song of trust)
Day 3   *Book II*—Psalms 42–43 (lament, deliverance and restoration); 46 (song of Zion); 51 (penitential psalm); 57 (lament, deliverance from enemies)
Day 4   *Book III*—Psalms 74 (community lament); 78 (historical psalm); 81 (festival liturgy); 88 (individual lament)
Day 5   *Book IV*—Psalms 90 (community lament); 93 (God as king, enthronement); 95 (God as king, liturgy of praise); 105 (history of God's deeds)
Day 6   *Book V*—Psalms 112 (wisdom psalm); 113 (hallelujah psalm); 119 (meditation on Torah); 130 (deliverance, individual lament); 150 (hymn of praise, doxology). Read and respond to "Marks of Faithful Community."
Day 7   Rest

THE RADICAL DISCIPLE

The radical disciple dares to own all the psalms, including the unfamiliar and those deliberately avoided. Memorize a psalm or a portion of a psalm that expresses emotions you consider negative so that when you need those words you have them.

PSALM OF THE WEEK

Pray Psalm 103 aloud daily. As you pray, picture others in your group who also are praying it. Pause to reflect as verses and sections remind you of situations in your own life or in the life of your faith community.

PRAYER

Pray daily before study:
"I have complete confidence, O God;
    I will sing and praise you!
Wake up, my soul!
    Wake up, my harp and lyre!
    I will wake up the sun" (Psalm 57:7-8, TEV).

Prayer concerns for this week:

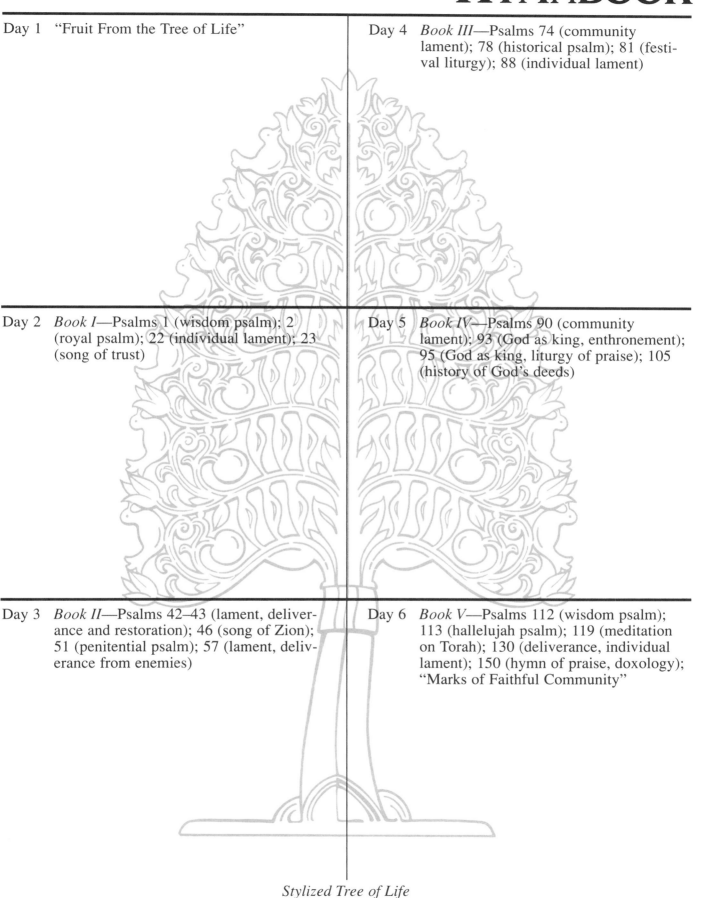

Day 1   "Fruit From the Tree of Life"

Day 2   *Book I*—Psalms 1 (wisdom psalm); 2 (royal psalm); 22 (individual lament); 23 (song of trust)

Day 3   *Book II*—Psalms 42–43 (lament, deliverance and restoration); 46 (song of Zion); 51 (penitential psalm); 57 (lament, deliverance from enemies)

Day 4   *Book III*—Psalms 74 (community lament); 78 (historical psalm); 81 (festival liturgy); 88 (individual lament)

Day 5   *Book IV*—Psalms 90 (community lament); 93 (God as king, enthronement); 95 (God as king, liturgy of praise); 105 (history of God's deeds)

Day 6   *Book V*—Psalms 112 (wisdom psalm); 113 (hallelujah psalm); 119 (meditation on Torah); 130 (deliverance, individual lament); 150 (hymn of praise, doxology); "Marks of Faithful Community"

Stylized Tree of Life

DISCIPLE

FRUIT FROM THE TREE OF LIFE

Tradition attributes many of the Psalms to David. As a boy he was a shepherd musician, singing songs and playing the harp. He calmed the anxious heart of King Saul with the soothing sounds of his music. When he danced in ecstasy before the ark of the covenant, he may have sung some of his own hymns. Several Psalms reflect his life experiences. Following David's adultery with Bathsheba and his contrived murder of her husband Uriah, he may have prayed,

"Have mercy on me, O God,
    according to your steadfast love; . . .
Wash me thoroughly from my iniquity,
    and cleanse me from my sin" (Psalm 51:1-2).

Over seventy-two psalms are attributed to David, some perhaps out of his creative mind, others written in his honor.

The Psalms, as we have them in our Bibles today, must have been written, shaped, transmitted, and used repeatedly over a period of more than a thousand years. Hints of the songs of Miriam (Exodus 15:21) and Moses (15:1-18) survive in the historical poems (Psalms 78; 106). Ancient Canaanite songs that once praised the baals were converted to praise Almighty God (29). Antique language in Psalm 18 indicates the psalm probably comes from or shortly after the time of David. Songs of David, songs for the coronation of kings, songs for the annual festivals emerged across the years.

Later, after the destruction of Jerusalem, psalms of the Exile appeared.

"By the rivers of Babylon—
    there we sat down and there we wept
    when we remembered Zion. . . .
How could we sing the LORD's song
    in a foreign land?"(137:1-4).

After the return from exile, Israel rebuilt the Temple and wrote new songs. Without a monarchy they prepared *enthronement* psalms, which declared God alone to be their king. They sang *hallelujahs* to celebrate their return.

Psalm Headings or Superscriptions

Flip through the Psalms, glancing at the headings. Besides the many references to David (and sometimes to an activity of David that relates to the message of the psalm), look at other notations. Look for liturgical instructions: *To the leader: with stringed instruments* (Psalm 4); *for the flutes* (5); *a Song at the dedication of the temple* (30); *for the memorial offering* (38); *a Song for the Sabbath Day* (92).

Maskil (52) and *Miktam* (56) seem to be technical musical terms or perhaps types of psalms. The *Sons of Korah* or the *Korahites* were descendants of the levitical songwriters and singers beginning in David's time and after the Exile (42; 44–49). A collection of twelve psalms carries the title *Asaph*, ancestor of a prominent guild of Temple musicians (50;

On this eighth-century B.C. stone wall relief from Turkey, four musicians march and play a small drum, two lyres, and a flute (pipe), instruments often mentioned in the Psalms.

73–83). *Jeduthun* (39), *Heman* (88), and *Ethan* (89) were three of the Levites given charge of the Temple music by David. Traditional tunes have names like *The Deer of the Dawn* (22), *Lilies* (45), and *The Dove on Far-off Terebinths* (56). The so-called *Songs* tend to be praise and thanksgiving psalms (65; 66).

The prayer "Give the king your justice, O God" is attributed to Solomon (72). Psalm 90, written both for worship and instruction, appropriately honors Moses. Some psalms describe their suitable use: *A prayer of one afflicted* (102). The *Songs of Ascents* were especially fitting as chants for the throngs of pilgrims who made their way up the slopes to Jerusalem for the festivals (120–134). The notation *Selah* in the text probably indicates a pause, an instrumental interlude within the singing of the psalm, or perhaps congregational response.

The closing psalms, 146–150, lack superscriptions but are known as doxologies or litanies of praise—hallel—for they begin and end with "Hallelujah!" translated, "Praise the LORD." They were known by heart and were and still are sung at all the annual festivals.

Hymnbook

The book of Psalms became the official hymnbook of the Second Temple, built between 520–515 B.C., following the people's return from exile. The New Testament quotes or alludes to the Psalms more than any other Old Testament book. It contains over one hundred quotations from more than sixty psalms. As with Torah and Prophets, Jesus quoted often from the Psalms. On the cross, he prayed Psalm 22, "My God, my God, why have you forsaken me?" (22:1; Matthew 27:46; Mark 15:34). Peter cited Psalms 16, 132, and 110 at Pentecost. Paul saw suggestions of Christ's messiahship in the Psalms and referred to them over thirty times. John, in Revelation 19, rejoices in the hallels and hallelujahs.

In the early Christian church, psalms were an integral part of worship. Both Jewish and Gentile Christians read psalms as Scripture, recited them as prayers, and sang them as hymns. Across the centuries, monks and mystics have chanted psalms as part of their daily discipline. Christian hymnals are crowded with quotations, allusions, and poetic images from the psalms. Christians of all theological persuasions can pray or sing the psalms. Christians and Jews can say them together as Scripture. Psalms cross all barriers.

The book of Psalms, as it came to be structured, consists of five books or units, drawing on the authoritative symbolism of the five books of Moses (Torah). So Israel has five books of the Law from Moses and five books of Psalms from David. Slight hints of difference in content from book to book may be detected in the changing nature of the superscriptions. Doxologies, like benedictions, tend to close the books: 41:13;

Several groups of praise psalms are called "hallels" because they use the Hebrew verb *hallel* throughout. Combined with *Jah* for the first letter of the name of God, *hallelujah* means "Praise the LORD."

Psalms 113–118 are known as the "Egyptian Hallel" because they praise God for the mighty deeds of the Exodus. These psalms were used at the great festivals of Sukkoth, Passover, Shavuoth, and later Hanukkah. Psalms 113–114 are sung before the Passover meal and 115–118 after the meal. The hymn Jesus and his disciples sang after the Last Supper may have been all or part of Psalms 115–118 if the meal was indeed a Passover meal (Matthew 26:30; Mark 14:26).

Psalm 136 is known as the "Great Hallel." It is sung or recited to begin morning prayers on sabbaths and festivals and during the Passover Seder. Psalms 104–106 and 146–150 are other groups of hallels.

Groupings of Psalms

Book I (Psalm 1–41)
Book II (Psalm 42–72)
Book III (Psalm 73–89)
Book IV (Psalm 90–106)
Book V (Psalm 107–150)

DISCIPLE

72:19; 89:52; 106:48. As in a hymnbook, psalms are grouped by theme or mood; yet each is unique, each message slightly different. Content of each book tends to progress from plea to promise, from lament to praise; but exceptions are obvious.

Psalms 1–89 (Books I, II, and III) seem to have been in place prior to Psalms 90–150 (Books IV and V). David's name is more prevalent in the earlier books, the laments more prominent. Because Books IV and V (Psalms 90–150) enthrone God, not princes, as king of Israel and because these latter books stress praise and thanksgiving and include the songs of ascents, the hallels, the doxologies, they are mostly attributed to the post-exilic period.

Scholars have built systems or categories, into which they placed each psalm. Scholars in antiquity tried to make each psalm fit a life experience of David. Modern scholars have listed psalms according to types—laments, stories of salvation history, songs of thanksgiving, hymns of praise, songs of trust and meditation, psalms that reflect the wisdom of Proverbs or the truth of Torah. But the Psalms are so rich and varied, so complex and diverse they tend to cross over the categories. Each psalm has intrinsic power to stand on its own. More than that, two people can say the same Psalm at the same time and experience a different spiritual insight.

Psalms a Way of Praying

The Psalms are not merely a collection of prayers; they are a way of praying. By singing, chanting, reading the Psalms, we not only pray; we learn how to pray. We are in a school of prayer—learning, growing, but never graduating because each psalm brings new challenges, each reading gives fresh meaning.

We learn there are different ways of praying, different kinds of prayer. These historic hymns aid us in expressing every conceivable emotion—joy, sorrow, awe, fear, loneliness, self-righteousness, guilt, remorse, love, anger, pride, despair, hate, gratitude. Nothing is held back. We experience God's presence and God's absence but never God's rejection. God may seem silent, or God's response may be delayed; but the God of these songs of faith never shuts the door on us. God lets us cry, plead, shout, even scream—lets us feel whatever we feel, say whatever we need to say.

So the Psalms teach us about God, about ourselves, about our relationship with God. They are communal, even when they express isolation or loneliness. They are community hymns, even when spoken in the words of a solitary individual. Standing together as mourners at a graveside, we say, "The LORD is my shepherd, I shall not want"; but we say it in unison and feel the presence of others. We learn who we are; we sense our shared humanity.

We will not truncate the prayers or leave out the angry, rage-ridden passages. Not only will we pray *for* the sick, the guilty, the enraged; we will pray *with* them, for from time to time, that is who we are. God wants honest prayers, not prayers dressed up in their Sunday best. After all,

"Even before a word is on my tongue,
O LORD, you know it completely" (139:4).

We may not be angry right now, but we can help express the feelings of those who are. We may not be confessing our sins today, but we might tomorrow. Today we stand beside and pray with those who will stand beside and pray with us next time.

Hebrew Poetry

We learned a lot about Hebrew poetry in Job, Song of Solomon, and especially Proverbs. We learned not to expect rhyme and meter, although the verses often have cadence. Especially in Proverbs, we noted that *parallelism* distinguishes Hebrew poetry. The two lines say essentially the same thing.

"Praise the LORD, all you nations!
Extol him, all you peoples!" (Psalm 117:1).

Parallelisms drive the point home, causing the words to cling to memory. The Hebrew psalms have been translated into all modern languages. Had they been built on rhyme or meter, the poetic force would have been lost in translation, but their parallelism preserves the poetic beauty and the power in every language. What a wonderful provision!

Sometimes the poet uses *antithetical parallelism*. The second line is a negative expression of the first:

"The LORD watches over the way of the righteous,
but the way of the wicked will perish" (1:6).

A *stair-step parallel* has the second line saying again the meaning of the first line but going beyond it:

"Smoke went up from his nostrils,
and devouring fire from his mouth;
glowing coals flamed forth from him" (18:8).

The stair-step verses are strong in the Songs of Ascents (120–134). As pilgrims made their way up the paths to Jerusalem, they sang these short, easily memorized songs. Like A, B, C, three poetic phrases stair-stepped along with their footsteps. Notice how each phrase builds on the preceding phrase but carries the thought further:

"He will not let your foot be moved;
he who keeps you will not slumber.
He who keeps Israel
will neither slumber nor sleep" (121:3-4).

Sometimes the parallel is simply *word pairs* like day and night, sun and moon, sea and land. These word pairs made the poem easy to remember. They provided a framework on which to construct an entire Psalm.

"The sun shall not strike you by day,
nor the moon by night" (121:6).

Repetition reinforces the idea and adds to the emotion. In Psalm 121, we hear the word *keep* like the beat of a drum:

"The LORD is your keeper. . . .

DISCIPLE

The LORD will keep you from all evil;
  he will keep your life.
The LORD will keep
    your going out and your coming in" (121:5-8).

Power increases when the *first word* is repeated, as the word *praise* in Psalm 150:

  "Praise the LORD!
Praise God in his sanctuary;
  praise him in his mighty firmament!" (150:1).

When the last word or phrase ends one line and begins the next, the form adds emphasis, as in

    "break forth into joyous song and sing praises.
Sing praises to the LORD with the lyre,
    with the lyre and the sound of melody" (98:4-5).

Sometimes two words or phrases are put together side by side for greatest possible effect. "My God, my God, why have you forsaken me?" (22:1). Many songs use a *refrain*. "His steadfast love endures forever" completes each verse in Psalm 136. Picture the priest calling out the verses and the worshipers shouting the refrain as they walked around the Temple.

All poetry delights in *figures of speech*—metaphors, similes, hyperbole—picture language. The Psalms abound in such imagery.

    "In the heavens he has set a tent for the sun,
  which comes out like a bridegroom from his
      wedding canopy,
  and like a strong man runs its course with joy" (19:4-5).

Of course all language about God is metaphor.

    "The Lord is my rock,
  my fortress, and my deliverer" (18:2).

We can say God is *like* something.

    "Your righteousness is like the mighty mountains,
  your judgments are like the great deep" (36:6).

We can make meaningful allusions.

    "Walk about Zion, go all around it,
    count its towers,
  consider well its ramparts;
    go through its citadels,
  that you may tell the next generation
    that this is God" (48:12-14).

Sometimes we don't know whether to take a poetic phrase literally or figuratively. When "the sea looked and fled," the waters actually backed up so the Hebrews could escape slavery, but "the mountains skipped like rams" must allude to the feelings in the hearts of the freed slaves (114:3-4). Language forms often convey double meanings, even meanings different to different people. "How very good and pleasant it is / when kindred live together in unity" (133:1) refers to peace within a family; but it may also plead for reunion between the Northern and Southern Kingdoms, focused on the Temple.

In picture language, much can be said in a short space. Each word, each image is loaded with meaning. Extraneous

A *metaphor* is a poetic statement of comparison that says one thing *is* another. A simile makes a comparison by saying one thing is *like* another, or *as* one thing is, so is another. A *hyperbole* is an exaggeration that emphasizes a quality or characteristic. An *allusion* is a reference that is unexplained because it is assumed to be so well-known that readers need no explanation.

words are omitted. "The LORD is my shepherd" says a bookful. Sometimes the figure of speech exaggerates for effect:

> "For he commanded and raised the stormy wind,
>   which lifted up the waves of the sea.
> They mounted up to heaven, they went down
>   to the depths" (107:25-26).

What a storm!

Sometimes the poems *personify,* as "Death shall be their shepherd" (49:14). Often an *enemy* is described, but generally with a double meaning. The enemy can symbolize distress, danger, disease, loneliness, or abandonment.

When praying a psalm, individually or corporately, make it your own. Let the sins be your sins; the diseases, your diseases; the troubles, your troubles. Let the enemies, even if they are called Edomites or Amorites, be your enemies. Name your enemies in your mind, whether they are persons or systems, whether they are addictions or temptations. Put your own name, your own personal tragedies, your own enemies into your psalm prayers. The psalm is yours; the prayer is yours.

MARKS OF FAITHFUL COMMUNITY

Day by day, week by week, the Psalms express the full range of human emotions. They help us bring our complete human experience into God's presence. We know God welcomes us, whether we are joyful and whole or broken and tired, thankful or resentful, grief-stricken or glad.

What emotions do you find most difficult to express to God?

_____

_____

How do the psalms help you express those emotions? What particular psalms?

_____

_____

What characterizes your own praying? What do your prayers include?

_____

_____

What does it mean to you to know that when you pray the psalms you are joining others who are also praying the psalms?

_____

_____

IF YOU WANT TO KNOW MORE

Write a psalm that fits your spiritual life at present, using such devices of Hebrew poetry as parallelism, the stair-step parallel, refrain, word pairs, repetition of words.

Being faithful community, we pray, knowing God welcomes us and knowing nothing we say or feel is outside that welcome.

MOURN

"Why are you cast down, O my soul,
   and why are you disquieted within me?
Hope in God; for I shall again praise him,
   my help and my God."

—Psalm 42:5-6

15 Songs of Pain

OUR HUMAN CONDITION

Being anything other than positive, upbeat, is not acceptable. So we put on a happy face, say all the right things, drive the pain inside, and turn on ourselves.

ASSIGNMENT

When people are sad, they need sad songs. Laments express anger, loneliness, grief, pain. Try to get inside these feelings because on Day 6 you will write a personal lament.

Day 1   *Individual Lament*—Psalms 3; 4; 31 (deliverance); 39 (healing); 71 (an aged person in distress); 77 (deliverance from trouble)

Day 2   *Community Lament*—Psalms 12 (help in faithless times); 80 (Israel's restoration); 85 (restoration of God's favor); 94 (appeal to God the avenger of the righteous); 126 (deliverance from national misfortune); 137 (lament for Jerusalem)

Day 3   *Penitence*—Psalms 6 (healing); 32 (thanksgiving for forgiveness); 38 (plea for healing and forgiveness); 103 (thanksgiving for God's goodness); 131 (submission to God's will)

Day 4   *Trust*—Psalms 11 (confidence and trust in God); 63 (delight in God's presence); 91 (assurance of God's protection); 121 (confidence in God's care); 139 (known to God)

Day 5   *Torah, Wisdom*—Psalms 19 (God's glory in creation and the Law); 37 (retribution for

the wicked); 49 (transience of life and wealth); *Liturgies*—Psalms 82 (God's judgment on pagan gods); 115 (greatness of God)

Day 6   Read and respond to "Fruit From the Tree of Life" and "Marks of Faithful Community." Write your personal lament.

Day 7   Rest

PSALM OF THE WEEK

Pray Psalm 143 aloud daily. Make the psalm your own. Each day name your enemy—cancer cells, tension in the family, depression, insecurity about the future. Keep the enemy in mind as you pray.

PRAYER

Pray daily before study:
   "Even if I go through the deepest darkness,
      I will not be afraid, LORD,
      for you are with me" (Psalm 23:4, TEV).

Prayer concerns for this week:

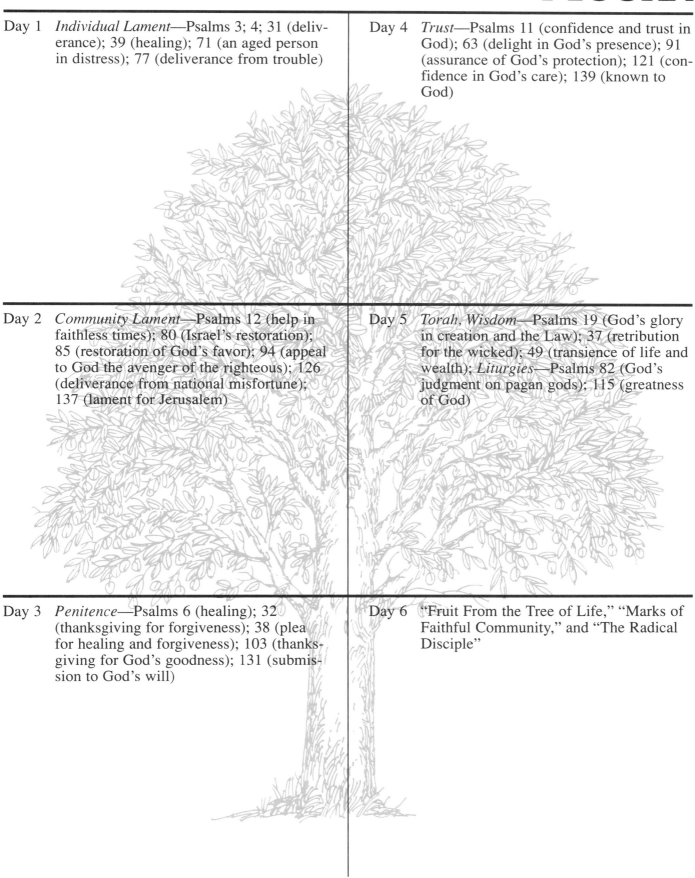

Day 1   *Individual Lament*—Psalms 3; 4; 31 (deliverance); 39 (healing); 71 (an aged person in distress); 77 (deliverance from trouble)

Day 2   *Community Lament*—Psalms 12 (help in faithless times); 80 (Israel's restoration); 85 (restoration of God's favor); 94 (appeal to God the avenger of the righteous); 126 (deliverance from national misfortune); 137 (lament for Jerusalem)

Day 3   *Penitence*—Psalms 6 (healing); 32 (thanksgiving for forgiveness); 38 (plea for healing and forgiveness); 103 (thanksgiving for God's goodness); 131 (submission to God's will)

Day 4   *Trust*—Psalms 11 (confidence and trust in God); 63 (delight in God's presence); 91 (assurance of God's protection); 121 (confidence in God's care); 139 (known to God)

Day 5   *Torah, Wisdom*—Psalms 19 (God's glory in creation and the Law); 37 (retribution for the wicked); 49 (transience of life and wealth); *Liturgies*—Psalms 82 (God's judgment on pagan gods); 115 (greatness of God)

Day 6   "Fruit From the Tree of Life," "Marks of Faithful Community," and "The Radical Disciple"

Almond Tree

DISCIPLE

FRUIT FROM THE TREE OF LIFE

Can we go before God in our full humanity, carrying with us the full range of human experience? Can we be ourselves in prayer, yelling out our bitterness, crying our eyes out in grief? Or in ecstasy, can we shout "God is good" and not be embarrassed?

Can we do it together? Can we pray together when one of us is angry, the other reconciled? When one of us is grief-stricken, the other strong as a youth ready to run a race? The Psalms say, "Yes!" The Psalms run the emotional gamut from despair to ecstasy. Because the Psalms are communal, even the ones that speak personally or individually, we touch one another's feelings when we pray. One person may be up, another person down, but we pray together before God whose "steadfast love endures forever."

We tend to cut the psalms, reading or singing those verses that are upbeat and positive. Many hymnals and prayer books use selections so they can eliminate angry phrases. Praise choruses focus on the majesty of God, but they generally omit bitter, dark nights of the soul. Why do we cut and paste? Is it because we think we should be nice before God, leaving our ugly thoughts at home? Because we want our worship to be pleasant? Because we think God will not approve our negative feelings? Or because we really don't want to share the negative emotions others are experiencing?

The Hebrew title of the Psalter is *tehillim,* meaning "praises," and having the same root word as *hallel* or *hallelujah,* which means "praise God." Everything, even the laments, are praises to God. We bring our entire existence into communal worship so that our lives might be gathered up in praise. Here we tackle the tough parts, the Scriptures seldom read, laments that cry out with despair, weep in grief, scream with rage. How can they be praise?

Laments

The word *lament* means a complaint or plea for help. Laments generally follow a pattern: a call, such as "O Lord"; a description of the trouble; a plea for God to respond, often with reasons why God should act; a statement of trust that God is listening; and a concluding vow or act of praise. Not all lament psalms include each element, but most keep the spirit and the movement of this pattern. Study Psalm 80 for the classic form.

Another way of explaining the lament is to say that the first statement represents security, order, trust—even if it only names or blesses God. Even if the first words are a frightened cry, they tell of a remembered stability—health, peace, social tranquillity. Things are going well. No surprises.

Suddenly, something bad happens. A break. Someone or something causes disorder, pain, loss of place or direction. When the sky falls on us, we often go into shock, denying such a thing could happen. We feel alone, isolated. Anger oozes out. Oh, how the rage explodes in the laments!

Often, in agony, we try to bargain. If God will do this, we will do that. We claim we've been good and don't deserve what has happened. The laments seek to postpone, to put off the trouble, plead for an act of grace, ask for release. When such appeals fail—if God seems asleep—the laments express deep depression.

"I am a worm, and not human;
scorned by others, and despised by the people"
(Psalm 22:6).

We grasp for earlier reliable securities, but they are gone. We feel betrayed. We can't go back; we are afraid to go forward. But the Psalms lead us on, even as we look over our shoulder or drown in a sea of tears.

The laments are spoken in community. We are not alone. We pray the prayers among the covenant people. A mysterious healing begins to take place. Surrounded by steadfast love, we move toward acceptance, reconciliation, adjustment, new direction. A surprising rush of positive emotions flood in—wonder, release, insight, courage, healing, forgiveness, deliverance. As we pray the lament, we realize—sometimes reluctantly—that while we cannot go back to the earlier security, we can be led into a new way of seeing life and its relationships, into a new form of trust in God.

"Steadfast love and faithfulness will meet;
righteousness and peace will kiss each other. . . .
The LORD will give what is good" (85:10, 12).

Judgment

We may be surprised at the oft-repeated plea for judgment: "Judge me, O LORD my God, according to thy righteousness" (Psalm 35:24, KJV).

The coming of God's judgment is cause for celebration.

"Then shall all the trees of the forest sing for joy
before the LORD; for he is coming,
for he is coming to judge the earth" (96:12-13).

When you and I think of judgment, we generally remember prophets like Amos who forecast the "day of the Lord" as a time of retribution. Or we think of Jesus' description of judgment, which he likened to a shepherd separating the sheep from the goats (Matthew 25:32). But the pleas in the Psalter are for equity, for fair play. They ask God to set things right. The Psalms plead for the incorruptible judge to come and right the wrongs. Earthly powers have distorted justice: The rich have too much, the poor too little. When God comes, justice will be fully and permanently established. Human beings will have their full rights as children of God. The righteous judge will restore respect to the downtrodden, rights to the helpless, full humanity to the oppressed.

Almond Tree

DISCIPLE

Occasionally, God is the accuser (6:1), and sometimes the prayer wants no part of judgment:

"Do not enter into judgment with your servant,
for no one living is righteous before you" (143:2).

We need to distinguish between being "righteous" and being "in the right" in a specific matter. *Righteous* means being fair, being just; and *in the right* means demanding privilege. The psalmists know we are not blameless, yet we can be wronged in a particular time and place. We have the right and the need to cry out for justice.

Curses

The most difficult verses to read or pray are the curses. We have been taught by Christ to turn the other cheek, pray for our enemies, return good for evil. Hebrew Scriptures warn against harboring bitterness, shouting vile slogans, meting out unfair retribution. "You shall not hate in your heart anyone of your kin. . . . You shall not take vengeance or bear a grudge against any of your people, but you shall love your neighbor as yourself" (Leviticus 19:17-18).

"Do not rejoice when your enemies fall,
and do not let your heart be glad when they stumble"
(Proverbs 24:17).

Even modern society refrains from spewing out vindictive language, preferring to coat over such feelings with a veneer of civility.

But the Psalms get angry. When we read the poignant Psalm 137, we are surprised, even shocked, at the vindictive spirit that says the people will be happy who can pay back those Edomites who assisted Babylon in ravaging Jerusalem.

"Happy shall they be who take your little ones
and dash them against the rock" (137:9).

We need to acknowledge that most of us have not seen enemies bash our own children's heads against the rocks, as did those who experienced the destruction of Jerusalem—and we need to ask if our reaction would be so different. We say we do not understand. Yet in our modern era of napalm bombs, gas chambers, ethnic cleansings, orchestrated starvation, millions of people have experienced just such horrors.

We must admit that violent anger does well up in the human heart when atrocities occur. Injured people become furious and resentful. The cry for revenge is no stranger to us. We read it daily in newspapers and hear it in newscasts—and at times even join it. If our argument is correct that God wants our full humanity—the way a good parent receives an upset child—then we can come to God in prayer, even with foul curses on our lips. The Psalms make sure we are human before we are holy. Thank God not all our prayers are given yes answers, not all our bargaining wins, not all our human expressions bring fire from heaven.

The plea for God to avenge is more than a catharsis. Our

cry turns retribution over to God where it belongs. We cannot get even; usually we don't have the power. If we did, one act of violence would bring another. The scales are never balanced. The final arbiter of justice is God. Our angry prayer takes it out of our hands. Vengeance is God's prerogative. Torah teaches, "Vengeance is mine" says the Lord (Deuteronomy 32:35).

Enemies

The Psalms, especially the laments, rail against "enemies." Those enemies, in national or community laments, are usually unnamed, although sometimes they refer to neighboring nations like the Edomites or mighty empires like the Babylonian Empire. Keep in mind that Israel was set down in a land already inhabited, so conflict with neighbors was inevitable. Remember too that the tiny country was the bridge across which great armies raced to attack one another.

Israel was both a nation and a religion. Enemies in war were seen as enemies of the king, the people, the Temple, the religion—as enemies of God. So the prayers plead with God to

> "Stir up your might,
>   and come to save us!" (80:2).

Sometimes the "enemies" were individual people, neighbors with cutting words or cruel behavior. "I am the scorn of all my adversaries" (31:11). A trusted friend turned vicious:

> "It is not enemies who taunt me—
>   I could bear that. . . .
> But it is you, my equal,
>   my companion, my familiar friend" (55:12-13).

Although a specific enemy may be named, the name quickly became symbolic, even for the psalmists. The Edomites and others became a metaphor for all other foes. A sickness can be a "battle"; a storm can be soldiers of the enemy. Who or what is seeking to undo us? Is it prejudice that blocks our way, the pains of the past, the injustices of the future? "Enemies" can be an economic downturn, a factory layoff, a bank foreclosure. "Enemies" can be addictions to gambling, drugs, alcohol, pornography, and tobacco that would destroy us. A liar is not merely a person across the street but also an advertising campaign. The question is not who were the psalmist's enemies but who are our enemies. The question is not what is wrong with the psalmist but what is wrong with us.

Name in your mind those things that are trying to defeat you. Put a title on forces that could bring you down. As you read the Psalms, specify who or what are your enemies. Find a psalm that is related especially to your situation.

DISCIPLE

Injury and Disease

The psalmist believes both sickness and health come from the hand of God. Of course, the wickedness of enemies or vindictiveness of neighbors can cause injury; personal sins can result in suffering. But all are perceived as divinely driven. Sickness is believed to be the result of somebody's sin:

"O LORD, be gracious to me;
   heal me, for I have sinned against you" (Psalm 41:4).

If God is not the direct cause of the sickness, then God is at least asleep or forgetful. "How long, O LORD? Will you forget me forever?" (13:1). Psalm 88 is a desperate plea for healing that ends in frustration.

The Psalms do not forget to be thankful when health returns.

"Bless the LORD, O my soul,
   and do not forget all his benefits—
who forgives all your iniquity,
   who heals all your diseases" (103:2-3).

Do not ask what were the iniquities or diseases of the psalmist; ask what are your iniquities or diseases, and ask for healing.

Death

Old Testament Scriptures offer little or no hope for life after death. Life was life; death was death. Sheol, the place of the dead, was a shadowy place, a dim place of vapors where the dead resided. The psalmist, in pleas for deliverance, reminds God that people cannot offer praise when they go to Sheol. "Do the shades rise up to praise you?" (Psalm 88:10). The Old Testament writers were concerned about right and wrong, good and evil, life and death, here and now. The Psalms understood that the human goal is to love God—not for reward, not for eternal life, but for God's glory and human happiness. The psalmist pants after God, hopes to enjoy the Lord's house "all the days of my life" (27:4).

Thus God, who is just, had to perform justice in this world and give punishment in this life. The debate raged between the wisdom of Proverbs, which saw right rewarded and wrong punished, and the teacher in Ecclesiastes, who countered that he had seen the wicked prosper and the righteous scorned. The Psalms struggle with the same issue, but always in the context of this life.

Stability and Change

The Psalms support both priest and prophet, both stability and change. They enrich worship, provide order. But psalms are prophetic too, challenging the establishment. Certainty that things are not yet right pulsates within the orderly worship service. Praise is laced with concern for the poor. The Psalms plead for God to give the king justice and compassion. Priest and prophet, stability and change sing together.

The Psalms reflect the brokenness of the world, but they hold on to the God who is just and caring. Often a psalm will urge God to act now because injustice cries out for correction. Hurry up, God; we don't have forever. "Answer me quickly, O LORD; / my spirit fails" (143:7). Sometimes psalms urge patience. Many an injury, many a grievance needs more time in which God can act.

"I wait for the LORD, my soul waits,
    and in his word I hope;
my soul waits for the Lord
    more than those who watch for the morning" (130:5-6).

Many a psalm closes with a yieldedness, a faith, a quiet trust that places life, with all its mysteries, in God's hands.

"The LORD will keep
    your going out and your coming in
    from this time on and forevermore" (121:8).

MARKS OF FAITHFUL COMMUNITY

We pray the Psalms as part of the covenant community. Together, we express our anger, our grief, our loneliness before God. God receives our negative feelings and offers assurance of hope, healing, and joy.

Think about why you choose to read certain psalms and to avoid others. What assumptions about Scripture underlie your choosing which psalms you read?

_____

_____

Recall a time of personal trouble. How did you express your feelings to God? What did you ask of God?

_____

How did your experience of trouble affect your view of life and its relationships, and your view of God?

_____

Being faithful community, we take God's Word with us into pain and trouble and let the psalms of lament be our voice.

THE RADICAL DISCIPLE

The radical disciple learns to express the full range of emotions to God. Write a personal lament. Base it on a past or present trouble. Include these elements: a call, description of the trouble, plea for God to respond, statement of trust that God is listening, a vow or expression of praise.

IF YOU WANT TO KNOW MORE

Most hymnals include a Scripture index. Use that index in your congregational hymnal to identify hymns based on psalms of lament from daily reading assignments. Read some psalms and their related hymns. Look also for psalms of lament in the Psalter selections for congregational responsive reading.

PRAISE

"Praise the LORD!
Praise God in his sanctuary;
    praise him in his mighty firmament!
Praise him for his mighty deeds;
    praise him according to his surpassing greatness!"

—Psalm 150:1-2

16 Songs of Joy

OUR HUMAN CONDITION

Life is an uphill struggle. Our bodies ache; our jobs are stressful; the weather is uncomfortable. Children are a heavy responsibility; aged parents are a burden. What is there to be joyful about?

ASSIGNMENT

Rise up each morning with words of a psalm in your mind and on your lips. Early in the week memorize Psalm 146:1-2 and say it aloud, even shout it, daily when you wake.

Day 1 *Lord of History*—Psalms 33; 106; 136 (God's great deeds); *Thanksgiving*—Psalms 145; 146 (praise for God's care)

Day 2 *Thanksgiving*—Psalms 18 (royal psalm, king's thanksgiving for victory); 34; 92 (individual thanksgiving after deliverance from enemies); 107 (community thanksgiving for pilgrims); 124 (community thanksgiving for national deliverance)

Day 3 *Praise*—Psalms 8 (God's glory); 100 (all nations praise the Lord); 104 (hymn to the Creator); 148 (all creation praise the Lord)

Day 4 *Trust*—Psalms 27 (trust for deliverance); 62; 125 (confidence in God's protection); 131 (submission to God's guidance)

Day 5 *Praise*—Psalms 111 (God's great deeds); 112 (a wisdom psalm); *Hallels*—Psalms 113–118 ("Egyptian Hallel," festival hymns of praise to God); *Liturgy*—Psalm 122 (praise, prayer for Jerusalem); *Enthrone-*

ment—Psalm 98 (praise for God's kingship); *Doxology*—Psalm 150 (everything praise the Lord)

Day 6 Read and respond to "Fruit From the Tree of Life" and "Marks of Faithful Community."

Day 7 Rest

THE RADICAL DISCIPLE

The radical disciple praises God. Write your own psalm of thanksgiving. Use Psalm 103 as your model. You may want to name God's victories and blessings in your life.

PSALM OF THE WEEK

Psalm 100 calls all nations to praise the Lord. Pray Psalm 100 aloud daily with a globe or world map in view, calling on different countries and areas of the world by name to praise the Lord.

PRAYER

Pray daily before study:
    "May the peoples praise you, O God;
        may all the peoples praise you!
    May the nations be glad and sing for joy,
        because you judge the peoples with justice
        and guide every nation on earth" (Psalm 67:3-4, TEV).

Prayer concerns for this week:

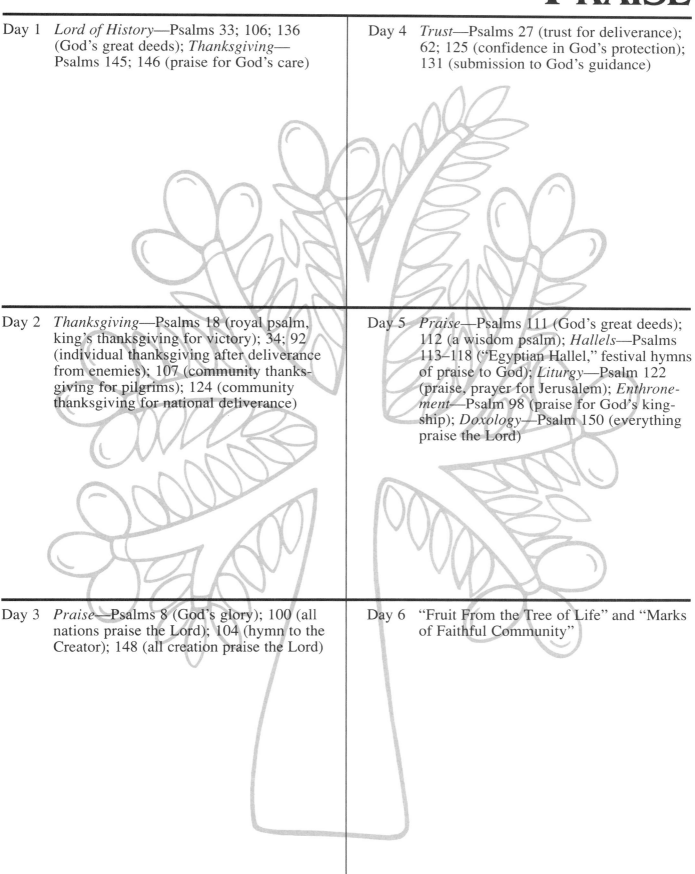

Day 1 *Lord of History*—Psalms 33; 106; 136 (God's great deeds); *Thanksgiving*—Psalms 145; 146 (praise for God's care)

Day 4 *Trust*—Psalms 27 (trust for deliverance); 62; 125 (confidence in God's protection); 131 (submission to God's guidance)

Day 2 *Thanksgiving*—Psalms 18 (royal psalm, king's thanksgiving for victory); 34; 92 (individual thanksgiving after deliverance from enemies); 107 (community thanksgiving for pilgrims); 124 (community thanksgiving for national deliverance)

Day 5 *Praise*—Psalms 111 (God's great deeds); 112 (a wisdom psalm); *Hallels*—Psalms 113–118 ("Egyptian Hallel," festival hymns of praise to God); *Liturgy*—Psalm 122 (praise, prayer for Jerusalem); *Enthronement*—Psalm 98 (praise for God's kingship); *Doxology*—Psalm 150 (everything praise the Lord)

Day 3 *Praise*—Psalms 8 (God's glory); 100 (all nations praise the Lord); 104 (hymn to the Creator); 148 (all creation praise the Lord)

Day 6 "Fruit From the Tree of Life" and "Marks of Faithful Community"

Stylized Tree of Life

DISCIPLE

FRUIT FROM THE TREE OF LIFE

So much to be grateful for! Creation itself is grounds for our gratitude. What is more natural than for the creatures to bless the Creator? The Psalms emerge from an outdoor people who tended gardens and pruned vineyards, fertilized fruit trees, and fought off wild animals. For farmers and keepers of herds, weather, seasons, wind, rain, sun, and moon are the stuff of existence.

Neighboring peoples, sustained by those same rhythms, worshiped fertility gods—gods of sexual procreation and agriculture. Israel did not worship the nature gods—the sun god, the moon god, or the gods of thunder and lightning. They worshiped their Designer and Creator, the God who created the heavens and the earth. Nor do the Psalms praise nature as if nature were God. Nature is God's handiwork. God is Creator, not the creation. The sun is not God, but light can be his garment. The wind can be a messenger, the waves a rebuke, the thunder a divine voice. Israel perceived sun and moon, summer and winter—all of life—as the work of God. Even psalms that praise God for other reasons often slip in a few verses of gratitude for creation.

"Praise is due to you, O God. . . .
You visit the earth and water it . . .
     you provide the people with grain. . . .
     the hills gird themselves with joy . . .
     the valleys deck themselves with grain,
     they shout and sing together for joy" (Psalm 65:1-13).

Not all allusions to nature are limited to things that benefit humankind. God is the Creator and Sustainer of all.

"The young lions roar for their prey,
     seeking their food from God" (104:21).

They, like us, receive their daily food from God. They are part of the mystery.

Salvation History

Israel loves to retell its story, for there is great power in remembering God's past victories. The Psalms carried the memory of their escape from Egypt on the wings of prayer. Sometimes the psalmists extolled God's saving power in history (Psalm 105), sometimes bemoaned the ancestral grumblings and lack of faith (106). But they gave the credit for rescue to the Creator.

"O give thanks to the God of gods . . .
who struck Egypt through their firstborn . . .
and brought Israel out from among them. . . .
who led his people through the wilderness . . .
and gave . . . land as a heritage, . . .
a heritage to his servant Israel" (136:2, 10-11, 16, 21-22).

God is Lord not only of Israel's covenant history; God is Lord of all human history. God not only governs Israel but also rules the nations.

"The LORD brings the counsel of the nations to nothing;
    he frustrates the plans of the peoples. . . .
The LORD looks down from heaven;
    he sees all humankind" (33:10, 13).

The Psalms also praise God for the Law, the religious teachings and instructions. Psalm 19 begins with a Creation theme, then moves to Torah.

"The heavens are telling the glory of God;
    and the firmament proclaims his handiwork. . . .
The law of the LORD is perfect,
    reviving the soul" (19:1, 7).

Torah is grounded in Creation. God's laws work because they are built into God's orderly creation.

Liturgy

Many psalms served as liturgies for special occasions. When a new king was crowned, the throngs filled the Temple to pray a royal or coronation psalm such as Psalm 110. Solomon and his successors were crowned with Psalm 72. The Lord puts the king on the throne (110:1), but the people will offer themselves willingly when the king has need (110:3). The king will be "a priest forever according to the order of Melchizedek" (110:4), the mysterious priest who blessed Abraham (Genesis 14:18-20). The kings are supposed to be righteous.

"Now therefore, O kings, be wise. . . .
Serve the LORD with fear" (Psalm 2:10-11).

The king in Psalm 101 pledges to be just, to "walk with integrity of heart," to reject "an arrogant heart," and to "look with favor on the faithful in the land." He continues, "No one who practices deceit / shall remain in my house" (101:1-2, 5-7). At public ceremonies, the covenant with God was always affirmed. The king was not absolute sovereign. God was Lord, and all the people stood within that covenant.

When the exiles returned under Cyrus and the Persian kings, they were allowed to rebuild the wall of Jerusalem, rebuild the Temple, and offer sacrifices. But they were not allowed to have a king, so the enthronement psalms emerged, songs like 93, 98, and 99. These prayer songs place God on the throne of Israel, much as earlier coronation psalms had placed the king on the throne.

Every time the Jews praised God as king, they fanned flames of distrust in the minds of their political overlords. If God was their king, they were a free people in their hearts, no matter who held governing power over them.

Humankind

Remembering that God gave Adam and Eve dominion over the earth, the psalmist sings that God has crowned humankind "with glory and honor" (Psalm 8:5-6).

If every woman, man, and child is only "a little lower than God" (8:5), then all human beings—the weak and the strong,

Disciple

the wealthy and the indigent, the able and the impaired—are a special creation. Woven through the Psalms is the theme of compassion. So whether we are praying a lament, offering a song of thanksgiving, remembering Israel's rescue, or shouting a doxology, concern for the poor inevitably emerges.

"O LORD, you will hear the desire of the meek;
    you will strengthen their heart, you will incline your ear
to do justice for the orphan and the oppressed" (10:17-18).

In the glorious doxologies, praise pours forth because

"The LORD watches over the strangers;
    he upholds the orphan and the widow" (146:9).

Sometimes the psalmist is "poor"—perhaps in spirit, perhaps in resources.

"As for me, I am poor and needy,
    but the Lord takes thought for me" (40:17).

No question where God's heart is.

"He delivers the needy when they call,
    the poor and those who have no helper.
He has pity on the weak and the needy" (72:12-13).

Why Express Gratitude?

Why do the Psalms invite us, even command us to praise God? Why do they offer themselves as vehicles for praise? We are most human and happy when we praise something beautiful, something good, something life-giving. When we praise the good, our enjoyment is made complete. When we experience joy, beauty, overwhelming truth, love, the upsurge of appreciation completes the experience. So whenever we come into the presence of the holy, we not only honor the true, the beautiful, the One who loves us; we delight in acknowledging the object of our gratitude. And in that mysterious process, we are blessed.

Praise seems to open the door of our hearts to God's presence. In adulation, we invite God to draw near, to manifest beauty and love to us, to invade our being. With joy and gladness we "enter his gates with thanksgiving, / and his courts with praise" (Psalm 100:4). But what does our gratitude point to? Often to creation, to life itself. We are thankful for the breath of our lungs and the beat of our hearts.

"O LORD, our Sovereign,
    how majestic is your name in all the earth!" (8:1).

Joy

Sometimes the Psalms explode in a symphony of joy, gladness, and exultation. As pilgrims by the thousands entered Jerusalem, they sang,

"Make a joyful noise to the LORD. . . .
    come into his presence with singing. . . .
    Give thanks to him, bless his name.
For the LORD is good" (Psalm 100:1, 2, 4-5).

They sang the songs of ascents as they traveled (120–134).

Notice that Psalm 124 even gives instructions for the response:
> "If it had not been the LORD who was on our side
>> —let Israel now say—
> if it had not been the LORD who was on our side"
>> (124:1-2).

They must have called it out phrase by phrase, perhaps helping the miles go by.

Every male Jew was expected to participate in the three pilgrimage festivals to the Temple—Pesach (Passover and Feast of Unleavened Bread), Shavuoth (Feast of Weeks), and Sukkoth (Feast of Booths). Keep in mind that, even though they raised animals as well as crops, meat was not a staple. Sheep were too precious for their wool to be slaughtered often for food. Oxen were needed to plow. Some meats were forbidden. Bread, fruit, and vegetables were the regular diet. So the festivals were feasts. Only certain portions of the sacrificed animals were burned on the altar. Most of the meat was given to the families for feasting. Pilgrims could smell the meat roasting from a thousand family fires as they entered the city. Festivals were celebrations, fellowship with family and friends, eating, singing, dancing—and praising God.

During the festivals, they sang the hallels (113–118)—sometimes called the Egyptian Hallel—remembering freedom from slavery. The hallels carried joy for Israel's people across the centuries. Israel, of course, should praise the Lord; but so should everyone, Gentiles too.
> "Praise the LORD, all you nations!
>> Extol him, all you peoples!" (117:1).

The choirs King David established, the musical instruments, and the priests and Levites who would lead—all the people would shout, "Praise the Lord!" Jesus would have sung these hallels when he went to the Temple with his family at age twelve and as a man. He would have sung them with the disciples at the Passover meal (Matthew 26:17-30).

Doxologies

The concluding hymns, like the hallels, are expressions of praise (Psalms 146–150). They are hallelujahs, sung at the annual festivals. They sound the note of thanksgiving.

Apparently written after the return from exile, when Israel no longer had kings, the praise psalms remind the people to put their trust in the God of Jacob. The God of Jacob executes justice for the oppressed, gives food to the hungry, watches over strangers, upholds the orphan and the widow (146). God heals the brokenhearted.

In Psalm 148, everyone, everything is invited to praise the Lord, not only the sea monsters but inanimate objects, "fire and hail, snow and frost" (148:8). Francis of Assisi based his "Canticle of the Sun" on this psalm, making sun and wind his praise brothers, moon and waters his praise sisters. Not just everything that breathes but everything that God created will

This brown jasper seal bears the image of a type of lyre known as a *kinnor,* having two uneven arms and twelve strings. The seal dates from the seventh century B.C., and its inscription reads "(Belonging) to Macadanah, the king's daughter."

DISCIPLE

praise the Lord. No wonder human beings are expected to care for the earth. "You have given them dominion over the works of your hands" (8:6). No wonder ecology is part of praise.

Everyone is called to praise the Lord. "Young men and women alike, / old and young together!" (148:12). Time to dance! Break out the melodies with tambourine and lyre. "Let the high praises of God be in their throats" (149:6). The final doxology was carefully chosen to conclude both the fifth group of psalms and the entire book. In the Temple, with musicians and choir, with cymbals crashing, the shout goes up:

"Let everything that breathes praise the LORD!
Praise the LORD!" (150:6).

MARKS OF FAITHFUL COMMUNITY

Praise takes us out of ourselves. In praise we ask nothing, offer nothing but ourselves. We come into the presence of God together. We remember and celebrate together.

List two or three of your favorite praise psalms and say why they are particularly meaningful for you.

What past actions of God cause you to praise God?

What is the power in praise? How does praising God affect you?

If genuine praise of God has little to do with how we feel, what enables you to praise God in the difficult times?

IF YOU WANT TO KNOW MORE

Many psalms are omitted from our study. Read the long but powerful meditation on the law of God, Psalm 119.

Francis of Assisi's "Canticle of the Sun" can be located easily at a public library or on the internet. Locate and read it.

Being faithful community, we praise God because God is worthy of praise, whatever our life situation.

DISCIPLE

JOHN

REVELATION

INCARNATION

"The Word became flesh and lived among us, and we have seen his glory, the glory as of a father's only son, full of grace and truth."

—John 1:14

17 The Word Became a Human Being

OUR HUMAN CONDITION

We hope for something new and something different, but when it comes and it doesn't match our expectations, it surprises us, confuses us, and puts us on the defensive.

ASSIGNMENT

Get a feel for the entire Gospel of John. Read the headings. See how the Word and the wisdom of God in the Old Testament become the Word made flesh in the New Testament. Read the Prologue aloud daily. Compare the four Gospel accounts of John the Baptist.

Day 1 Glance through the whole Gospel. Read the headings. Read John 1:1-18 (the Word became flesh) aloud. Genesis 1:1–2:3 (God's Word creates); Exodus 19:16–20:21 (God's word of law to Moses)

Day 2 Read John 1:1-18 aloud. Isaiah 40:1-8; 55:1-11 (God's Word stands forever, accomplishes its purposes)

Day 3 Read John 1:1-18 aloud. Proverbs 8:22-31 (wisdom with God at Creation); Wisdom of Solomon (Apocrypha) 6:12–9:4 (description and benefits of wisdom)

Day 4 Read aloud and try to memorize John 1:1-18. John 1:19-51 (testimony of John the Baptist, the Son of God, Jesus' first disciples); Matthew 3 (repent, the Kingdom has come near); 9:14-17 (new wine, new wineskins)

Day 5 Read aloud and try to memorize John 1:1-18. Luke 3:1-20 (bear fruits worthy of repentance); 7:18-35 (John the Baptist, more than a prophet); Mark 1:1-14 (Jesus baptized, tempted); 6:14-29 (Herod and death of John); Exodus 12:21-27 (Passover lamb)

Day 6 Read and respond to "Fruit From the Tree of Life" and "Marks of Faithful Community."

Day 7 Rest

PSALM OF THE WEEK

Each day's assignment calls for reading John 1:1-18 and the psalm of the week aloud. On Day 1 read aloud Psalm 33 followed by John 1:1-18. On subsequent days alternate the sequence of reading. Think about the question, What does the Word / word of God make happen?

PRAYER

Pray daily before study:
  "Your word, O LORD, will last forever;
    it is eternal in heaven.
  Your faithfulness endures through all the ages;
    you have set the earth in place, and it
      remains" (Psalm 119:89-90, TEV).

Prayer concerns for this week:

INCARNATION

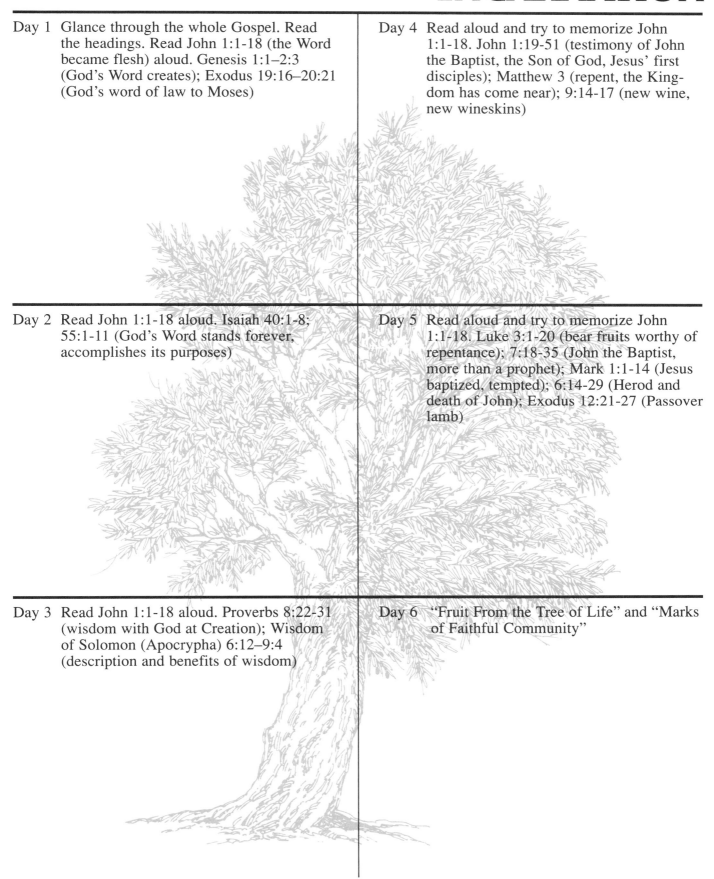

Day 1 Glance through the whole Gospel. Read the headings. Read John 1:1-18 (the Word became flesh) aloud. Genesis 1:1–2:3 (God's Word creates); Exodus 19:16–20:21 (God's word of law to Moses)

Day 4 Read aloud and try to memorize John 1:1-18. John 1:19-51 (testimony of John the Baptist, the Son of God, Jesus' first disciples); Matthew 3 (repent, the Kingdom has come near); 9:14-17 (new wine, new wineskins)

Day 2 Read John 1:1-18 aloud. Isaiah 40:1-8; 55:1-11 (God's Word stands forever, accomplishes its purposes)

Day 5 Read aloud and try to memorize John 1:1-18. Luke 3:1-20 (bear fruits worthy of repentance); 7:18-35 (John the Baptist, more than a prophet); Mark 1:1-14 (Jesus baptized, tempted); 6:14-29 (Herod and death of John); Exodus 12:21-27 (Passover lamb)

Day 3 Read John 1:1-18 aloud. Proverbs 8:22-31 (wisdom with God at Creation); Wisdom of Solomon (Apocrypha) 6:12–9:4 (description and benefits of wisdom)

Day 6 "Fruit From the Tree of Life" and "Marks of Faithful Community"

Olive Tree

DISCIPLE

FRUIT FROM THE TREE OF LIFE

John's Gospel, symbolized by the eagle, flies so close to heaven we scarcely can follow its flight, then swoops so near to us we almost can distinguish its features. Often it glides silently, then suddenly shrieks, shocking our sensibilities. The words are so simple yet the thoughts so profound that scholars spend their lives pondering them.

The Social Setting

Apparently John's Gospel emerged from a community of faith clustered around John the disciple. Motivated by missionary zeal and fear of persecutions, these Jews who confessed Jesus as Messiah seem to have moved to the urban seaport of Ephesus. They were a small beleaguered band of Jewish Christians amid a large Jewish community (estimate, fifty thousand) in the fourth largest city (estimate, five hundred thousand to a million people) in the Roman Empire.

The beloved disciple, we recall, had been given the care of Mary, Jesus' mother, by our Lord from the cross. Ancient traditions identify that disciple as John and claim John did just that—care for Mary while teaching as an "eyewitness," living to a ripe old age, and building up a community of faith.

At first the believers were Jews among Jews, for various sects and ideological groups had existed within Judaism—conservative Sadducees who did not believe in a final resurrection, scholarly Pharisees and scribes who did, zealots who wanted to rebel against Rome, priests and Levites who offered sacrifices in the Temple and cooperated with Rome, communities like the Essenes at Qumran in the desert, and the new sect, Jews who believed Jesus to be Messiah. But when Rome burned the Temple, leveled Jerusalem, and slaughtered hundreds of thousands of Jews in A.D. 70, Judaism was changed dramatically. The sacrificial system was gone forever. Judaism turned to the synagogue for survival. Religious leadership gravitated to rabbis, often Pharisees and scribes who were students of the Scriptures.

For a time the Jews who believed in Jesus still participated in religious ceremonies and festivals, circumcising, keeping sabbath, studying Torah, praying the Psalms, attending synagogue. But tension naturally developed as Jewish Christians read Scripture through Christ-filled lenses, met in their homes for the Lord's Supper, questioned food restrictions, and included Gentile believers in their fellowship. Eventually they were put out of the synagogues, causing pain and distress. John's Gospel reflects this pain. When the Gospel recalls those persons who feared being "put out" of the synagogue—the blind man's parents (9:22) and some Jewish authorities (12:42)—it must reflect their own fears and painful sense of rejection. To be cut off from the Jewish community meant social ostracism, loss of relationship with family and friends, economic reprisals, religious dislocation. Jesus alone was

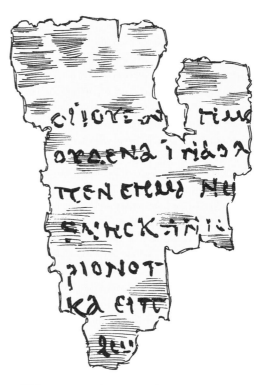

INCARNATION

their hope; the tiny Jewish Christian fellowship, their support.

New converts were invited not only to accept Jesus but to cross a line of separation into a new community. That act of faith meant a transferring of allegiance, leaving all status behind. They may have taken courage from the memory of such prominent men as Joseph of Arimathea and Nicodemus, who had risked public shame by placing the body of Jesus in the tomb.

Did this community of faith know about Paul's converts? Had they heard Paul preach or read his letters? Were they acquainted with the teachings of Jesus from other sources? Had they read the Gospels of Matthew, Mark, and Luke that had begun to circulate? Possibly so, at least they knew that "Jesus did many . . . signs in the presence of his disciples, which are not written in this book" (20:30). (Recall that John's Gospel was written considerably later than Paul's letters and several years after the other Gospels.) But this community of faith had its own eyewitnesses, its own understandings. These Christians framed their Gospel to make their own unique witness.

So in an alien and often hostile society related to both Greece and Rome, set in a largely rejecting Jewish community, John and his friends carefully crafted a witness to be read by Jew and Gentile alike: "These [words] are written so that you may come to believe [may continue to believe] that Jesus is the Messiah, the Son of God, and that through believing you may have life in his name" (20:31).

The Prologue

John's Gospel contains no birth stories, no Bethlehem, no King Herod, no shepherds. Instead a poem prologue announces the theme: "In the beginning was the Word" (John 1:1). The Greek word *logos,* or "Word," has deep scriptural and philosophical roots. In Genesis, God *spoke* creation into existence. The Psalms pick up this creational idea:

"By the word of the LORD the heavens were made . . .
   he spoke, and it came to be" (Psalm 33:6, 9).

Logos contains the creative act in Genesis, but it holds even more. In wisdom literature, *logos* is a means of creation. Wisdom, the preexisting *logos,* is personified as the one who helped God design the universe.

"I was there when he set the sky in place . . .
I was there when he laid the earth's foundations.
I was beside him like an architect" (Proverbs 8:27,
      29-30, TEV).

Greek philosophers considered *logos* to be "idea" or "thought." The Jewish philosopher Philo in the first century A.D. taught that *logos* was the idea in the mind of God through which God acted. Educated Gentiles would have understood the concept of *logos* as God's idea.

So the creating word from Genesis, wisdom from Proverbs,

This papyrus fragment from a copy of John's Gospel in Greek was found in Egypt and dates from A.D. 125–150. It is the earliest known copy of any part of the New Testament.

DISCIPLE

and the "idea" from the philosophers are all caught up in the meaning of the word *logos*. "The Word [*logos*] was with God, and the Word was God" (John 1:1). "And the Word became flesh and lived among us" (1:14). The Word became Jesus. Why this theological complexity? Because on one hand, almighty God did not abandon the throne of heaven. Jesus prayed to "the Father"; yet on the other hand, the very essence of God was in Jesus—"the Father and I are one" (10:30).

Incarnation

The notion of enfleshment offends Jew and Gentile alike. Both could believe in God "out there," but neither could easily accept God "down here." The Word became enfleshed. God became one of us, a human being—hungry, thirsty, tempted, yet without sin (Hebrews 4:15).

In John's Gospel, when people confront Jesus, they confront God. The Word "lived among us"—literally, "tented" or "tabernacled" among us (John 1:14). Jesus explained or interpreted God. Jesus made God known to us. Our Gospel's prologue proclaims that Jesus laid bare the heart and mind of God, and in doing that he brought not Law but love. Jesus brought and brings "grace upon grace" (1:16) to humankind.

The Prologue introduces two key words used throughout the Gospel—*light* and *darkness*. They have opposite meanings—no middle ground, no ambiguity. To live in light is life; to live in darkness is death. The darkness of unbelief tries to snuff out the light, but the light shines on.

John the Baptist testified to the light. Many admired this tough prophet of the wilderness. He had his own disciples. In fact, he had disciples long after his death. Paul met disciples of John the Baptist in Ephesus (Acts 19:1-7). But the Baptist's powerful witness was this: He was not Messiah. He was baptizing with water for repentance; Jesus is the Lamb of God and will baptize with the Holy Spirit. And like the best man at a wedding, he rejoices for the Bridegroom (John 3:29). John the Baptist encouraged his own disciples to transfer loyalties.

Come and See

In John's Gospel disciples of John the Baptist were among the first to follow Jesus—a nameless disciple and Andrew. Then Andrew brought his brother Simon. Next Jesus called Philip, and Philip invited Nathanael. To Nathanael's words, "Can anything good come out of Nazareth?" (1:46), Philip replied "Come and see." The key phrase is "come and see." Like many words in this Gospel, these words have a double meaning: Come and see where Jesus is staying, but also come, learn, listen, abide. Experience the relationship of Father and Son, of Son and disciple. Find out for yourself. "Come and see" with your own eyes of faith. Significantly, John's Gospel doesn't list the twelve disciples by name. It refers to them only a few times as "the twelve." Disciples, men and women, are being attracted continually to Jesus. The "twelve" are not a tight band but the core of those who are beginning to believe. Disciples are a growing fellowship of followers of Christ. The invitation to discipleship need not be manipulative, obscure, or emotional. What we do, we do in the full light of day. Come and see.

Write a brief paragraph, explaining what the words *come and see* have meant in your life.

_____

_____

_____

MARKS OF FAITHFUL COMMUNITY

God came to us in Jesus. God became one of us in Jesus. Those words sound simple, but their meaning is not. How do you understand "the Word became flesh"?

_____

_____

What about the divine-human Jesus draws you to him?

_____

_____

What about the divine-human Jesus pushes you away?

_____

_____

What does allegiance to the divine-human Jesus require of us?

_____

_____

Being faithful community, we receive and claim the teaching of the community that Jesus is God in the flesh.

THE RADICAL DISCIPLE

The radical disciple lives in a pluralistic society and at the same time believes that Jesus is the unique Word of God.

IF YOU WANT TO KNOW MORE

To understand some of the differences between the Gospel of John and the other Gospels, read the introduction to John in several versions of the Bible. Pay particular attention to the historical setting, purpose, and themes.

NEW BIRTH

"Very truly, I tell you, no one can enter the kingdom of God without being born of water and Spirit. What is born of the flesh is flesh, and what is born of the Spirit is spirit."

—John 3:5-6

18 Born of Water and Spirit

OUR HUMAN CONDITION

We are born, and we die. In between we attend to our physical needs. What can give life to our living? What can give purpose to our dying?

ASSIGNMENT

John calls Jesus' miracles "signs" that point to who Jesus is. Watch for signs and for people's reactions to them.

Day 1 John 2:1-12 (water into wine, first sign); Psalm 51 (prayer for cleansing from sin)

Day 2 John 2:13-25; Matthew 21:12-17; Mark 11:15-19; Luke 19:45-48 (cleansing the Temple); Psalm 69:9 (zeal for your house); Isaiah 56:6-8 (a house of prayer); Jeremiah 7:8-11 (a den of robbers)

Day 3 John 3 (Nicodemus comes to Jesus, must be born anew, the one from heaven); Jeremiah 31:31-34 (a new covenant); Ezekiel 18:30-32; 36:22-28 (a new heart and a new spirit)

Day 4 John 4:1-42 (Jesus and the Samaritan woman, worship in spirit and truth); 2 Kings 17:21-41 (Samaritans continued idol worship)

Day 5 John 4:43-54 (official's son healed in Capernaum); Matthew 8:5-13 (centurion's servant healed in Capernaum)

Day 6 Read and respond to "Fruit From the Tree of Life" and "Marks of Faithful Community."

Day 7 Rest

PSALM OF THE WEEK

Pray Psalm 24 aloud. Reflect on the condition of your heart and hands as you approach God daily in worship.

PRAYER

Pray daily before study:
"In the assembly of all your people, LORD, I told the good news that you save us. You know that I will never stop telling it" (Psalm 40:9, TEV).

Prayer concerns for this week:

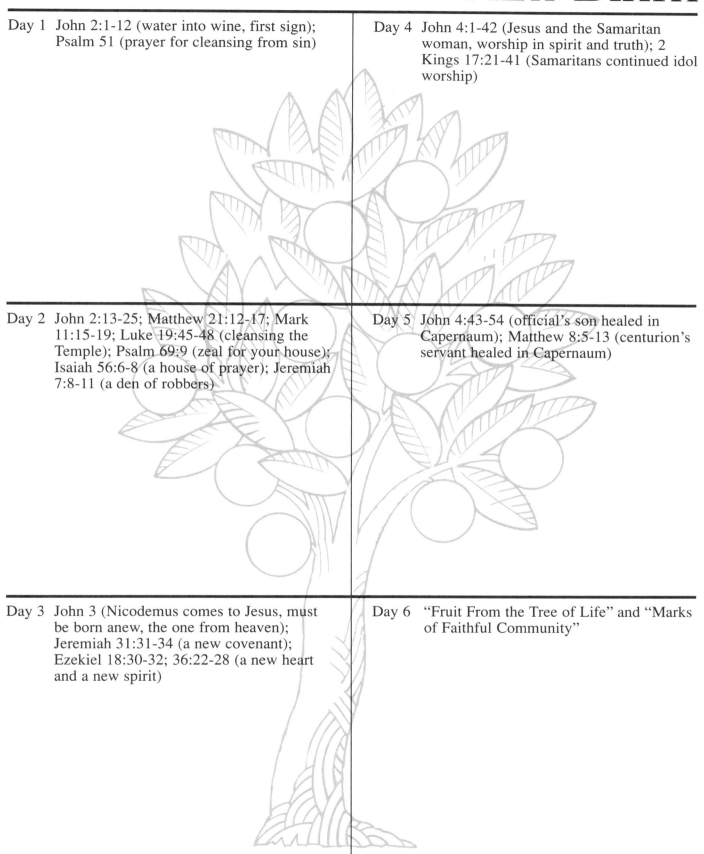

Day 1 John 2:1-12 (water into wine, first sign); Psalm 51 (prayer for cleansing from sin)

Day 4 John 4:1-42 (Jesus and the Samaritan woman, worship in spirit and truth); 2 Kings 17:21-41 (Samaritans continued idol worship)

Day 2 John 2:13-25; Matthew 21:12-17; Mark 11:15-19; Luke 19:45-48 (cleansing the Temple); Psalm 69:9 (zeal for your house); Isaiah 56:6-8 (a house of prayer); Jeremiah 7:8-11 (a den of robbers)

Day 5 John 4:43-54 (official's son healed in Capernaum); Matthew 8:5-13 (centurion's servant healed in Capernaum)

Day 3 John 3 (Nicodemus comes to Jesus, must be born anew, the one from heaven); Jeremiah 31:31-34 (a new covenant); Ezekiel 18:30-32; 36:22-28 (a new heart and a new spirit)

Day 6 "Fruit From the Tree of Life" and "Marks of Faithful Community"

Stylized Tree of Life

DISCIPLE

FRUIT FROM THE TREE OF LIFE

Jesus performed his first "sign" at a wedding feast in Cana. Questions abound. Nathanael came from Cana. Was a member of his family getting married? Why were Jesus and his disciples at the wedding? Why was Mary concerned about hospitality? Failure to provide food and drink was a heavy breach of etiquette. Families saved for a long time to feed their guests at the week-long wedding feast. Why did Jesus hesitate? In John's Gospel Jesus never lets people or events push him into action: His brothers urged him to go to a festival, but he waited (John 7:1-8). Mary and Martha pleaded with him to come when Lazarus was dying, but he delayed (11:3-6). And his mother Mary asked him to help with the wine supply, but he questioned her (2:3-4). In John's Gospel Jesus wants to make sure his actions fit the Father's timing and purpose. He wants to be completely ready for when and how he is to meet his death.

Gentile readers of John would not know the purpose of the six stone jars standing there. So John explains (2:6) that the Jews had purification rites and ceremonial cleansing of hands and vessels. The jars were large, holding twenty to thirty gallons each. Think about it. A hundred and fifty gallons or so of water changed into wine—and the best wine at that! God acts generously, extravagantly.

Cleansing the Temple

Passover was actually the ceremonial meal held on the first day of the Feast of Unleavened Bread. It followed the week of preparation. But the whole festival came to be called Passover. Thousands of religious pilgrims crowded the Temple.

In the Synoptic Gospels (Matthew, Mark, and Luke), Jesus cleansed the Temple near the end of his ministry; but John wanted to make certain readers understood that the Son of God challenged religious practices that went against the teaching and spirit of Scripture from the start. Travelers from afar could not bring their own animals to the Temple for sacrifice, so they had to buy animals at the festival. Money with images of caesar was forbidden in the Temple, so Roman money was changed into Temple coins. But more was at stake than confusion and noise, more even than commissions or Temple taxes. The system of animal sacrifice was being challenged by the Lamb of God whose own self-sacrifice would take away the sins of the world. Jesus claimed that God, who was profoundly present in the Holy of Holies in the Temple, would now reside in his body, which would be destroyed and raised again in three days. His listeners did not understand, of course—nor did his disciples until after the Resurrection—but the major confrontation had begun (John 2:22).

Stone jars such as these found in a first-century house in Jerusalem were used to store water for ceremonial washing. The "six stone water jars" at the wedding in Cana may have been like these (John 2:6).

Worship and Law

Two aspects of Jewish religion had their source in Moses: *Worship*—Tabernacle, sacrifices on the altar, festivals, songs of praise, and priests; and *Law*—the Ten Commandments, Torah, regulation of daily life, sabbath, and Pharisees. Part of Torah told the people how to build the Tabernacle, how priests should dress, what animals should be slain. Part of Torah told them how to treat the poor, how marriage and family life should be conducted, what rules would hold the community together.

Sometimes in the Scripture, worship and Law flow together, as when the priest Ezra read the Law in the square before the Water Gate. Sometimes worship and Law are in conflict, as when prophets such as Amos denounced emphasis on ritual rather than on righteousness and justice.

> "I hate, I despise your festivals,
> and I take no delight in your solemn assemblies"
> (Amos 5:21).

The Pharisees were laymen, lawyers and scribes, those who studied and interpreted both written and oral law. They were admired by the common people. The word *Pharisee* meant "separated ones," though it can also mean "interpreters." Josephus (A.D. 37–100?), the Jewish general and historian, claimed there were about six thousand Pharisees in the first century A.D. The Pharisees wanted to know the Law, but more, they wanted to do the Law—fully, completely. So the priests were concerned primarily with Temple worship, the Pharisees with applying the Law in everyday life.

Nicodemus's Night Visit

Nicodemus was a Pharisee. His peers had chosen him to serve in the Sanhedrin—the seventy elders, priests, aristocrats, and Pharisees, plus the high priest who presided, making seventy-one. The Sanhedrin governed as much of Israel as the Romans would allow. They were divided into three groups or subcouncils that could hear most legal matters as a proper quorum. Nicodemus, probably in his midyears, was an acknowledged leader of a group of Jews who "wanted to do it right."

At Passover time spring was in the air. The love poems from the Song of Songs were being read in the Temple. The earth was being reborn. Passover celebrated God's deliverance of Israel from slavery. What a time for Nicodemus to visit Jesus!

John's Gospel says Nicodemus came to Jesus at night. Why at night? To get away from the press of Passover crowds? To talk quietly with the rabbi in the evening—a traditional time to discuss religious matters? No. For John, the night represents darkness, confusion, doubt, sin, and death. Throughout the Gospel, darkness is contrasted with light, as death is contrasted with life.

DISCIPLE

During Passover Nicodemus no doubt had watched Jesus heal, heard him teach. He began respectfully, perhaps even deferentially, "Rabbi, we know that you ..." Why did Nicodemus say "we"? The Sanhedrin had not yet acted formally. He must have meant his group of Pharisees.

So when Jesus said, rather abruptly, "No one can see the kingdom of God without being born from above," "born anew" (John 3:3), Jesus was thinking not only of a man but of a system, of a way of practicing religion. In other words, Jesus said, you, Nicodemus, and Judaism must be born again.

"How can anyone be born after having grown old? Can one enter a second time into the mother's womb and be born?" (3:4). Nicodemus understood only the literal. In John's Gospel people tend to see only the physical or obvious, seldom the spiritual or the hidden meaning. Jesus' response to Nicodemus's question explains further: "I tell you, no one can enter the kingdom of God without being born of water and Spirit" (3:5). Why did this scholar of Scripture not grasp the spiritual concept of new birth? The words *ruach* in Hebrew and *pneuma* in Greek refer to "wind" or "spirit." God is the one who breathes the breath of life, the wind of the spirit—a prominent expression in sacred Hebrew writings. Nicodemus had studied Ezekiel: "A new heart I will give you, and a new spirit I will put within you; and I will remove from your body the heart of stone and give you a heart of flesh" (Ezekiel 36:26). Nicodemus had sung the psalms:

"Create in me a clean heart, O God,
    and put a new and right spirit within me" (Psalm 51:10).

Signs and teachings alone would not convert this Pharisee. "Just as Moses lifted up the serpent in the wilderness, so must the Son of Man be lifted up" (John 3:14). Nicodemus understood the historical reference. In the wilderness when the Israelites were dying of snakebites, Moses crafted a bronze snake and put it on a pole. "Whenever a serpent bit someone, that person would look at the serpent of bronze and live" (Numbers 21:4-9). But Nicodemus did not understand the allusion to the Son of Man "lifted up," because Jesus had not yet been "lifted up" on the cross. Jesus had not yet been "lifted up" in glorious Resurrection. The Son of Man had not yet been "lifted up" in his ascent to the Father.

Not that night but later, Nicodemus would understand. In the Sanhedrin he bravely spoke up, asking his fellow Pharisees to obey their own law—to hear a person's own witness (John 7:50-52). Still later, on the day of the Crucifixion, when the Son of Man was "lifted up," Nicodemus brought spices and helped prepare Jesus' body for burial. It took a cross for Nicodemus to be born from above, born again.

Samaritan Woman

Jesus met Nicodemus at night; Jesus met the Samaritan woman at high noon. The contrast is literally darkness and

NEW BIRTH

light. Nicodemus, a Jew, a male, had a distinguished name. He was a power player at the heart of the establishment. The Samaritan, a woman, is never referred to by name. She was a member of a marginalized people. Throughout history she is known simply as "the Samaritan woman" or "the woman at the well." Nicodemus walked back into the night, bewildered, confused, without understanding. The woman, in broad daylight, abandoned her water jar and ran back to her city proclaiming Jesus as the Promised One.

Despite being thought of as outsiders, the Samaritans thought of themselves as the true keepers of the faith; and they believed history bore them out. They reached back in memory to Abraham, whose first stop in the land of promise was at Shechem, between Mount Ebal and Mount Gerizim. They revered Jacob, who dug a well near Shechem and watered his flocks. Samaritans were descendants of Northern Kingdom Israelites who intermarried with people imported by Assyria after the fall of Israel in 722/721 B.C.

The Samaritans considered only the Pentateuch, the first five books of the Bible, authentic Scripture. They scorned the Pharisees' attempt to modernize and interpret the Law. Most important, they never accepted the Temple in Jerusalem. Their ties were to Mount Gerizim, which had preceded Mount Zion in Israel's religious heritage. The Samaritans built a temple on Mount Gerizim in the fourth century B.C.

When Nehemiah rebuilt the wall of Jerusalem and Ezra restored the covenant community, the Samaritans opposed them and tried to get Persia to stop the restoration of the Temple and Jerusalem.

In 111/110 B.C. some Judeans under John Hyrcanus, high priest and ethnarch of Judea, attacked Samaria and burned the Mount Gerizim shrine to the ground.

Against this background, John's Gospel says, "He had to go through Samaria" (John 4:4). Jesus did not have to go through Samaria, of course. Jews normally traveled from Judea to Galilee by way of the Jordan Valley, precisely so they wouldn't go through Samaria. Jesus' need rested in his obedience to the Father's will.

High noon. A Jewish man dared to talk to a Samaritan woman at a public well. Unthinkable. Jesus crossed every social barrier. Normally, in the Near East, a woman would not converse with even a male relative in public. "How is it that you, a Jew, ask a drink of me, a woman of Samaria?" For Gentile readers, John adds, "Jews do not share things in common with Samaritans" (4:9). That is, they do not associate with or eat and drink together.

Jesus deepened the conversation slowly, for the woman, like Nicodemus, at first thought only in literal terms. Jesus asked for a drink, then spoke of "living water." Notice the double meaning. Living water can mean fresh spring water, but it can also mean the water of God's Spirit. "Ho, everyone who thirsts, come to the waters" (Isaiah 55:1).

NOTES, REFLECTIONS, AND QUESTIONS

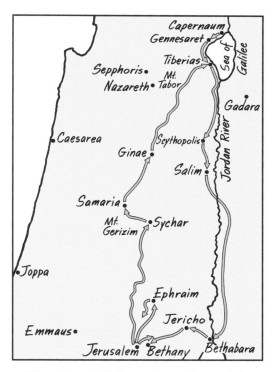

When Jesus left Jerusalem and traveled to Galilee, he went north through Samaria. When he went again to Jerusalem, he followed the route of the Jordan River, first west of the river and then east of the river, crossing it again to approach Bethany and Jerusalem from the east.

DISCIPLE

"Sir, you have no bucket," she replied. She was still on the physical plane, like Nicodemus referring to the mother's womb. When Jesus spoke of water that would gush up to eternal life, she asked for it so she wouldn't have to come to the well every day with a water jar on her head. She still didn't get it. Jesus continued, "Go, call your husband." She replied, "I have no husband." Jesus honored her by saying she had told the truth. When Jesus told her she had had five husbands and now lived with a man who was not her husband, she concluded he was a prophet.

Was the woman immoral? Such often has been the popular portrait. Perhaps she was barren, divorced by one man after another. Perhaps she, like Tamar, was caught in the levirate law; how many times had she been a widow? Perhaps with no dowry or family, she was destitute and had simply found a place to survive. Some scholars have suggested that her trip to the well at noon, instead of during the cool morning or early evening hours when other women would be drawing water, indicates she was ostracized. Without doubt, she was marginalized, alone.

Jesus was not offended; yet he knew all about her, just as he had known the hearts of those who had seen his signs in Jerusalem (2:25). Remember, Nicodemus said, "we know"—but he did not know. Jesus accepted the woman as she was.

At first the woman had said "Sir" but then "prophet." She lifted up her eyes to Mount Gerizim, looked down at Jacob's well, and spoke the ancient hostility: Mount Gerizim or the Jerusalem Temple? Which is the right place to worship God?

Neither mountain would hold power, for "God is spirit, and those who worship him must worship in spirit and truth" (4:24). That would happen only when Messiah came. "I am he," said Jesus (4:26). Recall that Moses asked God for the divine name. God responded, "I AM WHO I AM" (Exodus 3:14). In Jesus the woman confronted "I AM," God in human form, the Word made flesh.

The woman became a witness to her city—and to us. She invited the people to "come and see," an invitation for all to experience Jesus. In spite of any doubts she may have had, she gave her testimony with enthusiasm. And John's Gospel reports, "They left the city and were on their way to him" (John 4:30).

Jesus had departed Jerusalem because of suspicion, cynicism, and anger toward him. But now he stayed in Samaria because "many Samaritans . . . believed in him because of the woman's testimony" (4:39). Spurned by his own people, Jesus received the faith of "outsiders": "We know that this is truly the Savior of the world" (4:42).

Recall that the disciples asked Jesus if he had food to eat. His food, he said, was "to do the will of him who sent me" (4:34). That's what he was doing as he led the woman into new life, as he gave her "living water." Then Jesus looked out on the fields, perhaps green with growing barley or wheat, and said—again with double meaning—you say "four months" until harvest, but I say, "The fields are ripe for harvesting" (4:35). The faith of the Samaritan converts showed the harvest had begun.

MARKS OF FAITHFUL COMMUNITY

Jesus offers new life to the living. Think about the people and events in this week's readings in John. What was new about the life Jesus offered in those Scriptures?

_____

_____

Different versions of the Bible translate Jesus' word to Nicodemus in John 3:3 as "born again," "born from above," or "born anew." How do you understand each of those terms?

_____

_____

_____

Which one of these three terms best describes your experience of new life in Christ?

_____

THE RADICAL DISCIPLE

The radical disciple bears witness to the new life in Christ through daily acts of faithful living. How do you think your experience of new life is evident to those around you?

IF YOU WANT TO KNOW MORE

"Being born of water and Spirit" (John 3:5) is interpreted in various ways. Study the phrase in several commentaries and prepare a report of two to three minutes to give to the group.

Being faithful community, we see life as both physical and spiritual, and while we exist in the physical, we live in new life graciously offered by God in Christ Jesus.

BREAD

"I am the bread of life. Whoever comes to me will never be hungry, and whoever believes in me will never be thirsty."

—John 6:35

19 Bread of Life

OUR HUMAN CONDITION

We respond to our ever-present hungers by seeking more excitement, more pleasures, more possessions, more recognition. The basics are not enough.

ASSIGNMENT

Jesus reveals himself through "I am" sayings in John. Begin to watch for the connections between the "I am" sayings and Old Testament Scriptures.

Day 1   John 5:1-24 (healing on the sabbath, as the Father so the Son); Matthew 12:9-14; Mark 3:1-6; Luke 13:10-17; 14:1-6 (sabbath healings)

Day 2   John 5:25-47 (testimony to Jesus' relationship to God); Deuteronomy 17:2-7; 19:15-21; Matthew 18:15-20; 1 Timothy 5:19 (two or three witnesses)

Day 3   John 6:1-15; Matthew 14:13-21; Mark 6:30-44; Luke 9:10-17 (feeding five thousand)

Day 4   John 6:16-21; Matthew 14:22-27; Mark 6:45-52 (walking on the sea); compare Psalm 107 (God stills the storm)

Day 5   John 6:22-71 (the bread of life, bread from heaven, the living bread); Exodus 13:3-10 (Feast of Unleavened Bread, sign of Lord's deliverance); 16 (bread from heaven, manna)

Day 6   Read and respond to "Fruit From the Tree of Life" and "Marks of Faithful Community."

Day 7   Rest

PSALM OF THE WEEK

Pray Psalm 65 aloud each day as thanks to God for daily bread. Sometime during the week enjoy bread and the psalm with another person. Let the taste, texture, and goodness of the bread remind you of the goodness of God.

PRAYER

Pray daily before study:
"We give thanks to you, O God,
   we give thanks to you!
We proclaim how great you are
   and tell of the wonderful things
      you have done" (Psalm 75:1, TEV).

Prayer concerns for this week:

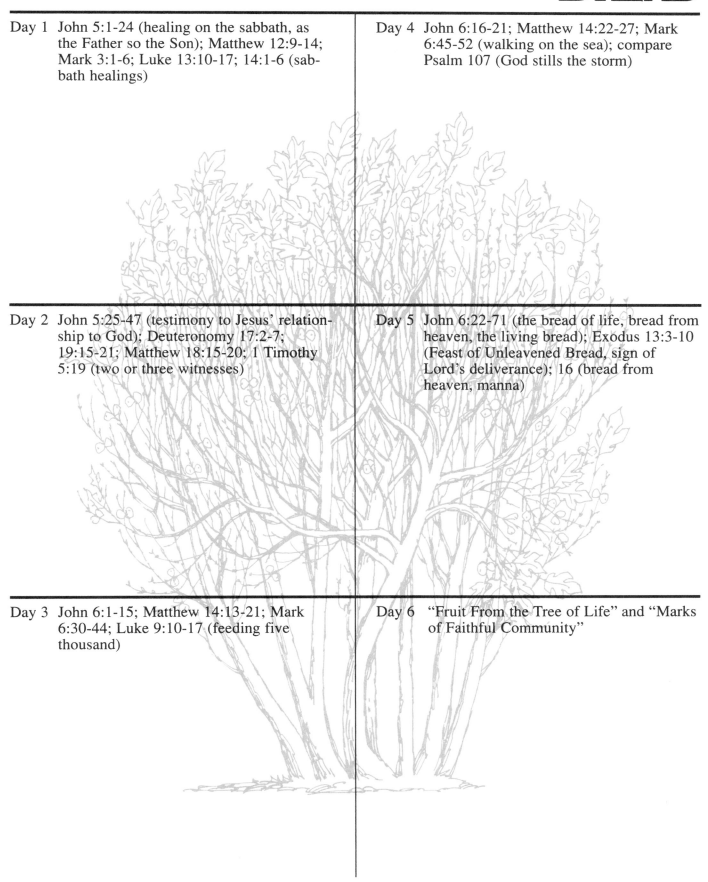

Day 1 John 5:1-24 (healing on the sabbath, as the Father so the Son); Matthew 12:9-14; Mark 3:1-6; Luke 13:10-17; 14:1-6 (sabbath healings)

Day 4 John 6:16-21; Matthew 14:22-27; Mark 6:45-52 (walking on the sea); compare Psalm 107 (God stills the storm)

Day 2 John 5:25-47 (testimony to Jesus' relationship to God); Deuteronomy 17:2-7; 19:15-21; Matthew 18:15-20; 1 Timothy 5:19 (two or three witnesses)

Day 5 John 6:22-71 (the bread of life, bread from heaven, the living bread); Exodus 13:3-10 (Feast of Unleavened Bread, sign of Lord's deliverance); 16 (bread from heaven, manna)

Day 3 John 6:1-15; Matthew 14:13-21; Mark 6:30-44; Luke 9:10-17 (feeding five thousand)

Day 6 "Fruit From the Tree of Life" and "Marks of Faithful Community"

Fig Tree

DISCIPLE

FRUIT FROM THE TREE OF LIFE

Sabbath was capstone of the covenant: "Israel keeps sabbath; God keeps Israel." But God's simple commandment to rest on the seventh day had been fortified by thirty-nine laws defining work, plus hundreds of rabbinic interpretations. The supporting regulations were called a "hedge" or "fence" to help people avoid sabbath violation.

In all four Gospels, when Jesus broke the sabbath rules, he used insights into Scripture, God's nature, and rabbinic interpretation to defend his actions.

In Matthew Jesus healed a man with a withered hand on the sabbath (Matthew 12:9-14; Mark 3:1-6; Luke 6:6-11). Religious opinion said the healing could have waited until the next day because the condition was not life-threatening. Jesus made a double appeal—first to rabbinic interpretation. If a sheep fell into a pit, you could pull it out. Might not the animal live until after sabbath? Then he appealed to the nature of God. Mark records Jesus as saying, "Is it lawful to do good or to do harm on the sabbath, to save life or to kill?" (Mark 3:4). The God of Israel gives life, healing, joy. God made the sabbath "for humankind, and not humankind for the sabbath" (2:27).

In Luke Jesus healed a woman who had not been able to stand up straight for eighteen years (Luke 13:10-17). When the synagogue leader objected, Jesus called him a hypocrite for two reasons: Rabbinic interpretation of the Law would allow someone to untie an ox and lead it to water on sabbath. Why not allow Jesus to "untie" a person? But more, the children of Abraham celebrated the God who had set them free from Egypt. Why didn't the leaders rejoice over an Israelite who had been "set free"? All three Synoptic Gospels record Jesus' words "The Son of Man is lord of the sabbath" (Matthew 12:8; Mark 2:28; Luke 6:5). God's compassion rules the sabbath.

"Do You Want to Be Made Well?"

In John Jesus gravitated to the sick and infirm. From among all the sick people at the pool of Beth-zatha (Bethesda), Jesus chose a tough case—a man ill for thirty-eight years (John 5:2-18). Apparently occasional bursts of air or water from some underground source caused the water to bubble. According to 5:4, which is not in all ancient manuscripts, people thought an angel stirred the water and it would heal.

Jesus asked abruptly, "Do you want to be made well?" (5:6). The man's answer—"I have no one to put me into the pool" (5:7)—hints of self-pity, unaccepted responsibility, and misplaced blame on others. Jesus went straight to the point— no prerequisite faith, no washing in the pool, no dependence upon others. He gave the man three commands: "Stand up"; "take your mat"; "walk" (5:8). John's Gospel makes clear obedience is essential for faith.

This man, ill for thirty-eight years, was healed, able to walk—and he was in trouble. He was carrying his mat as instructed; but that meant he was working on the sabbath, a specific violation. Now the reaction: Instead of praising God that a marvelous healing had taken place, the religious leaders said, "It's against the law to carry your mat on the sabbath." Instead of congratulating the man on being whole, the Pharisees asked, "Who told you to take up your mat and walk?"

What is the heartbeat of Torah, the law of Moses? God is righteous and full of compassion. In focusing on intricate sabbath regulations, the religious officials missed the point of the Law. They saw the legislation, but they missed the Legislator. Again, Jesus drew upon rabbinic understanding. Did God quit work on the seventh day? Yes and no. God in Genesis rested on the seventh day. Without rest, life becomes a meaningless blur. Rest recognizes God's care. Rest is an act of faith. Yet God obviously is causing babies to be born, crops to grow, prayers to be answered, even on sabbath. So God is still working, sustaining and giving life—seven days a week. "He who keeps Israel will neither slumber nor sleep" (Psalm 121:4). Jesus appealed to this understanding of God's character by saying, "My Father is still working, and I also am working" (John 5:17).

Of course, this reference to his relationship with the Father caused further controversy. In John Jesus' healings are followed by careful discourse. After restoring the sick man to health, Jesus explained he had come to give new life, eternal life now to all who would believe and obey him. Like the ill man, even the dead "will hear the voice of the Son of God and . . . live" (5:25).

When have you heard the words of Jesus Christ and been restored spiritually? physically?

The next time Jesus went to Jerusalem, people were still arguing about the earlier sabbath healing (7:19-24). When Jesus asked why some were looking for an opportunity to kill him, the crowd said he had a demon. So Jesus used yet another argument from Jewish law. Baby boys must be circumcised on the eighth day after birth (Leviticus 12:3). What if the eighth day fell on sabbath? Rabbinic law held that circumcision—with the work required—took precedence. Jesus, in true rabbinic form, asked if one part of the body could be cared for on sabbath to ensure wholeness, why should healing of the whole body not be allowed? Don't judge by superficial technicalities, Jesus taught; judge by what is right (John

DISCIPLE

7:24). Jesus was doing the redemptive work of God toward which the Law pointed. Did the leaders not sing the Psalms?

"The law of the LORD is perfect,
    reviving the soul . . .
the precepts of the LORD are right,
    rejoicing the heart" (Psalm 19:7-8).

Did they not praise God for healing?

"O LORD my God, I cried to you for help,
    and you have healed me. . . .
You have turned my mourning into dancing. . . .
    O LORD, my God, I will give thanks to you forever"
        (30:2, 11, 12).

Jesus revealed the heart of the God who gave the Law in the first place. Jesus' words and his works showed the glory of God in action.

In secular society, with frenzied activity; twenty-four-hour, seven-day merchandising; and endless entertainment, how can sabbath rest, with its healing power, be restored as a gift of God without reestablishing legalisms?

_____

_____

If not for society, at least for Christians?

_____

_____

Testimony

In John's Gospel Jesus' "signs" and "works" testify that he is from God. When Jesus' critics questioned his authority, he responded that he did nothing on his own and pointed to the Father.

Jesus reminded the Pharisees they had sent messengers to John the Baptist. "He testified to the truth" (John 5:33). Then the works, the signs, were testimony. In fact, Jesus' works were the work of God and therefore were the Father's testimony (5:36-38). Furthermore, if the Pharisees would read the Scriptures correctly, they would see that those Scriptures "testify on my behalf" (5:39). In other words, eternal life is in Jesus. "If you believed Moses, you would believe me, for he wrote about me" (5:46). Because of such testimony, the religious leaders should have believed; but they did not. They kept wanting more "signs."

Manna

In the Synoptic Gospels Jesus' ministry covers a single year, climaxing with his entry into Jerusalem. In John's Gospel Jesus taught and healed for three years. John has Jesus move back and forth between Galilee and Jerusalem. Three

BREAD

times he traveled to Jerusalem, at least twice to celebrate Passover.

God through Moses mandated the Feast of Unleavened Bread, Passover, so Israel would remember. Remember those four hundred years of slavery in Egypt. Remember that night when there was no time to knead the dough or let it rise. Release from oppression calls for celebration, a time to remember. That's why Jews search their homes, throw out every bit of yeast, and laugh and dance and pray—and eat unleavened bread. It is no small thing to be free!

The festival also recalled those forty wearisome years when their ancestors wandered in the wilderness, stomachs cramped with hunger, throats parched with thirst. They would have died in that barren desert if God had not provided manna, which means literally "What is it?" (Exodus 16:15). "It was like coriander seed, white, and the taste of it was like wafers made with honey" (16:31). This sweet substance had to be eaten the day it was gathered or it would spoil (16:19-20). It could not be saved up, except for manna gathered on the sixth day for sabbath food. Manna is the idea behind "Give us this day our daily bread" (Matthew 6:11).

Now notice the symbolism as Jesus fed the five thousand. Any Jew who had heard or read the books of Moses and had sung psalms would quickly relate the feeding of the five thousand to manna in the wilderness.

- Jesus and the disciples crossed the sea (Galilee). Had not Moses crossed the sea?
- They went to a "deserted place" (Matthew 14:13, 15) on the northeast shore of the Sea of Galilee, volcanic rock that is barren to this day. The Israelites went to the Sinai Desert.
- Everyone was tired, hungry, and far from any village. Just as with Moses in the wilderness, thousands of people needed food.
- Though all four Gospels report the story, only John's Gospel mentions barley, considered the food of the poor. The resources were meager—five tiny barley loaves and two salted, dried sardinelike fish. The situation seemed hopeless, just as in Exodus.
- Everyone had enough manna. Jesus had food left over, enough to fill twelve baskets. Is John giving us a double meaning again? Could Jesus "feed" the twelve tribes of Israel? Remember the one hundred fifty gallons of wine at the wedding in Cana? God is extravagant!
- As it does to this day, the warm air from the Sea of Galilee, 690 feet below sea level, rose and clashed with cold air coming down from Mount Hermon. In a matter of minutes, waves eight to twelve feet high rose and fell on that little lake (thirteen miles by eight miles). A strong wind was blowing (John 6:18). The strong wind remembered at Passover was the one that piled up the water, allowing the freed people to cross the Red Sea (Exodus 14:21-22).

NOTES, REFLECTIONS, AND QUESTIONS

The Feast of Unleavened Bread was one of three pilgrimage festivals that all Jewish males were required to celebrate. The Passover meal on the first day of the feast was originally a separate observance celebrating the angel of death's "passing over" the Israelite homes that had been marked with the blood of a lamb, and so represented the salvation of the firstborn. The three major festivals required a great deal of preparation, and all necessary work had to be finished before the festival began; so the week before a festival came to be called the "week of preparation" and the day before it the "day of preparation." In New Testament times, all preparation had to be finished by 3:00 P.M. on the day before a festival began. The lambs to be eaten at the Passover meal were killed on the day of preparation.

DISCIPLE

- The story reaches its climax when the people, after seeing the sign, followed Jesus to Capernaum. They wanted more food, just as the Israelites had wanted more food. But besides food, they also wanted to make Jesus king (John 6:15). He had rejected that political temptation when he had struggled with Satan after his baptism (Matthew 4:8-10). So Jesus withdrew from them (John 6:15).

Now the people complained, just as their ancestors had complained in the wilderness. They wanted more food, and they wanted another sign. Jesus now offered himself as the "bread from heaven." The "sign" had been done. It pointed to him. But when Jesus spoke of the "true bread from heaven," the people made the same mistake the Samaritan woman made when she asked for more water so she wouldn't need to go continually to the well. "Sir," they said, "give us this bread always" (6:34).

With his audacious claim, "I am the bread of life," Jesus moved the discussion from physical bread that God provides to the spiritual "bread" that gives abundant and eternal life. "Whoever comes to me will never be hungry, and whoever believes in me will never be thirsty" (6:35).

His listeners had not seen the cross. They had not experienced the Resurrection. They were confused. Jesus did not feed them again physically.

When Jesus said in the synagogue, "Unless you eat the flesh of the Son of Man and drink his blood, you have no life in you" (6:53), many followers who heard it complained. Jews were forbidden to eat blood, for the life is in the blood. So the crowds scattered, leaving only the faithful twelve who said with Peter, "Lord, to whom can we go? You have the words of eternal life" (6:68).

The crowd could not comprehend the deeper meanings. To "eat" and "drink" meant to trust Jesus, to follow him, to obey him, to feed on his spirit—to believe. When John's Gospel was written, Holy Communion was at least implied in the words *eat* and *drink*. For a generation or two, Christians had been eating the bread and drinking the cup as a "participation" in the body and blood of Christ. The Christian community understood the meaning of spiritual unity and of eating the body and drinking the blood as the synagogue listeners never could.

How would you explain "Those who eat my flesh and drink my blood abide in me, and I in them" and "will live forever" (6:56-58)?

_____

_____

_____

MARKS OF FAITHFUL COMMUNITY

Recall Jesus' question to the ill man: "Do you want to be made well?" (John 5:6). Consider your own life—your weaknesses and ailments. What answer would you give if Jesus asked you the same question?

_____

_____

Consider the health of your congregation. What answers would you as a congregation give if Jesus asked the congregation the same question?

_____

_____

What would be the cost of healing for you? for your congregation?

_____

_____

We know God provides the beat of our heart and the breath of our lungs. We pray, "Give us this day our daily bread," and express gratitude for life itself.
What do Jesus' words "I am the bread of life" mean to you?

_____

_____

How are you nourished by the bread of life?

_____

_____

THE RADICAL DISCIPLE

The radical disciple hears the hard sayings of Jesus and does not turn away. What teachings of Jesus in this week's Scripture did you find difficult?

IF YOU WANT TO KNOW MORE

Christian denominations understand the Lord's Supper differently. In a Bible dictionary or dictionary of church history, look for meanings particular to the terms _Eucharist, Holy Communion, the Lord's Supper._

NOTES, REFLECTIONS, AND QUESTIONS

Being faithful community, we seek nothing less than "the food that endures for eternal life," Jesus the living bread.

GUIDANCE

"I am the light of the world. Whoever follows me will never walk in darkness but will have the light of life."

—John 8:12

20 Light of the World

OUR HUMAN CONDITION

For the most part we determine the course of our lives. We don't need anyone to guide us. We'll find our own way.

ASSIGNMENT

Pay attention to how John contrasts light and darkness, sight and blindness.

Day 1 John 7:1-52 (festival of booths, living water); Leviticus 23:33–24:4 (festival of booths, tabernacle lamp with light burning regularly); Deuteronomy 16:13-17 (pilgrimage festivals)

Day 2 John 7:53–8:11 (woman caught in adultery); Leviticus 20 (penalties for violating holiness code)

Day 3 John 8:12-59 (light of the world, Jesus and Abraham, *I am*); Exodus 13:17-22; Numbers 14:1-25 (pillar of cloud by day, fire by night); Exodus 40 (lampstand and lamps in tabernacle, cloud of Lord by day, fire in cloud by night)

Day 4 John 9 (man born blind, Jesus the light of life)

Day 5 John 10:1-21 (Jesus the good shepherd, the gate, life abundant); Ezekiel 34 (God the true shepherd of Israel)

Day 6 Read and respond to "Fruit From the Tree of Life" and "Marks of Faithful Community."

Day 7 Rest

THE RADICAL DISCIPLE

Having seen the light of Christ, the radical disciple becomes a bearer of that light. Each day this week, decide where, how, and to whom you will take the light of Christ.

PSALM OF THE WEEK

Read Psalm 27 aloud daily—in daylight if possible. And each day follow the urging of verse 14: "Wait for the LORD." Sit silently, listening for God. Meditate on the safety, comfort, and guidance found in light.

PRAYER

Pray daily before study:
"Your word is a lamp to guide me
    and a light for my path.
I will keep my solemn promise
    to obey your just instructions" (Psalm 119:105-106, TEV).

Prayer concerns for this week:

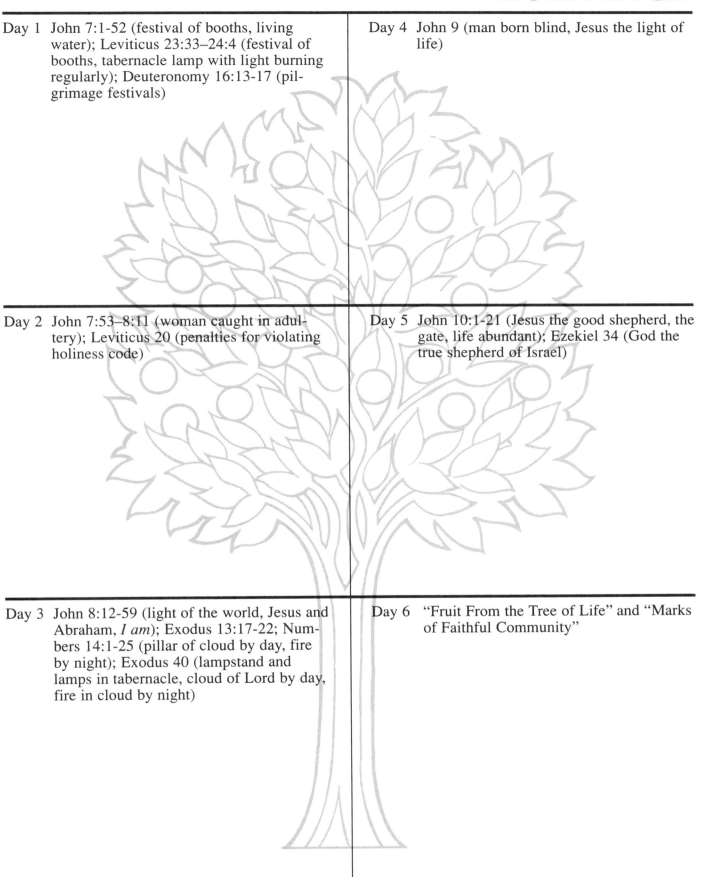

Day 1 John 7:1-52 (festival of booths, living water); Leviticus 23:33–24:4 (festival of booths, tabernacle lamp with light burning regularly); Deuteronomy 16:13-17 (pilgrimage festivals)

Day 2 John 7:53–8:11 (woman caught in adultery); Leviticus 20 (penalties for violating holiness code)

Day 3 John 8:12-59 (light of the world, Jesus and Abraham, *I am*); Exodus 13:17-22; Numbers 14:1-25 (pillar of cloud by day, fire by night); Exodus 40 (lampstand and lamps in tabernacle, cloud of Lord by day, fire in cloud by night)

Day 4 John 9 (man born blind, Jesus the light of life)

Day 5 John 10:1-21 (Jesus the good shepherd, the gate, life abundant); Ezekiel 34 (God the true shepherd of Israel)

Day 6 "Fruit From the Tree of Life" and "Marks of Faithful Community"

Stylized Tree of Life

DISCIPLE

FRUIT FROM THE TREE OF LIFE

The Feast of Booths or Tabernacles is Thanksgiving, harvest festival, vacation, family cookouts, pilgrimage to the Temple, feasting, singing, dancing, all rolled into one great week-long celebration. It begins on the fifteenth of the month of Tishri (September-October), under a full harvest moon, when the last crops are being brought in. Rooted deep in ancient agricultural history, the Feast of Booths marks the end of one growing year and the beginning of the next. Called "Sukkoth" in Hebrew, it is one of the three pilgrimage feasts mandated by the law of Moses (Leviticus 23:34-44; Deuteronomy 16:13-17).

The autumn crops come mostly from vines and trees—grapes, the last figs, green and ripe olives, citron. Five months of hard work during the dry season have ended; hopes for the new year begin. People thank God for the harvest. Then they begin praying for rain for the coming year. They read the scroll of Ecclesiastes to remember that life still has toil and trouble but is good.

Sukkoth recalls the wandering in the desert—those forty years when Israel dwelt in the Sinai waiting for entrance to the Promised Land. Those were the days when they lived not in houses but in tents. Even the place of worship was a tent. God led the people with a cloud by day and a pillar of fire by night. Some rabbis called this time the "honeymoon years," when Israel was in love with God, under a mutual covenant, trusting God for life itself.

During the festival, people lived in "booths." They built simple makeshift booths with roofs of tree branches. They had to be able to see three stars through the branches so they would know when sabbath began.

Three Processions

Like Passover, the Feast of Booths brought hundreds of thousands—perhaps as many as two million—pilgrims to Jerusalem. Each day there were three processions. In the first, male worshipers carried a citron (similar to a lemon) in their left hand, a *lulav* or bundle of branches (three myrtle, two willow, and one palm) in their right. As they marched around the altar, they sang the "Egyptian Hallel" (Psalms 113–118) while the priests offered the thanksgiving sacrifices. When a response occurred in the psalms, the men raised their arms with the fruit and the branches and shouted, "His steadfast love endures forever" (118:1-4).

In the second great procession, men, women, and children followed the high priest from the Temple courtyard area down to the pool of Siloam. Water for this pool flowed from the Gihon Spring, just outside the city walls. Called "living water," it was unlike collected cistern water, for it flowed directly from the hand of God—this natural spring gushed intermittently. The priest filled a pitcher from the pool of

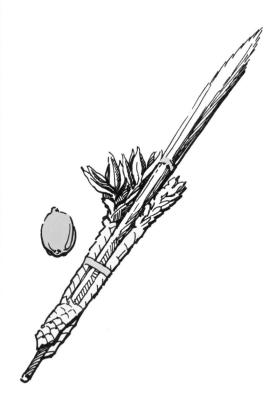

Part of the Feast of Booths (Sukkoth) ceremonies is the waving of tree branches in rejoicing before the Lord (Leviticus 23:40). This ceremonial object, called a *lulav*, has a palm branch, two willow branches, and three myrtle branches bound together. Alongside it is an *etrog*, a member of the citrus family, also used in the celebration.

Siloam, led the procession back up the slope, through the Water Gate, into the sacred courtyard area, then poured the water at the base of the altar. As the priest poured the water, the people remembered when God, through Moses, brought water from the rock in the desert.

The third procession took place at night. The priests and Levites erected four seventy-five-foot-high lampstands in the women's courtyard. The wicks placed in the oil of the lamps were made from worn-out robes of the priests. When these lamps were set aflame, every home in Jerusalem could see the light. On the last night of the festival, the people carried torches and danced the night away. They remembered God's guiding the people in the wilderness by a pillar of fire.

Jerusalem was astir. At earlier festivals Jesus had caused turmoil with his healing and teaching. So people were talking. Would he come? Would he teach? Would he heal? What would happen if he did come? His brothers in Galilee urged him to join them in the pilgrimage. But Jesus declined. Instead of entering the city with the vast opening-day throngs when everyone was watching for him, Jesus slipped quietly into the city, midfestival, and began to teach (John 7:10, 14).

Tested in the Temple

Jesus, not the woman caught in adultery, was the issue. The accusers were setting a trap. If Jesus said, "Stone her," he would violate Roman law, because capital offenses required Roman courts. A stoning would also seem to go counter to Jesus' message of forgiveness. If Jesus said, "Let her go," his decision would be in direct conflict with the law of Moses. The religious leaders brought the woman to test Jesus, "so that they might have some charge to bring against him" (John 8:6).

Adultery involves two people. If they had caught her in the act, where was the man? The law of Moses required that both man and woman be put to death (Leviticus 20:10). And where were the witnesses? The would-be protectors of public morals were breaking their own codes. Bringing the woman before an uncertified rabbi in the Temple courts, shaming her, "making her stand before all of them" (John 8:3) ignored several legal requirements for just treatment.

Interpreters have wondered what Jesus wrote on the ground. Was it the sins of those men standing around him? Perhaps he wrote their names along with their sins, beginning with the most respected. But when Jesus bent down, he humbled himself. By not speaking, he refused to respond to their charges. His silence, his bending down, his writing in the dirt changed the interaction. When they "kept on questioning him," Jesus responded, "Let anyone among you who is without sin be the first to throw a stone at her" (8:7).

The test was over. The men had been judges; now they were humbled. The woman had been an object; now she was a person. Everyone was invited to break with old ways—the

The oldest manuscripts of the Gospel of John omit 7:53–8:11, the story of the woman caught in adultery. Other manuscripts add this section after 7:36 or at the end after 21:25.

DISCIPLE

men with legalism and judgmentalism, the woman with sin and sexual immorality. Jesus said to her what he had said to the ill man made well: "Go . . . and from now on do not sin again" (8:11). Jesus offered grace and mercy but also required accountability of the scribes and Pharisees and of the woman.

The Light of the World

Imagine this night: The great lamps are filled with oil and set afire; the torches are lit so the Temple courtyard is aglow with light. Jesus spoke: "I am the light of the world" (John 8:12). The "I AM" who spoke to Moses is speaking now.

Then a man blind from birth. Jesus and his disciples saw him. The disciples wondered aloud whose sin had caused the tragedy: The man had been born blind—hardly his sin, perhaps the sin of his parents. Jesus was clear and abrupt. "Neither this man nor his parents sinned; he was born blind so that God's works might be revealed in him" (9:3).

Although it was sabbath, Jesus said he must work "while it is day" (9:4), saying in effect, God's work would be revealed through him. He was participating in God's redemptive work, and the time was short.

Jesus spat on the ground, made mud (a sabbath violation), put it on the sightless eyes, then said, "Go, wash in the pool of Siloam" (9:7). Every day during the festival this blind man had heard throngs sing their way to Siloam to carry the "living water" back to the altar. What symbolism! From the hand of God who gave water to the man's ancestors in the wilderness came "living water" to heal his eyes and let him see.

Typical of John's Gospel is this threefold account—a "sign," discussion among the people, then the teaching of Jesus. The miraculous healing of the man born blind spurred the authorities into action. They questioned the man, then his parents, then questioned him again. They tried to get him to praise God and denounce Jesus, but he refused. The parents were careful not to defy the authorities lest they be "put out of the synagogue" (9:22). The blind man—still nameless— became increasingly bold. He even asked the authorities if they wanted to become believers. In anger they denounced this "sinner" and drove him from the synagogue. Jesus had "heard that they had driven him out," and went and found him (9:35). The man became a believer: "'Lord, I believe.' And he worshiped him" (9:38).

The expulsion of the man from the synagogue and Jesus' exchange with the Pharisees who, though confronted with the light, remained blind (9:39-41) set the stage for John's next teaching.

The Good Shepherd

"I AM" speaks again. Jesus said, "I am the good shepherd. The good shepherd lays down his life for the sheep" (John 10:11). The prophet Ezekiel criticized the kings and priests who were supposed to be good shepherds of the people: "You shepherds of Israel . . . have been feeding yourselves! Should not shepherds feed the sheep? You eat the fat, you clothe yourselves with the wool, you slaughter the fatlings; but you do not feed the sheep. You have not strengthened the weak, you have not healed the sick, you have not bound up the injured, you have not brought back the strayed, you have not sought the lost, but with force and harshness you have ruled them" (Ezekiel 34:1-6). So, "thus says the Lord GOD: I myself will search for my sheep" (34:11)—God, the true shepherd! And Jesus says "I am." "I am the gate for the sheep" (John 10:7). What did he mean? Using imagery every rural person would know, Jesus pictured a shepherd gathering his flock into a pen or cave. Laggard sheep would be called in by name. Wounded or sick sheep would be cared for. The shepherd would protect the sheep from wild animals or thieves by lying down in the opening. At night he literally would be the "gate." The sheep could come in and go out only through the gate.

The shepherd would lay down his life for the sheep.

MARKS OF FAITHFUL COMMUNITY

John's Gospel uses the mighty work that God in Christ performed for the man born blind to show that Jesus will give light to our paths. As the Prologue announced, "The true light, which enlightens everyone, was coming into the world" (John 1:9).

Being faithful community, we choose to be diligent witnesses to the light of Christ.

Reflect on these verses from this week's Scripture: "Your word is a lamp to guide me / and a light for my path" (Psalm 119:105, TEV) and "If you continue in my word, you are truly my disciples; and you will know the truth, and the truth will make you free" (John 8:31-32). How have these verses become true for you in your experience of studying Scripture through DISCIPLE?

_____

_____

How do you seek and recognize "light" for your daily life?

_____

Identify areas of your life in which you currently need more light, more guidance.

_____

IF YOU WANT TO KNOW MORE

To study the image of the shepherd in Scripture, use a Bible concordance to look up verses that include the word *shepherd*. Be aware of how the role of shepherd is variously depicted.

BELIEVE

"I am the resurrection and the life. Those who believe in me, even though they die, will live."

—John 11:25

21 The Coming Hour

OUR HUMAN CONDITION

We move between life and death, not sure what to believe about either. We look for groups or ideas that promise to free us from our uncertainty.

ASSIGNMENT

Events begin to move quickly now. Pay attention to what Jesus does and why. Ask yourself what John intends to say in the way he reports the events. You will need a Bible with the Apocrypha for reading the background on the Feast of Dedication.

Day 1   John 10:22-42 (festival of Dedication); 1 Maccabees 4:36-59, Apocrypha (cleansing and rededication of the Temple)
Day 2   John 11:1-54 (the resurrection and the life, Martha's confession, raising of Lazarus); Daniel 12 (time of the end, resurrection hope); Job 19:23-29 (faith in a Redeemer)
Day 3   John 11:55–12:11 (anointing at Bethany)
Day 4   John 12:12-36 (Jesus enters Jerusalem on donkey, Jesus' hour); Matthew 21:1-17; Mark 11:1-11; Luke 19:28-44 (to fulfill prophecy, weeping over Jerusalem); Zechariah 9:9-10 (Prince of Peace); Isaiah 62 (salvation of Zion); Luke 13:31-35 (sorrow for Jerusalem)
Day 5   John 12:37-50 (belief and unbelief, came not to judge but to save); Isaiah 6 (Isaiah's vision)
Day 6   Read and respond to "Fruit From the Tree of Life" and "Marks of Faithful Community."
Day 7   Rest

PSALM OF THE WEEK

Pray Psalm 116 aloud daily after reading the assigned Scriptures. Listen for different meanings in the psalm against the background of the day's Scripture.

PRAYER

Pray daily before study:
"LORD, you will always be proclaimed as God; all generations will remember you" (Psalm 135:13, TEV).

Prayer concerns for this week:

162

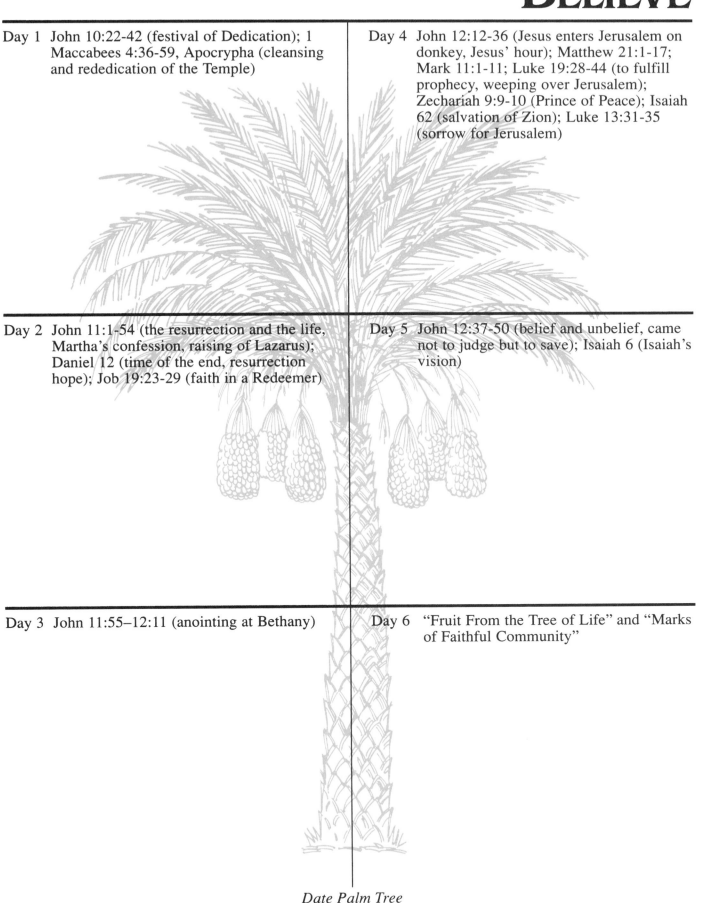

Day 1   John 10:22-42 (festival of Dedication); 1 Maccabees 4:36-59, Apocrypha (cleansing and rededication of the Temple)

Day 4   John 12:12-36 (Jesus enters Jerusalem on donkey, Jesus' hour); Matthew 21:1-17; Mark 11:1-11; Luke 19:28-44 (to fulfill prophecy, weeping over Jerusalem); Zechariah 9:9-10 (Prince of Peace); Isaiah 62 (salvation of Zion); Luke 13:31-35 (sorrow for Jerusalem)

Day 2   John 11:1-54 (the resurrection and the life, Martha's confession, raising of Lazarus); Daniel 12 (time of the end, resurrection hope); Job 19:23-29 (faith in a Redeemer)

Day 5   John 12:37-50 (belief and unbelief, came not to judge but to save); Isaiah 6 (Isaiah's vision)

Day 3   John 11:55–12:11 (anointing at Bethany)

Day 6   "Fruit From the Tree of Life" and "Marks of Faithful Community"

Date Palm Tree

DISCIPLE

FRUIT FROM THE TREE OF LIFE

John's Gospel doesn't waste words. So why mention "the festival of the Dedication" (John 10:22)? Why say "It was winter"? Because the setting is essential to understand what Jesus was about to say and do.

Dedication and Winter

Although not dictated by Scripture, the Feast of Dedication (Hanukkah) has nevertheless become a powerful Jewish celebration. It holds in memory the rededication of the Temple after it had been profaned by the Seleucids in 167 B.C. The eight-day festival begins on the twenty-fifth of Chislev (November/December) and recalls the day the Temple was desecrated. Antiochus IV (Epiphanes) in 167 B.C. launched yet another attack on Egypt; only this time the Egyptians were strengthened by newfound allies, the Romans. Ashamed, embarrassed, Antiochus retreated in haste through Judea. Believing that the Jewish high priest had turned traitor, and needing a victory banner to carry back to his capital in Syria, Antiochus sacked Jerusalem. He desecrated the Temple by sacrificing pigs and slaughtering priests on the altar. He erected a statue dedicated to Zeus in the Temple. He outlawed the Jewish festivals, sacrifices, and religious practices.

A family called the Hasmoneans, whose leader was Judas Maccabeus, gathered Jewish patriots, defeated the Syrians, recaptured the city, and purified and reconsecrated the altar (1 Maccabees 4:52-58, Apocrypha). Purification required seven days, then an eighth day to celebrate. For a time Hanukkah focused on the military victory; but by the end of the first century A.D., it had lost its military emphasis. Under the Romans any hint of an armed force was forbidden. So the celebration came to recall a small jar of consecrated oil that during purification burned miraculously for eight days until new oil could be pressed and consecrated. Hence, this celebration uses a candlestick, called a menorah, with eight branches and a center candle. Hanukkah is known as the Feast of Lights.

Why does John mention Solomon's Portico (John 10:23)? Because Herod the Great had modified and enlarged the north, west, and south parts of the Temple courtyard. The oldest part on the east, where Solomon's Portico was, dated back to Maccabean times—or according to Josephus, to Solomon's time. It was the historically authentic place to remember the desolation and to look across the Kidron Valley to the cemetery where the dead awaited "the last day." John reminds us, "It was winter" (10:22). Hanukkah occurs at the darkest time of the year, when the earth dies.

Jesus was in Jerusalem. An argument took place between Jesus and the religious leaders, "the Jews" (10:24-30). They were furious at Jesus' claim, "The Father and I are one" (10:30), and were ready to stone him. Soon Jesus would be

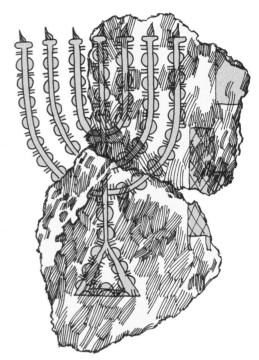

These fragments from a plaster wall of a house in Jerusalem date from the time of Herod (37 B.C. to 4 B.C.) and are the earliest representation we have of a Temple menorah. The two large fragments allow us to imagine the whole.

The Hanukkah menorah has eight branches, to hold one light for each of the eight days the miraculous oil burned during the purification and rededication of the Temple. A center branch holds the *shamash*, a ninth candle that is used to light the others.

killed. So John has prepared us for the story of Lazarus. The setting is full of images of death.

Lazarus

In other Gospels Jairus's daughter (Mark 5:22-24, 35-43; Luke 8:41-42, 49-56) and a widow's only son (Luke 7:11-15) are raised from the dead by Jesus. But John's account tells only of the raising of Lazarus, as if this dramatic event alone will be his witness—a mighty work done to the glory of God. In John's Gospel Jesus did his first sign at a wedding in Cana, his final sign at a tomb near Bethany. Just as Jesus' mother, Mary, had believed he could do something at the wedding, so Mary and Martha believed Jesus could do something for Lazarus.

When the sisters sent word that Lazarus was seriously ill, Jesus did not go. Jesus' delay was deliberate. He picked the hour for the sign and the time for his approach. Similarly, he selected the time for his death. "No one takes it [my life] from me, but I lay it down of my own accord" (John 10:18).

The Jews did not embalm, but perfumed and buried the body the day of death. Sometimes, even after burial, a comatose person might revive, "come back to life." The people believed the spirit of a person stayed near the body for three days, then departed.

Four days had passed since Lazarus had died. Mourners sang dirges. Martha and Mary felt grief's resentment and pain. These three single adults, sisters and brother, were among Jesus' closest friends. Their home had been a haven for him. They were disciples.

Jesus wept.

Why did Jesus weep? John's Gospel says Jesus was "deeply moved in spirit and troubled" (11:33, NIV). Was Jesus revealing his humanity, showing how much he loved Lazarus, showing the heart of God weeping when we weep? John's main concern usually is to show Jesus' divinity, the Son of God, rather than to show his humanity. Was Jesus weeping with disappointment that the crowd, even Martha and Mary, did not comprehend who he was? did not believe? Was Jesus sensing that to raise Lazarus would seal his own doom? Was he moved at the power of death—what the apostle Paul called "the last enemy" (1 Corinthians 15:26)?

Jesus did not pray to the Father for power to raise Lazarus, nor did he ask the Father to do it. He prayed a prayer of thanksgiving, grateful that the Father already had heard and answered him. The raising of Lazarus would be a sign that would cause many to believe (John 11:41-42),

Where was Jesus standing? At Lazarus's tomb, Jesus was near the cemetery on the Mount of Olives where Jews have been buried for centuries, awaiting "the last day"—the day of resurrection.

Where would Messiah appear? On the Mount of Olives, of

DISCIPLE

course, that high bluff overlooking Jerusalem from the east. Messiah would come from the east. When would Messiah appear? On the last day. Jews buried in the cemetery had carved on their tombstones a *tav,* the last letter of the Hebrew alphabet, to testify to their belief in resurrection on the last day.

So with symbols of death all around, Jesus proclaimed, "I am the resurrection and the life" (11:25). Not someday, but now. Not "I will be" but "I am." Martha had a "someday" perspective on resurrection. Jesus had a "now" perspective. In Jesus, resurrection life is already present. Only a few people seemed to grasp this message before Jesus' resurrection. Peter, according to Matthew's Gospel, professed, "You are the Messiah, the Son of the living God" (Matthew 16:16). The Samaritan woman said, "He cannot be the Messiah, can he?" (John 4:29). Now Martha gave her powerful testimony: "Yes, Lord, I believe that you are the Messiah, the Son of God, the one coming into the world" (11:27).

Lazarus proved an embarrassment to religious leaders. "When the great crowd of the Jews learned that he was there, they came not only because of Jesus but also to see Lazarus, whom he had raised from the dead. So the chief priests planned to put Lazarus to death as well, since it was on account of him that many of the Jews were deserting and were believing in Jesus" (12:9-11). The more powerful the witness, the more dramatic the gulf between belief and disbelief.

Passover

Momentum moves now to Passover, the Feast of Unleavened Bread. Once again Jesus and the disciples were in the home of Lazarus, Martha, and Mary in Bethany. Martha served a meal, but Mary did the unexpected. She had bought imported perfume. According to Judas, the cost was "three hundred denarii," about what a day laborer would earn in a year. Mary had been saving the perfume to anoint Jesus' body at his death. She had believed Jesus when he said his "hour" was coming. She anointed Jesus' feet with the perfume and wiped them with her hair. The rich fragrance filled the house. Judas is not called a thief in other Gospels; he is in John. He asked, "Why was this perfume not sold . . . and the money given to the poor?" (John 12:5).

Jesus' response seems threefold. First, the beauty of Mary's love gift should not have been ridiculed or spurned. Just as God gives extravagantly, so did Mary. We remember the wine at the wedding in Cana, the twelve baskets of bread gathered up from the miraculous feeding.

Second, the reference to "the poor" by Judas seems feeble indeed. According to John's account he was stealing from the "common purse" used to help the poor. Usually, people who object to a lavish love gift do not sacrifice for the poor.

More important, Mary recognized what everyone else

either ignored or refused to acknowledge. Jesus' hour had come. Jesus said as much: "You always have the poor with you, but you do not always have me" (12:8). If anyone were going to do him a kindness, it had to be now. But most significantly, the anointing signaled the glorification, the love of God poured out on the cross. Mary's lavish gift graphically symbolized the pouring out of Jesus' immeasurable love.

Jesus' time had come. "The hour has come for the Son of Man to be glorified.... Now my soul is troubled. And what should I say—'Father, save me from this hour'? No, it is for this reason that I have come to this hour. Father, glorify your name" (12:23, 27-28).

John's Gospel tells us to believe Jesus is the Son of God, the Word made flesh. Some people seem to believe but experience no transforming power. Others do. What is essential to believing?

Palm Sunday

Jerusalem was like a tinder box. Every Roman soldier was on alert. Religious pilgrims were pouring in from all over the world. Men, women, and children jostled shoulder to shoulder in the crowded streets. Even in faraway Rome, the emperor knew the unsubmissive Jews might rebel. And if they did, Passover would be the time.

Zechariah, like other prophets of Israel, had a vision of the day when enemies would be stripped of their powers and justice and peace would rule. Israel would no longer need chariots or war-horses, for Messiah would come, and Zion would "rejoice greatly" (Zechariah 9:9-10). Messiah would come as king, "triumphant and victorious." But how would he come, this strange king of peace? He would come humbly, riding "on a colt, the foal of a donkey" (9:9). Jesus intentionally drew upon this peaceful, lowly image in Zechariah; for he was trying to reinterpret messiah. He rode no white stallion, like a general leading his troops, but came as a quiet teacher, riding a colt, his feet nearly touching the ground. Jesus did not want people to call him "king" because of the popular misconceptions.

But the crowd waved palm branches from Jericho; they shouted "Hosanna! ... King of Israel!" (John 12:13) as if he might overthrow the Roman occupation as Judas Maccabeus had defeated the armies of Antiochus.

Only John's Gospel mentions that the branches waved for Jesus were palm branches—the symbol of national unity and freedom. The shouts were from the hallelujah psalms, the "Egyptian Hallel," in which they remembered freedom from Egypt, victory over enemies, the entrance of their victorious king. The enthusiastic cries were the exact words of Psalm

Date Palm Tree

DISCIPLE

118, "Blessed is the one who comes in the name of the LORD" (Psalm 118:26; John 12:13). The crowd sensed the liturgical moment.

> "Bind the festal procession with branches,
>   up to the horns of the altar" (Psalm 118:27).

Perhaps with this prophet of great power they could gain their long-sought liberty. They exploded with pent-up zeal.

As Jesus entered the city, the Jewish leaders must have recognized the potential for trouble, for messianic pretenders had sometimes raised up militant bands of followers only to incur Rome's wrath. In preceding years the Roman army had put down several messianic insurrections. A few years earlier, the Romans had slaughtered fifty thousand people quashing one rebellion. Later (A.D. 70) Rome would crush the defiant Jews, destroying the Temple forever, and leaving Jerusalem in ruins.

The religious leaders were supposed to keep civil order for the Roman authorities. No wonder, when the multitudes were streaming into the city praising Jesus, the Pharisees commanded Jesus, "Teacher, order your disciples to stop." Jesus answered, "I tell you, if these were silent, the stones would shout out" (Luke 19:39-40). Perhaps Jesus was recalling a messianic image from Isaiah: "For Zion's sake I will not keep silent" (Isaiah 62:1). Jesus, by word and deed, redefined *messiah,* but the people did not understand. The Palm Sunday entrance, even without swords, confronted and challenged the religious community and the Roman Empire.

Jesus knew his hour had come (John 13:1). His death was imminent. Earlier visits to Jerusalem had caused conflict. The Temple police had tried to arrest him (7:45-47). Jesus' raising of Lazarus resulted in many coming to believe in him. Greeks came to the festival wanting to see Jesus (12:20-22). The Pharisees were frustrated: "Look, the world [literally, the cosmos] has gone after him!" (12:19).

Jesus tried continually to interpret who he was. Earlier, when Nathanael, newly enlisted by Jesus, called him "Son of God" and "King of Israel," Jesus challenged Nathanael's thinking: "You will see greater things than these" (1:49-50). When the five thousand tried by force to make him king after the miraculous feeding, Jesus withdrew into isolation (6:15). John even modifies the text from Zechariah. The prophet had written "Rejoice greatly, O daughter Zion" (Zechariah 9:9), but John's Gospel replaces the opening phrase: "Do not be afraid, daughter of Zion" (John 12:15). The disciples were confused, the crowds were recklessly exuberant, the authorities sensed political crisis, but Jesus used the moment to teach about his forthcoming death—what he called his hour of glory. "Unless a grain of wheat falls into the earth and dies, it remains just a single grain; but if it dies, it bears much fruit" (12:24). Jesus could have toned down his message, stopped healing, shown more respect for organized religion. Instead, he gave up his life in obedient self-sacrifice, dying to bring forth a rich harvest. Think how many blind people have been given sight, how many people have been forgiven, how many children have been blessed, how many hungry have been fed by the "fruit," because the single grain fell into the earth. According to John's Gospel, Jesus' sacrificial death brings life abundant.

MARKS OF FAITHFUL COMMUNITY

We recognize death as part of life. Even when someone we love dies, we do not grieve as those who have no hope. Our hope is in Jesus. Jesus proclaimed, "I am the resurrection and the life" (John 11:25). Not someday, but now. Not "I will be" but "I am." Martha had a "someday perspective on resurrection. Jesus had a "now" perspective. In Jesus, resurrection life is already present.

How are you experiencing eternal life now?

Being faithful community, we live and die believing Jesus is the Messiah, the Son of God.

How do Jesus' words "I am the resurrection and the life" free you from uncertainty about life and death?

When Jesus speaks repeatedly of his "hour," what is he referring to? Why was it important for John to emphasize that Jesus was in control of his hour?

THE RADICAL DISCIPLE

"Unless a grain of wheat falls into the earth and dies, it remains just a single grain; but if it dies, it bears much fruit" (John 12:24). What must the radical disciple die to, let go of, in life in order to bear fruit?

IF YOU WANT TO KNOW MORE

To understand more fully the context of Jesus' final sign in John—the raising of Lazarus—do some research on Jewish beliefs about death, Sheol, and future resurrection. Information can be found in Bible dictionaries and commentaries as well as on the internet.

ABIDE

"Abide in me as I abide in you. Just as the branch cannot bear fruit by itself unless it abides in the vine, neither can you unless you abide in me."

—John 15:4

22 Power to Bear Fruit

OUR HUMAN CONDITION

We live with the illusion we are connected. Technology tells us so. But we feel isolated, cut off. We don't know our neighbors; we have little time for our families. We wither on the vine for lack of relationships that sustain.

ASSIGNMENT

Read slowly, thoughtfully. Jesus is giving intimate guidance to believers. Imagine Jesus speaking to you personally, just before his arrest.

Day 1 John 13 (Jesus washes the disciples' feet, a new commandment)
Day 2 John 14 (Jesus and God are one, promise of the Holy Spirit)
Day 3 John 15 (vine and branches, abide and bear fruit, love one another, warnings of persecutions, Spirit of truth)
Day 4 John 16 (Spirit will guide you, Jesus comforts his disciples, ask and receive)
Day 5 John 17 (Jesus prays for himself, his disciples, the church)
Day 6 Read and respond to "Fruit From the Tree of Life" and "Marks of Faithful Community."
Day 7 Rest

THE RADICAL DISCIPLE

Describe what for you would be an act of servanthood. Pray during the week for the enabling power of the Holy Spirit. Then act.

PSALM OF THE WEEK

Pray Psalm 80 aloud daily as a prayer for restoration of relationship with God. Think about what the community is asking of God and what the community is promising God in order for the relationship to be restored.

PRAYER

Pray daily before study:
"Your teachings are wonderful;
I obey them with all my heart.
The explanation of your teachings gives light
and brings wisdom to the ignorant"
(Psalm 119:129-130, TEV).

Prayer concerns for this week:

ABIDE

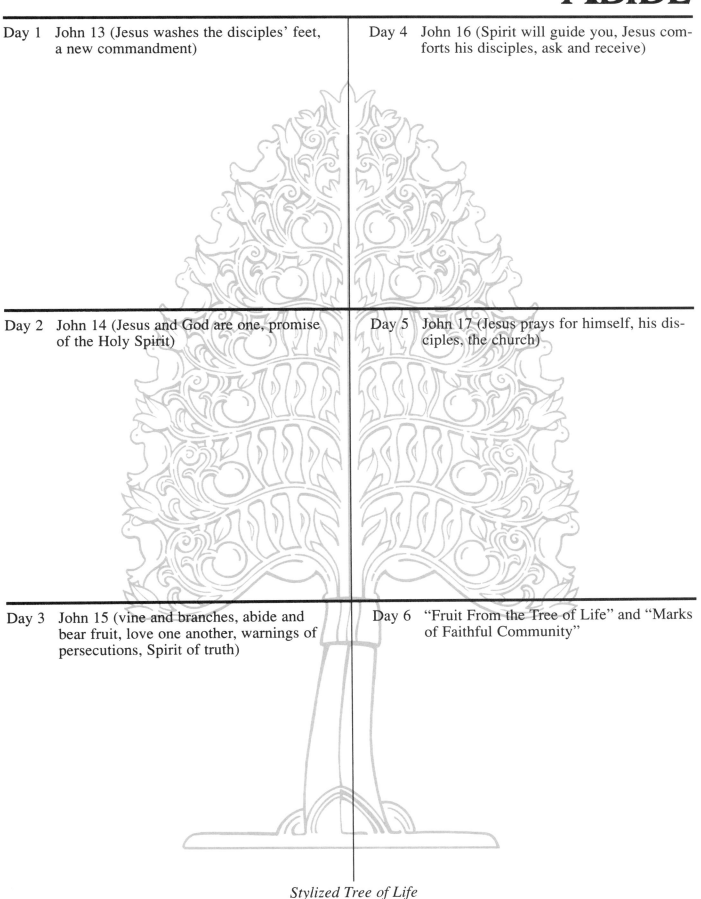

Day 1   John 13 (Jesus washes the disciples' feet, a new commandment)

Day 4   John 16 (Spirit will guide you, Jesus comforts his disciples, ask and receive)

Day 2   John 14 (Jesus and God are one, promise of the Holy Spirit)

Day 5   John 17 (Jesus prays for himself, his disciples, the church)

Day 3   John 15 (vine and branches, abide and bear fruit, love one another, warnings of persecutions, Spirit of truth)

Day 6   "Fruit From the Tree of Life" and "Marks of Faithful Community"

Stylized Tree of Life

DISCIPLE

FRUIT FROM THE TREE OF LIFE

As Jesus' ministry to the world closed, his ministry to the disciples began. The transition takes place in John 13:1. Jesus had signaled repeatedly that his "hour" was approaching. Now he confirmed that the time had come. Jesus had "loved his own"; now he was ready to show "them the full extent of his love" (13:1, NIV).

All four Gospels focus on the common meal. In the Synoptics Jesus ate the Passover meal the first evening of the Feast of Unleavened Bread. In John's account the meal was "just before the Passover Feast" (13:1, NIV). By John's timing Jesus' crucifixion occurred on the day of Preparation when the sacrificial lambs were being slaughtered at the Temple. No coincidence. For John, Jesus is the Lamb.

John's Gospel does not remind us of the cup of wine—the blood of Jesus poured out for the forgiveness of sins—or of the bread—his body, broken for his disciples. All three Synoptic Gospels and the testimony of Paul tell of the institution of Jesus' words for the Eucharist or Lord's Supper at the last meal. Holy Communion was central to the life of the earliest Christian fellowship. Immediately after Pentecost, believers "devoted themselves to the apostles' teaching and fellowship, to the breaking of bread and the prayers" (Acts 2:42). Paul not only quoted the words of Jesus that already had become institutionalized—"This is my body that is for you" (1 Corinthians 11:24)—he chastised his fledgling Corinthian church for not waiting for latecomers before eating (11:33-34).

Washing the Disciples' Feet

John, an eyewitness, had a special memory he didn't want the church to lose. He alone of the Gospel writers saves for the church that moment at the supper when Jesus washed the disciples' feet.

Tensions in Jerusalem were high. The lines were drawn between the authority of Jesus and the authority of the religious power structure. No doubt the disciples felt the strain. Judas had criticized Mary for wasting expensive perfume (John 12:4-5). John says, "The devil had already put it into the heart of Judas . . . to betray him" (13:2). At the meal, Jesus said so all could hear, "One of you will betray me" (13:21). Peter was told he would deny Jesus three times before the dawn (13:38). Matthew reports that shortly after supper, Jesus warned, "You will all become deserters" (Matthew 26:31).

A further word heightened the tension. Throughout John's Gospel, Jesus had carefully conducted his ministry according to the approaching hour. Several times Jesus avoided a confrontation because "his hour had not yet come" (John 7:30; 8:20). Now, at the supper, "Jesus knew that his hour had come" (13:1).

In this emotion-laden moment, Jesus stood up, took off his outer garment, tied a towel around his waist, poured water into a basin, and began to wash the disciples' feet (13:4-5). The role was that of a slave or servant in a wealthy home, of a child in a poor home—whoever had the lowest rank. Often the host would simply make water available so visitors could wash their own feet. Of course the washing was done before the meal, as guests arrived. But in the middle of the meal, Jesus "laid aside" his robe (13:4, KJV). (The verb is the same one used when Jesus said he would "lay down" his life.) Like a servant, Jesus knelt down and washed the disciples' feet. Jesus was sending a message. He wanted to leave behind a servant church focused and unified.

Peter, always impetuous, doesn't get it. Like Nicodemus with the birth, like the Samaritan woman with the water, Peter couldn't see the spiritual meaning. He turned full circle from "You will never wash my feet" to "not my feet only but also my hands and my head" (13:8-9). Peter was confused.

This washing was not baptism. It was an act of hospitality, of humility, of service. This act is not even an act of washing the feet of the world. Jesus wants his church made up not of those elbowing to get ahead but of those kneeling to honor one another. "So if I, your Lord and Teacher, have washed your feet, you also ought to wash one another's feet" (13:14).

The footwashing was an act of divine revelation. Jesus acted as host. As he washed their feet, Jesus welcomed the disciples in his Father's house. The footwashing was an extravagant act of love on the eve of the Crucifixion. It pointed to the ultimate extravagant act of love—grace upon grace (1:16).

Vineyard

Grapes, raisins, wine, and a thick syrup called honey were food staples in biblical Palestine. The climate and landscape were right for growing grapes, and vineyards were everywhere—large ones owned by the rich, tiny ones inherited by the poor.

Bible references to vineyards are everywhere too. Queen Jezebel had Naboth murdered to steal his inherited vineyard (1 Kings 21:1-16). The young maiden in Song of Solomon worked in the sun among the grapes until her skin was black as goat's hair used to make the tents of Kedar (Song of Solomon 1:5-6).

Often the vineyard symbolized God's people, Israel. Hosea called Israel "a luxuriant vine that yields its fruit" (Hosea 10:1). Jeremiah said God planted "a choice vine, from the purest stock" but it became "degenerate," "a wild vine" (Jeremiah 2:21). Ezekiel, as Babylon carried off the exiles, saw the vine "transplanted" and withering under the hot east wind (Ezekiel 17:7-8, 10). Isaiah described Israel as the vineyard of the Lord: God cleared the land of stones, dug it, and planted choice vines, carefully built a wall around it and a watchtower within it. God expected sweet fruit in great clusters. Instead, the vineyard yielded wild, sour grapes. So

DISCIPLE

God tore down the wall and let the vineyard be trampled,
> "For the vineyard of the LORD of hosts
>> is the house of Israel,
> and the people of Judah
>> are his pleasant planting;
> he expected justice,
>> but saw bloodshed;
> righteousness,
>> but heard a cry!" (Isaiah 5:7).

The psalmist maintains the metaphor:
> "You brought a vine out of Egypt. . . .
> You cleared the ground for it. . . .
> Why then have you broken down its walls . . . ?"
>> (Psalm 80:8-12).

Jesus turned this rich vineyard imagery into parable. He told the parable of the landowner who sent servants to collect the rent on his vineyard, the one he had prepared and planted. The tenants beat the first two servants and sent them away. The third one they killed. When the landowner sent his "beloved son," his heir, to collect the rent, the tenants killed him too. Now the point of the parable: The landowner will "destroy the tenants and give the vineyard to others" (Mark 12:1-9). The early church clearly understood the parable as a reference to the rejection and crucifixion of Jesus.

The True Vine

In his final farewell to his disciples, Jesus kept the vineyard metaphor but transformed it. No longer is Israel the vineyard; now Jesus is the vine: "I am the true vine," said Jesus (John 15:1). The vinegrower, the vine, and the branches make up the metaphor—the Father who "planted"; Jesus, the vine; and disciples, the branches. A vine exists for one purpose—to bear great clusters of ripe fruit. Disciples are meant to live "in Christ" and to bear the fruit of discipleship.

Some vines show promise of fruit; others do not. Worthless branches are pruned away so the vine's energy can flow into the fruited branches. The whole point—for vinegrower, vine, and branches—is the fruit. And the fruit is the same for the branches as it was for the vine, the same for disciples as it was for Jesus' earthly ministry—to invite people to hear, believe, and obey the Word. The fruit is to witness to Nicodemus so he can be born from above, to witness to the woman at the well so she can experience Messiah, to help an ill man walk and carry his mat. To point others to him who is "the way, and the truth, and the life" (14:6).

Jesus knew disciples could be drawn to other loyalties. Branches lying on the ground can root themselves, but those roots are shallow. Separated from the central vine, they lose their vitality. They bear little fruit. They usually die. "Those who abide in me and I in them bear much fruit, because apart from me you can do nothing" (15:5).

The prophet Ezekiel wrote that dead vines are worthless.
"Is wood taken from it to make anything?
  Does one take a peg from it on which to hang
    any object?" (Ezekiel 15:3).
The pruned, dry branches are not even good firewood, but
they must be disposed of. Sometimes a poor man or woman
would carry a bundle home for a quick flash fire under an
evening meal. The "branches" are not being punished; they
simply are cut away as worthless, nonproductive.

Think about your congregation. What fruit are you bearing?

When and where are you most effective in making disciples?

Because *prune* means both "to cut" and "to clean," Jesus
gave the dramatic assurance, "You are already clean because
of the word I have spoken to you" (John 15:3, NIV). Disciples of all generations have heard these words with gratitude.
We are clean not because we are good but because we are
pronounced forgiven and cleansed by God's Word.

The relationship between the Father and the Son provides
the key to the image of the vine. The Father and the Son are
one because the Father sent the Son in love and the Son is
fully obedient in love. Jesus' mission was to show that love to
the world. We are beginning to understand "God so loved the
world that he gave his only Son, so that everyone who
believes in him may not perish but may have eternal life"
(3:16). But the picture is complete only when disciples abandon their love for the world, love the Son, and express that
same love to one another. "Abide in my love" (15:9). If we
do, several things will happen.
- We will be able to bear fruit, thereby glorifying the Father
  (15:8). The amazing promise is that disciples will do
  "greater works" than Jesus did, because he goes to the
  Father (14:12).
- We will be able to pray, as Jesus prayed, and have our
  prayers answered, as Jesus' prayers were answered (15:7).
- We will know Jesus as friend and other disciples as friends.
  When Jesus washed the disciples' feet, he used master-
  servant language. But with his death approaching, he said,
  "I do not call you servants any longer, because the servant
  does not know what the master is doing; but I have called
  you friends, because I have made known to you everything
  that I have heard from my Father" (15:15).
- We will experience joy—joy that is in the heart of God, joy
  greater than pleasure, joy deeper than happiness, joy that is
  "complete" (15:11).
- We will experience hatred from "the world." The "world"
  hated the goodness, the love, the witness of Jesus. The

DISCIPLE

world will hate those who abandon their allegiance to the world and give their loyalty to the Son of God. John's beloved community learned firsthand the prophecy "They will put you out of the synagogues. . . . those who kill you will think that by doing so they are offering worship to God" (16:2).

The Paraclete

The Greek word for *Paraclete* (John 16:7) has several meanings. Different translations use "Advocate," "Counselor," "Comforter," or "Helper." All are correct, for the image is of a beloved attorney or counselor who is trusted, wise, and has your best interests at heart. The Paraclete is the Holy Spirit, the Spirit of truth.

- The Paraclete will come after Jesus leaves. The Paraclete's coming makes Jesus' going advantageous to the believer (16:7).
- The Paraclete will come from the Father in Jesus' name. As the Father sent Jesus, Jesus sends the Spirit (14:26; 15:26).
- The Paraclete will say what Jesus wants him to say as Jesus said what the Father wanted him to say (16:13-15).
- The Paraclete will help disciples remember all Jesus said and did, "remind you of all that I have said to you" (14:26).
- The Paraclete will teach and explain new things that disciples prior to the Crucifixion and Resurrection were not able to understand. Jesus still has much to teach us (16:12).
- The Paraclete will give you peace, not someday but now. As Jesus said to the disciples in the boat, so the Spirit will say, "Do not be afraid" (6:20; 14:26-27).
- The Paraclete will convict the world of its sin and show the world righteousness as Jesus did. Wherever Jesus' Spirit is present, judgment takes place, revealing light and darkness, life and death (16:8-11).
- The Paraclete is the Spirit of Jesus, the Spirit of truth. Jesus is the truth. The Holy Spirit will say and do only what Jesus would say and do (16:14).

The High Priestly Prayer

Only John's Gospel records the prayer Jesus offered just before going into the garden of Gethsemane. The church has called it the high priestly prayer because Jesus acts as intermediary. The prayer has three parts.

First, Jesus prayed for himself (John 17:1-5), acknowledging that the hour had come. Jesus wanted the cross to be showered with glory. The Father glorified the Son so the Son would glorify the Father. What does that mean? Often the church makes the Crucifixion tragedy and the Resurrection triumph. Blood and death on Friday, open tomb and life on Sunday. But John's message is glory in the whole event, especially the cross. There love is being expressed in its completeness, in its fullness. "I glorified you on earth by finishing the

work that you gave me to do" (17:4). Remember that Jesus said, "No one has greater love than this, to lay down one's life for one's friends" (15:13). Finishing was essential. John's testimony was clear: "Having loved his own who were in the world, he loved them to the end" (13:1). All the way. Completely. Only John records Jesus' saying from the cross, "It is finished" (19:30). Jesus offered himself back to the Father, back to the glory that once was his. The cross is glory.

But the heart of the prayer is for the disciples (17:6-19). Jesus is physically leaving them. He gave them his word of love and truth; he prayed that the Father would "protect them from the evil one" (17:15). Jesus did not pray that they would not suffer. He prayed that they would be faithful.

Then he prayed for believers yet to be, for those who would "believe in me through their word" (17:20-26). For us! The prayer is twofold—"that they may all be one" and "so that the world may believe that you have sent me" (17:21). Jesus had given his witness. His priestly prayer was that his followers would not falter, would care for one another, and through that love and unity give powerful and effectual witness to the world.

MARKS OF FAITHFUL COMMUNITY

With the example of footwashing, the image of a vine, and the promise of the Holy Spirit, Jesus equips a servant church—a church that abides in Jesus.

Abide is a word seldom used today. What other words or images express the idea of *abide* for you?

_____

_____

Being faithful community, we abide in Christ in order to bear the fruit of service.

What does discipleship shaped by the example of footwashing look like?

_____

_____

What does discipleship shaped by the image of the vine look like?

_____

_____

IF YOU WANT TO KNOW MORE

After rereading John 16, express your understanding of the function of the Holy Spirit through art, music, poetry, written prayer, dance, and so on. Consider where you might share it.

CROSS

"Carrying the cross by himself, he [Jesus] went out to what is called The Place of the Skull, which in Hebrew is called Golgotha. There they crucified him, and with him two others, one on either side, with Jesus between them."

—John 19:17-18

23 Where No One Else Can Go

OUR HUMAN CONDITION

We love ourselves. We build our lives around ourselves. Selfless love makes us uncomfortable. When offered to us, we don't know how to receive it; so we usually push it away.

ASSIGNMENT

Look for similarities and differences in the accounts of events in the Synoptic Gospels and John. Notice how Leviticus and Hebrews help to interpret the information in the Gospels.

Day 1   John 18:1-14 (betrayal and arrest); Matthew 26:30-56; Mark 14:26-50; Luke 22:39-53 (Gethsemane prayer, betrayal and arrest, Scripture fulfilled)
Day 2   John 18:15–19:16; Matthew 26:57–27:26; Mark 14:53–15:15; Luke 22:54–23:25 (Jesus before Caiaphas, Peter's denial, Jesus before Pilate, handed over)
Day 3   John 19:16-42; Matthew 27:27-66; Mark 15:16-47; Luke 23:26-56 (Crucifixion, casting lots for clothes, inscription, Joseph's tomb)
Day 4   Leviticus 17 (blood for atonement)
Day 5   Hebrews 10:1-25; 4:14-16 (Jesus' once-for-all sacrifice, Jesus our high priest)
Day 6   Read and respond to "Fruit From the Tree of Life" and "Marks of Faithful Community."
Day 7   Rest

THE RADICAL DISCIPLE

In our society the cross is displayed as a decorative accessory as often as a sacred symbol. Watch for crosses displayed in various ways during the week. What message did each cross convey to you?

PSALM OF THE WEEK

Locate art depicting the crucifixion of Jesus in books or on the internet. Choose a different image each day to accompany your praying Psalm 22 aloud. Or simply recall depictions you have seen of the Crucifixion as you pray the psalm.

PRAYER

Pray daily before study:
"Save me, O God!
   LORD, help me now!" (Psalm 70:1, TEV).

Prayer concerns for this week:

CROSS

Day 1   John 18:1-14 (betrayal and arrest);
Matthew 26:30-56; Mark 14:26-50; Luke
22:39-53 (Gethsemane prayer, betrayal
and arrest, Scripture fulfilled)

Day 4   Leviticus 17 (blood for atonement)

Day 2   John 18:15–19:16; Matthew 26:57–27:26;
Mark 14:53–15:15; Luke 22:54–23:25
(Jesus before Caiaphas, Peter's denial,
Jesus before Pilate, handed over)

Day 5   Hebrews 10:1-25; 4:14-16 (Jesus' once-
for-all sacrifice, Jesus our high priest)

Day 3   John 19:16-42; Matthew 27:27-66; Mark
15:16-47; Luke 23:26-56 (Crucifixion,
casting lots for clothes, inscription,
Joseph's tomb)

Day 6   "Fruit From the Tree of Life" and "Marks
of Faithful Community"

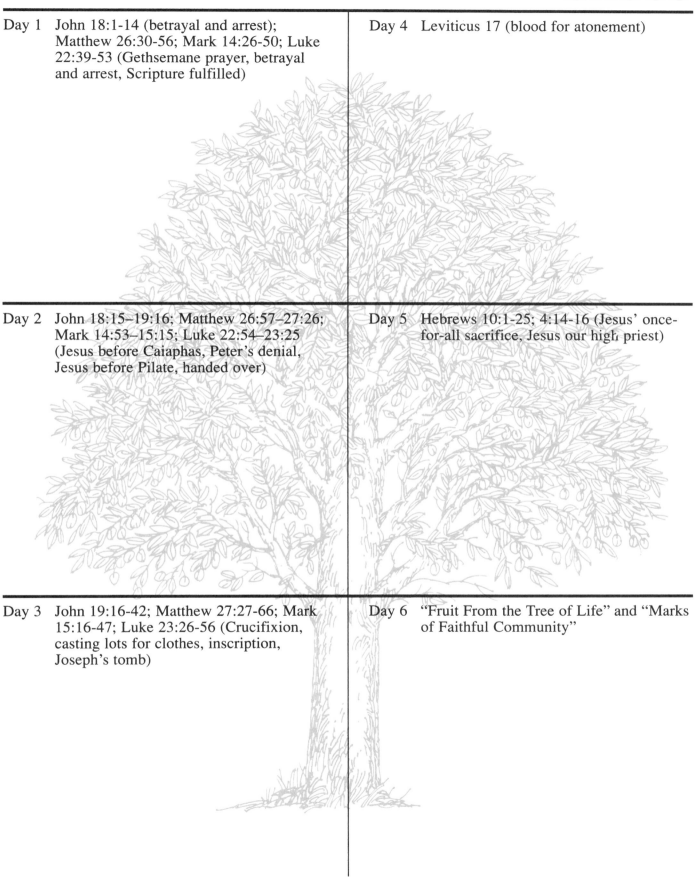

Almond Tree

DISCIPLE

FRUIT FROM THE TREE OF LIFE

Who caused the cross? Who killed Jesus? John's Gospel gives several answers, with different levels of meaning.

The world. "The world" rejected Jesus. The word *world* (cosmos) has two meanings: first, the universe including all humanity; and second, humanity's attitude of self-interest. With this second meaning, John is saying the world turned its back on Jesus. In the Prologue John states, "He was in the world . . . yet the world did not know him" (John 1:10). Light came into the world, but "people loved darkness rather than light because their deeds were evil" (3:19).

Sin. Sin, in John's Gospel, is not *sins,* the acts of breaking God's law. Sin is rejecting Christ and his ministry, refusing to accept his forgiveness, his healing, his shepherding love. The world, said Jesus, "hates me because I testify against it that its works are evil" (7:7). That hatred, confronted by Jesus' love, revealed sin. "Now they have no excuse for their sin" (15:22). When the light came, sin became visible. In some sense, human rejection of divine love—sin in all centuries—must be cause for the crucifixion of Jesus.

Religious Authorities in Jerusalem. John often refers to Jesus' immediate adversaries as "the Jews," but the term is complicated. The Greek word *Ioudaioi* can be translated "Judeans" or "Jews." A person in Galilee might refer to the people of Jerusalem—that is, the people of Judea—as "Jews." Jesus was a Jew. So were Mary and Martha, Peter and John. So were the five thousand who wanted to make Jesus king. So were the throngs at Passover who waved palm branches and shouted hosanna. But John's Gospel uses the phrase in a particular sense: By "the Jews," John meant the Jewish religious authorities in Jerusalem who clearly opposed Jesus. Unfortunately, across the centuries, Christians have misunderstood John's use of the phrase, taking it to mean all Jewish people. As a result of that misunderstanding, many Christians have tended to think of Jesus, the disciples, and most of the early church as non-Jews. For John the expression clearly points to the powerful Jewish establishment who held hands with Rome and governed the everyday life of the people.

Without doubt, John says the religious leaders were part of the human instrument that crucified Jesus. They sent a detachment of Temple police and Roman soldiers to the garden to arrest him, then took him to one authority after another. They brought the accusation to Pilate.

The irony is overwhelming. The leaders sent, at night, a small army to capture a man who had been teaching in the Temple. When Jesus said, "I am he" (18:5), he meant more than mere identification. Even as he gave himself up, he used the divine "I AM." But what was most ironic, these religious leaders periodically praised God as Lord and only king of Israel. They sang enthronement psalms in the Temple:

"The LORD is king; let the peoples tremble" (Psalm 99:1).

"O come, let us sing to the LORD; . . .

For the LORD is a great God,

and a great King above all gods" (95:1, 3).

When Pilate asked, "Shall I crucify your King?" they answered, "We have no king but the emperor" (John 19:15). In so doing, they denied their faith, their covenant commitment to God their only King, their identity as the people of God.

Roman Empire. The Roman Empire also played a part in the Crucifixion. Herod Antipas, Roman governor, had soldiers on the lookout for Jesus. Roman soldiers joined with Temple guards to arrest Jesus in the garden. (Only John's Gospel shows both Jewish police and Roman soldiers at the arrest.) Roman soldiers taunted him, stripped him, pressed thorns on his head, and gambled for his garments. The *Pax Romana* (Roman peace) was enforced by Rome's iron fist. Jewish authorities knew that one miscue on their part or one rebellion by a band of zealots could topple the Temple, strip them of power, even destroy the nation. The word that clinched the verdict was the word Rome feared most: He "claims to be a king." He "sets himself against the emperor" (19:12).

Pilate. Pilate played a part. When Jesus told Pilate he had no power over him "unless it had been given you from above" (19:11), Jesus may have meant from God, or he may have meant from the emperor. Or both. But Pilate knew well that his authority came from the emperor and rested on his ability to keep order in Judea.

Don't mistake Pilate for a nice guy. Political expediency and compromise governed his thinking. He disliked Jews. Whenever he thought he had to, he killed them by the thousands. He despised their religious government. In Jesus' trial, he granted their wishes yet humiliated them at the same time. He paid no attention to their charge that Jesus said he was God. That was their law, not politics. He made the accusers change their charge to sedition. His fear was not of Jesus, who had no soldiers. His fear was of an uprising followed by a necessarily heavy-handed Roman crackdown. Pilate's fear was that Rome would get word that the job was too big for him.

The religious authorities accused Jesus of claiming to be a king. Pilate would give them a king: Flog him. Dress him in purple. Put a crown of thorns on his head. The word *sat* in the phrase "sat on the judge's bench" (19:13) can mean "seated him." What a gesture that would have been, putting Jesus on the judge's bench. "Here is your King!" The double meaning for our Gospel is clear. They thought they were the judge, but they were being judged by the King.

Pilate went further. The procedure was to tie a charge or inscription around the criminal's neck, then nail it to the cross. Jesus said he was a king; they said he claimed to be a

DISCIPLE

king. So be it. The inscription read "Jesus of Nazareth, the King of the Jews" (19:19).

Satan. Satan played a role. Clearly in our Gospel, the battle is waged between principalities and powers. Jesus called Satan "the ruler of this world" (12:31). He called him "a murderer" and "a liar and the father of lies" (8:44). Jesus knew he fought against Satan; he knew full obedience to the Father would break Satan's powerful grip on the world. In his farewell talk with the disciples, Jesus said, "The ruler of this world is coming. He has no power over me" (14:30). Amid betrayal and denial, Jesus would stay faithful "to the end" (13:1). Amid lies, Jesus would speak truth. Amid hatred, Jesus would love. Satan's power would be broken when Jesus was "lifted up" on the cross.

God the Father. Did God the Father cause Jesus to be crucified? Christians, reading Hebrew Scriptures through their experience of Jesus, saw the sacrifice foretold. The prophet Isaiah wrote,

> "He was wounded for our transgressions,
>   crushed for our iniquities. . . .
> the LORD has laid on him
>   the iniquity of us all" (Isaiah 53:5-6).

Jesus saw Scriptures being fulfilled. So did the early church.

Jesus prayed Psalm 22 as he was dying. Parts of this ancient lament almost seem to be an eyewitness account of the Crucifixion, beginning with Jesus' own utterance, "My God, my God, why have you forsaken me?" (Psalm 22:1; Matthew 27:46). Notice how Jesus' experience fulfilled the psalm. The soldiers derided him, "Hail, King of the Jews!" (John 19:3). "All who see me mock at me" (Psalm 22:7). The soldiers gambled for his seamless robe (John 19:23-24). "They divide my clothes among themselves, / and for my clothing they cast lots." (Psalm 22:18).

The key to the question of God's involvement is to understand "the cup." Other Gospels record Jesus' agonizing prayer, "My Father, if it is possible, let this cup pass from me; yet not what I want but what you want" (Matthew 26:39; Mark 14:36; Luke 22:42). The "cup" in John's Gospel is the gift of the Father, freely accepted by the Son because drinking it was essential to the work God gave him to do: "Am I not to drink the cup that the Father has given me?" (John 18:11).

The mission given to Jesus required Jesus to drink the cup of suffering. The Father required the Son to be faithful and obedient unto death.

Jesus. What about Jesus' role? From the beginning of his ministry, Jesus knew his hour would come. He was not taken against his will; he made himself available. Jesus was in control of his life. "No one takes it [his life] from me, but I lay it down of my own accord. I have power to lay it down, and I have power to take it up again. I have received this command from my Father" (10:18). Jesus could have said no to his mission at any point. His going to the cross was the great love act of all time. The works and the witnesses were not enough. Remember, he told Nicodemus, "Just as Moses lifted up the serpent in the wilderness [to bring healing], so must the Son of Man be lifted up, that whoever believes in him may have eternal life" (3:14-15). In John's Gospel, the cross is love shining amid hatred, fidelity amid rejection. Glory is not Resurrection after humiliation; glory is love on the cross.

Now we understand what Jesus meant when he said, "Where I am going, you cannot come" (8:21). His cross was a place no one else could go, an act of love no one else could perform. In Crucifixion and Resurrection he would glorify the Father. The church, looking back, would understand. The cross was a once-for-all act of love by the Father through the Son for the world.

The Hour

In John's Gospel the Crucifixion took place on the afternoon of the day of Preparation. On that afternoon the Passover lambs were sacrificed, their blood drained, and the animals given to the families for the Passover meal. The Passover lambs were being sacrificed at the time of Jesus' death. He truly was the sacrificial Lamb.

When the sour wine was placed on Jesus' lips, the soldier used a branch of hyssop—the same plant used by the Israelites to put the blood of the Passover lamb on the lintels of their homes in Egypt. That blood caused the angel of death to pass over their homes, allowing their children to live. The symbolism is overwhelming. Now the church is remembering the words of John the Baptist: "Here is the Lamb of God who takes away the sin of the world!" (1:29).

MARKS OF FAITHFUL COMMUNITY

The faithful community understands that God in Jesus did what no one else could do. Even though the cross is shrouded in mystery, we are drawn to it, pulled by a love that forgives our sins, even breaks the power sin has over us.

We have difficulty comprehending how a man dying on a cross could have anything to do with our sins. We believe Jesus died, but we don't understand how his death affects our lives. What explanations satisfy you?

IF YOU WANT TO KNOW MORE

Find a hymnal and read the words of several hymns on the cross. What messages about the cross do the words convey?

Hyssop is a wild shrub with woody stems and small white flowers. Jesus on the cross was offered a sponge soaked with sour wine and held up to him on a branch of hyssop (John 20:28-30).

Being faithful community, we receive with gratitude the selfless love of God in Christ shown on the cross and proclaim it in our living.

"Jesus said to him, 'Have you believed because you have seen me? Blessed are those who have not seen and yet have come to believe.'"

—John 20:29

24 Weeping Turned to Witness

OUR HUMAN CONDITION

We believe only what we see; otherwise, we are skeptical. And convincing others to believe what they cannot see is nearly impossible. So why try?

ASSIGNMENT

Each Gospel has its own memory and its own emphasis. Try to discover the truths being lifted up. Pay attention to detail.

Day 1   John 20:1-18 (Jesus appears to Mary Magdalene); Matthew 28:1-10 (the stone rolled back); Mark 16:1-11 (the empty tomb); Luke 24:1-12 (the women and Peter at the empty tomb)
Day 2   John 20:19-31 (Jesus appears to his disciples, invites Thomas to believe); Luke 24:36-43 (Jesus appears to his disciples, eats fish)
Day 3   Mark 16:12-13; Luke 24:13-35 (Jesus appears to two, the Emmaus road, known in breaking of bread)
Day 4   John 21 (breakfast on a Galilee shore, feed my sheep, follow me)
Day 5   Matthew 28:16-20 (make disciples); Luke 24:44-49 (proclaim repentance and forgiveness); Acts 1:3-5, 8; 2:1-4 (Holy Spirit power)
Day 6   Read and respond to "Fruit From the Tree of Life" and "Marks of Faithful Community."
Day 7   Rest

PSALM OF THE WEEK

Celebrate the Resurrection through praying Psalm 98 aloud daily. Work out some hand motions to express the joy of the psalm and use them as you pray.

PRAYER

Pray daily before study:
"You are my God, and I give you thanks; I will proclaim your greatness" (Psalm 118:28, TEV).

Prayer concerns for this week:

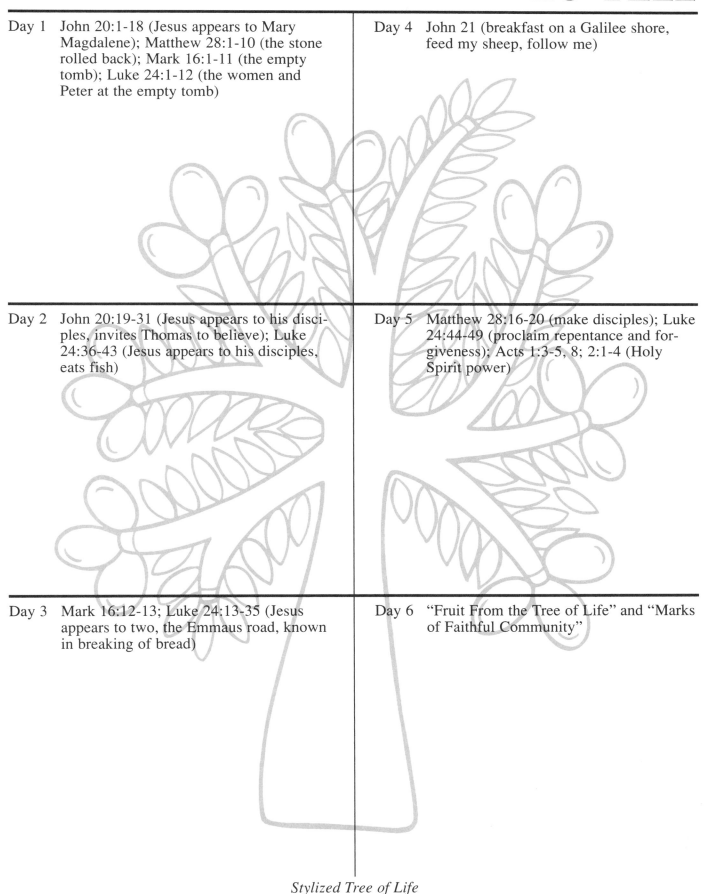

Day 1 John 20:1-18 (Jesus appears to Mary Magdalene); Matthew 28:1-10 (the stone rolled back); Mark 16:1-11 (the empty tomb); Luke 24:1-12 (the women and Peter at the empty tomb)

Day 2 John 20:19-31 (Jesus appears to his disciples, invites Thomas to believe); Luke 24:36-43 (Jesus appears to his disciples, eats fish)

Day 3 Mark 16:12-13; Luke 24:13-35 (Jesus appears to two, the Emmaus road, known in breaking of bread)

Day 4 John 21 (breakfast on a Galilee shore, feed my sheep, follow me)

Day 5 Matthew 28:16-20 (make disciples); Luke 24:44-49 (proclaim repentance and forgiveness); Acts 1:3-5, 8; 2:1-4 (Holy Spirit power)

Day 6 "Fruit From the Tree of Life" and "Marks of Faithful Community"

Stylized Tree of Life

DISCIPLE

FRUIT FROM THE TREE OF LIFE

Jesus knew where he came from and where he was going. He came from the Father and was returning to the Father. His glory was to do his Father's will, coming to completion in the offering of his life in love on the cross, in his Resurrection, and in his Ascension. Jesus came to reveal the source of life and to offer salvation to a dying world.

His actions, his words, and his ministry were not hidden but performed in broad daylight, often on a crowded hillside or in a synagogue. Even his Crucifixion was carried out beside a busy thoroughfare. To the high priest he said, "I have spoken openly to the world. . . . I have said nothing in secret" (John 18:20).

Jesus was not a spirit in a physical shell, not a divine apparition in a human mask. He was a human being who knew hunger and thirst, who wept at Lazarus's grave, who washed the feet of his followers. His pain was real. He actually died as we will actually die.

Resurrection Appearances

John did not record all the Resurrection appearances. He did not need to. Other Gospels told of Jesus' breaking bread at table in Emmaus (Luke 24:28-35) and the final commissioning of the eleven on the mountain in Galilee (Matthew 28:16-20). Besides, the Johannine community had John's eyewitness testimony as well as the testimony of others. Paul quoted the tradition: "He was raised on the third day in accordance with the scriptures, . . . he appeared to Cephas, then to the twelve. Then he appeared to more than five hundred brothers and sisters at one time, most of whom are still alive, though some have died. Then he appeared to James, then to all the apostles." Then Paul adds himself: "Last of all, as to one untimely born, he appeared also to me" (1 Corinthians 15:4-8).

John's Gospel is selective, to make his unique emphasis. In Resurrection form, Jesus kept his word. He had promised in his farewell teachings, "I will not leave you orphaned; I am coming to you" (John 14:18). So he did. The Resurrection appearances were not to unbelievers but to believers. "The world will no longer see me," but to "those who love me . . . I will love them and reveal myself to them" (14:19-21).

A Family of God

Jesus was creating a new family of God. Remember John's Gospel does not list "the twelve," nor is the expression often used. Rather, "the disciples" often refers to the gradual accumulation of believers. The Samaritan woman expressed faith. The blind man cried out, "Lord, I believe" (John 9:38). The gathering at the foot of the cross—Jesus' mother, her sister, the wife of Clopas, Mary Magdalene, and the beloved disciple—all were charter members of this new family.

Mary Magdalene was the first herald of the Resurrection on Easter morning. Luke records that Jesus had healed her of "seven demons." Mary Magdalene, along with some other women "who had been cured of evil spirits and infirmities," sometimes accompanied the disciples and gave them financial aid (Luke 8:2-3). We can picture Mary with her arm around Jesus' mother at the foot of the cross. While all the disciples except the beloved disciple fled, she stood steadfast. She waited until sabbath (Saturday) was over; then we see her hurrying to the tomb "while it was still dark" and finding the great stone had been moved (John 20:1).

Alarmed at seeing the open tomb, "she ran and went to Simon Peter and the other disciple, the one whom Jesus loved and said to them, 'They have taken the Lord out of the tomb, and we do not know where they have laid him' " (20:2). By saying "we," was she expressing for everyone the mystery of the empty tomb? She stood outside the tomb, weeping. When Jesus spoke to her, "Woman, why are you weeping?" (20:15), Mary Magdalene was focused momentarily on the physical. In the early hours, with both dimness of light and dimness of perception, she presumed Jesus to be the gardener. "Sir, if you have carried him away, tell me where you have laid him, and I will take him away" (20:15).

Witness

Jesus spoke one word. It was the word of life, the word of revelation, the ultimate word of love. He said, "Mary!" He called her by name. The good shepherd knows his sheep by name. "I know my own and my own know me" (John 10:14). Surely a part of our salvation is to believe in our hearts that the Lord knows us personally and individually, by name. Mary's response was immediate: " 'Rabbouni!' (which means Teacher)" (20:16). John wanted readers not only to hear the actual Aramaic word but also to know what it meant. Mary's words changed from "tell me where you have laid him" to telling others "I have seen the Lord" (20:15, 18).

Now she got the point, the point Jesus had made repeatedly—the same point John wanted the Resurrection appearances to emphasize. She was to proclaim the gospel message. She was to tell others. She was to bear fruit. "Mary Magdalene went and announced to the disciples, 'I have seen the Lord,' " and she told them what he had said to her (20:18).

The Body

The resurrected body of Jesus is a problem for scientific moderns, but it was a problem for Jesus' contemporaries too. Lazarus was brought back from the dead. Jesus was resurrected. Lazarus came forth covered with grave wrappings. Jesus left "the linen wrappings lying there" and the head cloth carefully "rolled up in a place by itself" (John 20:6-7). The grave cloths indicated that no one had taken Jesus away. Jesus

Small flasks like this tin-lead one, less than two inches across, were used by pilgrims to the Holy Land to carry home holy oil from the lamps above Jesus' tomb. This flask from the sixth century A.D. shows three women, the rotunda of the tomb built by Constantine above the burial site, and the inscription "The Lord is risen" in Greek.

DISCIPLE

left death behind. Just as no one took his life from him, so no one took his death from him; he walked away from it.

Lazarus would die again. Jesus was raised as Savior and Lord, with a new kind of body, a body that could be perceived as Jesus yet was clearly different. Jesus, in Resurrection form, was neither a soul nor a spirit, disembodied and ready to go to heaven; nor did he live in the former pre-Crucifixion physical body. He said to Mary Magdalene, "Do not hold on to me, because I have not yet ascended to the Father" (20:17). He had changed.

Why did John record that Jesus walked through locked doors? Was he emphasizing the mystery of Jesus' resurrected body? Was he recalling that the disciples were behind locked doors, fearful they too might be arrested?

John wanted readers to know that Thomas, who was not present for earlier appearances, was slow to believe. Jesus said to Thomas, "Put your finger here and see my hands. Reach out your hand and put it in my side" (20:27). The message: The Crucifixion was real; so was the Resurrection. Thomas was invited to touch the resurrected body. His response was a witness: "My Lord and my God!" (20:28). Thomas the doubter gave a most powerful confession. But Jesus, without discrediting Thomas, said, "Blessed are those who have not seen and yet have come to believe" (20:29).

What is the relation between seeing and believing?

Peace

When Jesus appeared to the disciples, he said, "Peace be with you" (John 20:19, 21, 26). These words were not simply a "shalom," a "hello" greeting. Rather, Jesus was reassuring them, as he had when the storm threatened their boat on the Sea of Galilee: "It is I; do not be afraid" (6:20). He was reaffirming his promise made in the farewell discourses: "Peace I leave with you; my peace I give to you" (14:27). It was one thing to say "Peace" as a greeting; it was quite another to say "Peace" after the Crucifixion. It was one thing to say "Peace" when they were moving about freely; it was another thing to say "Peace" when they were hiding behind locked doors. The peace of "shalom" now meant the Kingdom promise of justice, righteousness, and peace just as Isaiah said: "The wolf shall live with the lamb" (Isaiah 11:6). "Do not let your hearts be troubled. Believe in God, believe also in me" (John 14:1).

Holy Spirit

Luke concluded his Gospel with Resurrection appearances and began the book of Acts with the powerful Pentecost account—when the church received the Holy Spirit. John reported the giving of the Holy Spirit in a less dramatic but equally powerful way: "He breathed on them and said to them, 'Receive the Holy Spirit'" (John 20:22).

The expression "he breathed" calls to mind the expression used of God in Creation. "Then the LORD God formed man from the dust of the ground, and breathed into his nostrils the breath of life; and the man became a living being" (Genesis 2:7). The God who gave us breath gave us life abundant and eternal by breathing into us the Holy Spirit.

Jesus was equipping his followers to carry on his ministry in the world. The work of the Holy Spirit was to link the disciples to Jesus as Jesus was linked to the Father. Receiving the Holy Spirit is not merely an experience to be savored but a power to be used. Even as Jesus said, "Receive the Holy Spirit," he instructed, "If you forgive the sins of any, they are forgiven them" (John 20:23). "Repentance and forgiveness of sins is to be proclaimed in his [Messiah's] name to all nations" (Luke 24:47).

Breakfast on a Galilean Shore

By the end of John 20, the evangelist has proclaimed the full message of Incarnation, Atonement, Resurrection, and glorification. As if the scroll of testimony is full, though much more could be said, the Gospel seems to draw to a close. "Now Jesus did many other signs in the presence of his disciples, which are not written in this book. But these are written so that you may come to believe [may continue to believe] that Jesus is the Messiah, the Son of God, and that through believing you may have life in his name" (20:30-31).

But John 21 follows as though the faith community said, "Wait a minute!" A memory not retained in other Gospel accounts is a story so precious, so important, it must be added. Even the first words, "After these things," imply an addition after second thoughts (21:1).

The account is loaded with symbolism and double meaning. Jesus appears not in Jerusalem but in Galilee—a reminder he can appear anywhere. The disciples were fishing. They had fished all night—the time we remember as a sign of confusion. They had caught nothing. They had been called to bear fruit, but they were coming in empty-handed.

At daybreak—the light was coming—"Jesus said to them, 'Children, you have no fish, have you?' They answered him, 'No'" (John 21:5). They had no food, just as the five thousand had no food. Jesus would provide. "Cast the net to the right side of the boat" (21:6). Didn't Peter, the professional fisherman, know how to fish? Or could Jesus, standing on the shore, with morning's first light, see the shadow of a school of fish? Or is the Gospel saying that if the disciples wanted to make disciples, they had to do it Jesus' way?

They caught so many fish in their nets they scarcely could

DISCIPLE

haul them in. Memories of the hundred and fifty gallons of wine at Cana and the twelve baskets of leftovers at the feeding of the five thousand flood our minds.

The verb translated "to haul" (21:6) is the same one Jesus used for drawing people into faith. Simon Peter "hauled the net ashore" (21:11). It can mean to pull or to draw. "No one can come to me unless drawn [hauled in] by the Father who sent me" (6:44). "And I, when I am lifted up from the earth, will draw [haul in] all people to myself" (12:32).

When did we last hear of fish and bread? In the feeding of the five thousand, of course. When did we hear of a charcoal fire? When Peter stood in the high priest's courtyard warming himself by a charcoal fire and denied Jesus (18:18).

In the Near East, reconciliation often occurs at a meal. If enemies sit down and "eat salt" together, they are reconciled. Friendships are restored when bread is broken together. Covenants are made as people sit at the table. Fellowship at meals indicates intimacy, harmony, agreement.

Simon Peter

Something was amiss. Jesus was the host. At the last meal, he washed Peter's feet. Now Jesus drew Peter aside.

Jesus called him by name, but not the name he had given him, "Cephas," meaning Rock. Jesus called him, "Simon son of John," the name his mother had given him, the name he had before he became a disciple. Peter had always been impetuous. He tended to overreact. He alone jumped into the sea (John 21:7). He reacted to the footwashing (13:8-9). He cut off the slave's ear (18:10). Often he blurted out the thoughts of the other disciples as if he were their spokesman (6:68-69). Had Peter now returned to his old ways, his old self, even his old occupation? Had he reacted to recent events by returning to the place where Jesus had first spoken to him, "You are Simon son of John" (1:42)? "Do you love me more than these?" (21:15). Jesus was referring to that last supper when Peter wanted his whole body washed, when he echoed Jesus' words saying he would lay down his life for Jesus (13:37). "Yes, Lord; you know that I love you" (21:15, 16). No boast here.

Peter was hurt because Jesus asked him the third time, "Do you love me?" (21:17). The disciple responded, "Lord, you know everything." He now knew Jesus had read his heart, even before his denials.

Jesus, by his three questions, brought back the guilt and pain. Forgiveness and reconciliation were expressed in the form of relationship. The branch had to do what the vine intended. "Feed my sheep" (21:17).

The question, "Lord, what about him?" (21:21) clarified the fact that one disciple had one course of action, another disciple had another. Even today Jesus says, "What is that to you?''—what others are giving, what others are saying, what sacrifices others are making? "Follow me!"

How does your call to discipleship particularly fit you?

_____

_____

MARKS OF FAITHFUL COMMUNITY

The faithful community believes in the resurrected Christ and witnesses boldly to that victory with joy. We have a wonderful story to tell. Like someone who has read a good book or seen a great movie, we want to tell others. We are witnesses and evangelists.

What is it about the story of the Resurrection that empowers you to witness?

_____

_____

What is it about the story of the Resurrection that makes witnessing about it hard for you?

_____

_____

Some people say, "I witness by my life." When is a word also needed?

_____

_____

THE RADICAL DISCIPLE

The radical disciple risks taking the good news of the empty tomb where others hesitate to go. Where is that for you?

IF YOU WANT TO KNOW MORE

Tradition tells us that some of Jesus' disciples were martyred. Check the public library and internet for books and information on saints and martyrs to learn about the fate of the disciples.

Being faithful community, we believe in the resurrected Christ and witness boldly to that victory with joy.

UNITY

"Beloved, let us love one another, because love is from God; everyone who loves is born of God and knows God."

—1 John 4:7

25 Our Life Together

OUR HUMAN CONDITION

We want both to belong to the group and to think and act independently. What must we say yes to, and what can we say no to? What boundaries and benefits shape our relationship to others and to the group? What defines our life together?

ASSIGNMENT

Read the introductions to these letters in your Bible. Focus on breaches of harmony within the church, breaches over belief and behavior—arrogance versus humility, claims of sinlessness versus forgiveness, dissension versus love. Study Paul's pleas for unity.

Day 1   1 John 1 (Christ the Word and source of life); Romans 14 (do not judge one another or cause to stumble); Ephesians 4:1-16 (unity in the body of Christ)
Day 2   1 John 2–3 (knowing and obeying God, do not love the world, warning against antichrists, children of God)
Day 3   1 John 4–5 (spirit of truth and spirit of error, God is love, faith conquers the world)
Day 4   2 John (truth and love); 3 John (commendation for hospitality)
Day 5   Jude (judgment on false teachers, persevere)
Day 6   Read and respond to "Fruit From the Tree of Life" and "Marks of Faithful Community."
Day 7   Rest

PSALM OF THE WEEK

As oil is God's blessing on worship and dew is God's blessing on creation in Psalm 133, unity is God's blessing on community in the letters of John and Jude. As you read Psalm 133 aloud daily, think of expressions of unity in the life of your congregation experienced as blessing. How would you symbolize those expressions of unity?

PRAYER

Pray daily before study:
"Enable me to speak the truth at all times,
    because my hope is in your judgments.
I will always obey your law,
    forever and ever.
I will live in perfect freedom,
    because I try to obey your teachings"
        (Psalm 119:43-45, TEV).

Prayer concerns for this week:

UNITY

Day 1   1 John 1 (Christ the Word and source of life); Romans 14 (do not judge one another or cause to stumble); Ephesians 4:1-16 (unity in the body of Christ)

Day 4   2 John (truth and love); 3 John (commendation for hospitality)

Day 2   1 John 2–3 (knowing and obeying God, do not love the world, warning against antichrists, children of God)

Day 5   Jude (judgment on false teachers, persevere)

Day 3   1 John 4–5 (spirit of truth and spirit of error, God is love, faith conquers the world)

Day 6   "Fruit From the Tree of Life" and "Marks of Faithful Community"

Olive Tree

DISCIPLE

FRUIT FROM THE TREE OF LIFE

At first glance, the Johannine letters (1, 2, 3 John) seem a light touch. Phrases such as "little children, let us love" (1 John 3:18), "God is love" (4:16), and "walk in the light" (1:7) appear gentle, almost superficial. But a careful, between-the-lines study reveals that the early church was struggling to survive. It was tossing and turning, trying to be faithful. We know from secular history and from other Scripture that the church of the first century A.D. faced a hostile society. The Romans reacted forcefully to Jews and Jewish Christians with their stubborn loyalties. Nero lighted the streets of Rome with Christians' oil-soaked bodies (A.D. 64). The Roman general Titus captured Jerusalem and destroyed the Temple. After A.D. 70, as Judaism struggled to survive, the synagogues began to exclude non-Jews, including Jewish Christians.

Furthermore, the Greek and Roman culture set an alien stage for Christians. Greek philosophies and mystery religions spoke of secret knowledge and saving truths divorced from earthly life.

But with all these external forces facing the early Christians on every front, the letters of John and Jude focus clearly on the problems within the church. The issues were dissension, division, and desertion. These letters have one clear intent—to maintain the community's central belief in Jesus Christ and loyalty, harmony, and faithfulness within the fellowship.

The Family of God

The cluster of letters, often called the catholic (universal) or general epistles, includes James; First and Second Peter; First, Second, and Third John; and Jude. They exhort and encourage the newborn churches scattered in Asia Minor to be faithful both in belief and practice. The Johannine letters seem to flow from the experiences of the fellowship groups founded by John of the Gospel. Their appeal for love among the members (1 John 3:11) springs logically from the footwashing (John 13). The plea for unity echoes the prayer of Jesus "that they may all be one . . . so that the world may believe" (17:21).

The writer of Second John and Third John, and presumably of First John too, identifies himself as "the elder." His approach seems that of a trusted adviser and older respected leader. His appeal and authority come from spiritual and moral power to influence. Without doubt, he was immersed in John's Gospel and a long-time member of the churches shaped by John. He either was John the disciple or was guided by John's faith and thought.

His language is steeped in John's words: "Know the truth" (the implication being to walk in it) (John 8:32; 2 John 1, 4); "love one another" as a new yet timeless commandment (John

13:34; 1 John 2:7; 3:11); and "abide in" Christ (John 15:4; 1 John 2:6). References abound to "an advocate" (which in 1 John 2:1 refers to Christ, not to the Holy Spirit as in John 14:16-17), to the "world" of unbelief, to the joy among believers. Without knowledge of the Gospel of John we scarcely could interpret the Johannine letters.

Traditionally the word *letter* has been used to designate these documents, but First John seems more a discourse or sermon. It has no salutation or closing. Perhaps like the letter to the Ephesians, it was meant to circulate from group to group. Second and Third John clearly are letters, addressed to a specific fellowship or individual, dealing with particular problems. The normally secular greetings are included; yet as in Paul's letters, they are amplified with faith language ("Grace, mercy, and peace," 2 John 3). "The elect lady" seems to have been a home church with adult members as "her children" (2 John 1). Gaius appears to have been the leader of another home church (3 John 1).

The language throughout is family oriented. Only a respected elder could comfortably say, as Jesus had said, "little children" to the believers in the churches. Tenderness of expression imbues tough arguments and tense reproofs. "Beloved," "children," "young people," "fathers," "brothers and sisters" saturate the discourse. God as "Father" and Christ as "Son" are used continually, not to emphasize gender but to stress intimacy, warmth, parental affection. The family language is not a ploy to soften the audience. The gentle words help formulate the gracious message. The church is family.

In what ways do you think of your church fellowship as family?

_____

_____

The Danger

The ultimate enemy, of course, is evil, the "evil one" who has a hold on "the world." But the immediate danger is any breakdown within the fellowship. Jesus Christ has broken the evil one's hold on lives. Believers are free to walk in the light, in the freedom to love. But if the evil one slips into the fellowship, the saving work of Christ can be undermined.

When we read 1 John 2:18, we are not surprised to hear "that antichrist is coming." Scripture speaks often of conditions of last days or last times. But suddenly we are confronted with an unusual expression, "now many antichrists have come" (2:18). Who were they? What did they do? Why the crisis? We have only hints for answers. "They went out from us" (2:19). Apparently their beliefs were different. Although they had left the fellowship, they continued to teach false ideas and lure others to their way of thinking. They were "false prophets," distorting traditional teaching. Were they

The term *antichrist* (from the Greek *antichristos*, meaning "against Christ" or "counterchrist") appears in the Bible only in 1 John 2:18, 22; 4:3 and 2 John 7. In these letters the antichrist is one who denies the human-divine nature of Jesus Christ. As early as the second century A.D., the term *antichrist* was connected with opponents of Christ—the "false messiahs and false prophets" of Matthew 24:24 and Mark 13:22 and "the lawless one" of 1 Thessalonians 2:3-10. Though the term *antichrist* does not appear in Revelation, these Christian writings saw the opponents of Christ in Revelation, especially the two beasts of Revelation 13, 16, 17, and 19, as antichrist.

DISCIPLE

honoring Jesus Christ as teacher but questioning his Lordship? Or were they denying that Jesus was fully human? "This is how you will be able to know whether it is God's Spirit: anyone who acknowledges that Jesus Christ came as a human being has the Spirit who comes from God. But anyone who denies this about Jesus does not have the Spirit from God" (1 John 4:2-3, TEV). The elder wrote to "the elect lady and her children" to beware of "deceivers," those who did not confess that Jesus Christ had come in the flesh (2 John 7-8).

About this time, in both Greek and Jewish circles, particularly among the intellectually elite, a spirituality developed that perceived the physical world—the world of flesh and matter—as lower, unclean, and evil. It taught that the material world was wicked, so the spiritually elite should abandon it. The Greek spiritualists had a secret knowledge, a *gnosis,* that lifted them out of a decaying material world. A heresy called *docetism* emerged that was to plague the church for centuries. Docetism means simply "to seem" or "to appear." The heresy believed Jesus was divine but did not actually become a human being. Rather, "the Word" only "seemed" or "appeared" to take on human form and become a human person. This philosophy thereby avoided the then-horrifying notion of God's Spirit or Word becoming flesh, of God's actual bleeding on a tree. He only "seemed" to suffer. To refute such thinking, the later creeds held on to Jesus' full humanity. He was "*born* of the Virgin Mary, *suffered* under Pontius Pilate, was *crucified, dead,* and *buried.*"

In today's world, dissenters probably would not deny Jesus' humanity but rather his divinity. What do you think?

Does docetism split theological hairs? Not to John and his followers. If the Incarnation—the true Word of God truly made flesh—is undercut, then the cross loses its atoning power. None but God can forgive sin. If the suffering was not Jesus in human reality loving "to the end" (John 13:1), then Christians have not been reconciled and we, like the world, are lost. That is why the elder called the dissidents "antichrist"; they were against the Savior. The elder called them "liars" because they did not hold to the essential truth. Their false teaching removed the cornerstone of salvation and made the gospel a lie.

If we believe Jesus was only divine and not human, he therefore did not suffer for us. If we think salvation comes through secret knowledge, if we have that knowledge, we do not need to be obedient. Thus dissension rooted in a lie grows into hatred. Hatred leads to murder (1 John 3:15). The Christian believer who has experienced the cleansing power of forgiveness through confession and the blood of Jesus (1:7)

Olive Tree

shows love toward sisters and brothers in the faith. "If we walk in the light as he himself is in the light, we have fellowship with one another" (1:7).

Hospitality and False Teachers

Love is God's initiative. The family being created is God's family. "We know love by this, that he laid down his life for us—and we ought to lay down our lives for one another" (1 John 3:16). Love is no mere sentimental emotion. Love takes on everyday practicality. If one Christian "has the world's goods and sees a brother or sister in need and yet refuses help" (3:17), that Christian denies the Lord. Members of the family are to help one another.

The elder praises Gaius for his hospitality. Gaius received the traveling witnesses, welcomed these Christian strangers who were without financial support (3 John 5-7). We offer the hospitality of Christ when we invite believers, strangers from other places, to our tables. By giving hospitality, "we may become co-workers with the truth" (3 John 8).

Still the elder warned against giving hospitality to false teachers. If they went beyond the teaching of Christ or denied the Word made flesh in Jesus, their teaching could destroy the fellowship. "Be on your guard, so that you do not lose what we have worked for, . . . for to welcome is to participate in the evil deeds of such a person" (2 John 8, 11).

According to Jude, false teachings flow into licentiousness. When believers pervert grace, they deny Jesus as "Master and Lord" (Jude 4). The danger, dramatized by "certain intruders" who "have stolen in among you," is that they bring anger, like Cain's anger toward his brother Abel (Genesis 4:1-8). They bring greed, like Balaam's prophecy for profit (Numbers 22–24). They bring a rebellious nature, like the Levite Korah, who led a rebellion against Moses (Numbers 16). Some are "grumblers," "malcontents," "scoffers" (Jude 16-18).

Who were the dreamers who "defile the flesh" (Jude 8)? Two kinds, apparently. Some said sexuality was impure. They were above it in a "spiritual" state. Others said sexuality was irrelevant to faith. They could participate in promiscuity ("they indulge their own lusts," 16) and not be faulted. These people were corrupting influences. They were "blemishes on your love-feasts" (12). These folk were not hungry for forgiveness or searching for salvation. Rather they were arrogant people, self-satisfied, self-serving. "They feast with you without fear, feeding themselves" (12). Their punishment will come from God; they will be like wandering stars that disappear into the darkness (13).

How can your church be open to sin-sick people and, at the same time, confront arrogant, divisive people?

NOTES, REFLECTIONS, AND QUESTIONS

DISCIPLE

What has caused division or dissension in your church?

Sin

The discussions about sin in these letters are as complex as sin itself. As in John's Gospel, sin is a denial of the revelation of God in Jesus Christ. It is seeing the light, then insisting on walking in darkness. A key idea is not to "deceive ourselves." Total disclosure of sin is required. Our openness meets Christ's blood. We are struggling with an authority break, our souls being wrenched from the world's control to Christ's control. "If we say that we have no sin, we deceive ourselves. . . . If we confess our sins, he who is faithful and just will forgive us our sins and cleanse us from all unrighteousness" (1 John 1:8-9).

Are believers then completely clean and blameless? Sometimes John seems to say so. "No one who abides in him sins; no one who sins has either seen him or known him" (3:6). Yet our observation of ourselves and others tells us that even in faith we do sin, and often. Our Lord taught us to pray, and we pray regularly for God to forgive us our sins as we forgive those who sin against us.

Perhaps John means that for believers, the authority and power of sin is broken. We live in a new relationship. But perhaps he sometimes overstates his case in an urgent plea for us to walk continually in love. He clearly knows even the children of light need fresh forgiveness. He explains, "I am writing these things to you so that you may not sin" (2:1). Aha! John holds the light of hope before our eyes. "But if anyone does sin, we have an advocate with the Father, Jesus Christ the righteous; and he is the atoning sacrifice for our sins" (2:1-2). So not only does the atoning sacrifice break the hold sin has upon us, but it offers fresh cleansing as we repeatedly repent.

Some readers think the elder made his message too easy by failing to lift up Jesus Christ's command to care for the neighbor or to love the enemy. But they forget it sometimes is harder to love a sister or brother than to love a stranger.

But God offers much to help us as we try to love one another. We have the gospel message: God's love was made clear to us in Jesus Christ. We have powerful testimonies—water, blood, the Spirit (5:6-8). The water refers to the cleansing water of baptism. The blood points to the sacrificial and glorifying love on the cross. The Spirit witnesses to the water and the blood; "the Spirit is the truth."

Friends in the church can help too. Not only are we to love sisters and brothers; they are to love us. Gaius was kind to visiting Christians (3 John 5-6). For every Diotrephes who excluded people from the church fellowship (9-10), there was a Demetrius who encouraged and did good (12).

The joy of Christian fellowship is like nothing the world offers. It is not glitzy pleasure but deep trust and inner assurance. But the greatest source of strength, enabling the believer to hold steady in love, is found in the majestic benediction that closes Jude. "Now to him who is able to keep you from falling, and to make you stand without blemish in the presence of his glory with rejoicing, to the only God our Savior, through Jesus Christ our Lord, be glory, majesty, power, and authority, before all time and now and forever. Amen" (Jude 24-25).

MARKS OF FAITHFUL COMMUNITY

Every community has a reason for being: For the Christian community that reason is Christ. We hold one another accountable in what we believe, how we love, and when we forgive by what was from the beginning—what was seen and what was revealed in Jesus Christ.

What do 1, 2, and 3 John hold to be true about Jesus?

_____

_____

What do you hold to be true about Jesus?

_____

What differences do you see in what John says and what you believe?

_____

How is your congregation intentional in relating what it *believes* about Jesus to what it *does* as the church?

_____

_____

What do we risk in terms of unity when we stray from the central beliefs that form the community?

_____

THE RADICAL DISCIPLE

When faced with new situations that call old assumptions, old commandments into question, the radical disciple views the situation with a clear eye, knows the limits of tolerance for change, and holds self and community to the central teaching of Christ.

IF YOU WANT TO KNOW MORE

To get some sense of the communities who received the Gospel of John and the Letters of John, compare words, phrases, and themes in the Gospel and the letters.

NOTES, REFLECTIONS, AND QUESTIONS

Being faithful community, we are shaped in our relationship to one another by the message we have heard from the beginning: Love one another.

SPEECH

> "How great a forest is set ablaze by a small fire! And the tongue is a fire. The tongue is placed among our members as a world of iniquity; it stains the whole body, sets on fire the cycle of nature, and is itself set on fire by hell."
>
> —James 3:5-6

26 The Power of the Tongue

OUR HUMAN CONDITION

People talk about people. Everybody does. Talk is easy. We don't always mean what we say. Our actions sometimes speak louder than our words, but not always. Everybody stretches the truth sometimes. Few people hold us accountable for what we say. We keep talking.

ASSIGNMENT

Read with an eye on your own behavior. James is a practical wisdom book. Look carefully at your life, especially your speech habits, as you study.

Day 1   James 1 (hearing and doing the word)
Day 2   James 2 (faith and works)
Day 3   James 3 (power of the tongue, true wisdom comes from God)
Day 4   James 4 (contrast between godliness and worldliness)
Day 5   James 5 (be patient, power of righteous prayer)
Day 6   Read and respond to "Fruit From the Tree of Life" and "Marks of Faithful Community."
Day 7   Rest

THE RADICAL DISCIPLE

During the coming week, listen. Listen for talk that tears down, belittles, degrades, undercuts—on radio and television and in movies; in conversations at home, at work, at play. Examine your own participation in such talk. Listen for positive uses of the tongue. Consider the relationship between your faith and your speech.

PSALM OF THE WEEK

Keep your own speaking in mind as you pray Psalm 141 aloud daily. Focus on 141:3. Memorize it and repeat it to yourself throughout the day as you choose the words you say.

PRAYER

Pray daily before study:
  "Help me to speak, Lord,
    and I will praise you" (Psalm 51:15, TEV).

Prayer concerns for this week:

Day 1   James 1 (hearing and doing the word)

Day 4   James 4 (contrast between godliness and worldliness)

Day 2   James 2 (faith and works)

Day 5   James 5 (be patient, power of righteous prayer)

Day 3   James 3 (power of the tongue, true wisdom comes from God)

Day 6   "Fruit From the Tree of Life" and "Marks of Faithful Community"

Stylized Tree of Life

DISCIPLE

FRUIT FROM THE TREE OF LIFE

The "tongue" may seem too narrow a focus for the theme of James, but think of the tongue as tied to the heart. When the heart is in harmony with God's grace, words of integrity, compassion, and praise come through the tongue. The "works," without which faith is dead, flow from the tongues of the faithful. Seen in that perspective, the tongue becomes a key instrument for Christian behavior.

As James is acutely aware, believers tend to take lightly their use of the tongue. Christians who would never kill someone often destroy lives with their mouths. People who would never cheat on their financial ledgers often lie with their lips. The letter of James challenges believers to speak more carefully in the workplace and at the dinner table. James, like wisdom in the Old Testament, deals with everyday life after the worship services are over.

The Teacher

Perhaps because James was a teacher, he knew the power of words. He wrote in elegant Greek, with balanced diction, rhetorical questions, quotations from and allusions to the Greek Old Testament, the Septuagint. No writer is more skilled with word pictures—the master teacher's craft. His metaphors march in measured beat to make a point. Just look at his picture language: The tongue needs to be bridled, restrained, like a spirited horse with a bit in its mouth. The tongue is like a small rudder guiding a great ship. The tongue is a fire, able, like a match, to set a forest ablaze.

James addresses both "brothers and sisters," and his figures of speech appeal to ordinary people in everyday life—fresh or brackish water, figs and olives and grapes, horses and ships. His comparing the taming of wild animals, birds, reptiles, and sea creatures with the more difficult taming of the tongue could be understood by all.

The authority for this letter is attributed to James, the brother of Jesus, a leader in the early Jerusalem church. Paul and Barnabas met with James and Peter to gain permission for their missionary work among Gentiles (Acts 15:1-29). Whether the book is by James's hand, or under his influence, or in his honor, we do not know. What we do know is James was revered and respected.

The book is more exhortation than letter. Except for the salutation, it lacks the usual characteristics of a letter. The greeting is to "the twelve tribes in the Dispersion" (James 1:1), presumably Jewish Christians scattered throughout the Mediterranean world, but perhaps to Christians everywhere. Most scholars think the writing came from first-generation or second-generation Christians, because the churches still seemed to be fellowship groups without much organization or administrative structure. Yet the problems they faced are the troubles of the church in all generations.

SPEECH

Wisdom

Discipline of the tongue resides deep in the wisdom tradition. Ancient sages knew the power of speech. Job and the wisdom writers knew integrity was a godly attribute and expressed itself in truthful speech. When Job professed his innocence before God, he asked, "Is there any wrong on my tongue?" (Job 6:30). The Teacher in Ecclesiastes recommended that a person not speak too much. "What the wise say brings them honor, but fools are destroyed by their own words. They start out with silly talk and end up with pure madness. A fool talks on and on" (Ecclesiastes 10:12-14, TEV). God grounded truth-telling in the heart of the commandments: "You shall not bear false witness against your neighbor" (Exodus 20:16). Psalms and Proverbs describe the tongue with violent images. The tongue "is like a sharp razor" (Psalm 52:2). "Rash words are like sword thrusts" (Proverbs 12:18). Lying lips, foolish talk, smooth seductive speech, backbiting—these weapons of evil divide families, bring down governments, bankrupt businesses, cause murder, start wars. No wonder the proverb declares the Lord hates "a lying tongue" (6:17). No wonder the psalmist vows,

"I will guard my ways
  that I may not sin with my tongue;
I will keep a muzzle on my mouth" (Psalm 39:1).

But the tongue can generate great good as well. Proverbs points out that, while rash words can cut, wise words can heal (Proverbs 12:18), and "a gentle tongue is a tree of life" (15:4). The "capable wife" of Proverbs has on her tongue "the teaching of kindness" (31:26). A word of absolute integrity is like a house built on a rock foundation. James quotes the Sermon on the Mount almost word for word when he writes, "Do not swear, either by heaven or by earth or by any other oath, but let your 'Yes' be yes and your 'No' be no, so that you may not fall under condemnation" (James 5:12; Matthew 5:34-37).

Wisdom in James

James is often called the wisdom teacher of the New Testament. Like the sages, he gives a reasoned view of life. But he writes from a perspective different from that of the Old Testament writers. While the wisdom of Proverbs is grounded in creation—the way things are—James's wisdom is grounded in Jesus Christ—the way things are coming to be. The Teacher in Ecclesiastes rejected the mad dash for pleasure and the frantic accumulation of worldly goods as foolishness, a chasing after wind. James rejects worldly values as in conflict with the way Jesus lived and taught. Job used as his frame of reference the Mosaic law, with its emphasis on justice. James appeals to a "royal law," to the gospel, the law of love of neighbor. Instead of merely making sense of this life, James wants Christians to live in a way that assures their receiving the crown of life.

Stylized Tree of Life

DISCIPLE

James sees the world differently from the way the world sees itself. "The world" tends to see existence as a system in which people strive for success by competing against one another. Social status is important; possessions take priority; suffering is avoided; pleasure is pursued feverishly.

In James's view, the social system is turned upside down. The poor are lifted up; the rich are asked to serve. All are equal, yielding to one another in the fellowship. We give generously because God gives generously in a world that seems afraid there isn't enough to go around. In a world of lies, believers tell the truth because "he gave us birth by the word of truth" (James 1:18). In a world of anger, believers are "quick to listen, slow to speak, slow to anger; for . . . anger does not produce God's righteousness" (1:19-20). In a world of social climbing, James would approve of Paul's admonition, "outdo one another in showing honor" (Romans 12:10). The community of faith is living out a new joyful social order of equally valued persons.

No New Testament writer is more critical than James when believers fall back into worldly thinking, particularly regarding treatment of the rich and the poor. If the church defers to the person in "fine clothes," with "gold rings," it becomes a club, not a community. If the poor person "in dirty clothes" comes in and is humiliated with demeaning words—"stand over there" or "sit here on the floor"—the fellowship is violated (James 2:3, TEV). Believers live under "the royal law": "You shall love your neighbor as yourself" (2:8; Leviticus 19:18). Showing partiality is breaking the laws of God as surely as committing murder or adultery is breaking the laws of God (James 2:9-11). In their speaking and their acting, believers will be judged by "the law of liberty" (2:12), that is, by the gospel.

The Clean Heart

James is no mere moralist, admonishing believers to watch their mouths. He knows the heart must be changed. Although James emphasizes outward "works," he understands works emerge from faith. He agreed with Jesus' words to Nicodemus, "You must be born from above" (John 3:7), and the words Jesus spoke to his followers, "You have already been cleansed by the word that I have spoken to you" (15:3). James insists that pure, clean speech comes from our lips because God has given us "birth by the word of truth" (James 1:18). Like a clean spring from which pure water gushes forth, purified hearts can produce words of integrity and praise.

Trying to live godly lives together may bring suffering, for believers will be living in contrast to and conflict with the ways of the world. "Whenever you face trials of any kind, consider it nothing but joy" (1:2). Why? Because testing produces endurance, and endurance will lead to maturity.

"If any are hearers of the word and not doers, they are like those who look at themselves in a mirror; for they look at themselves and, on going away, immediately forget what they were like" (James 1:23-24). A bronze mirror such as this one could be polished to a high sheen to provide a dark or dim reflection.

SPEECH

We must not fall back into "envy and selfish ambition" (3:16), enmity and conflict. The friend of the world is an enemy of God. The ways of the world lead to death. Be patient, like a farmer waiting for a crop, for "the coming of the Lord is near" (5:8). Remember Job, who "showed endurance" and the Lord proved "compassionate and merciful" (5:10-11).

Faith Without Works

Some scholars have wanted to set James against Paul, with James stressing "works" and Paul emphasizing "faith." Martin Luther seemed to fall into that trap. Although James and Paul come at the issue in different ways, both know believers are saved by faith in God's grace in Christ but must live out that faith in their behavior.

Admittedly, James makes his case intensely, but he is pleading with the faith community. Intellectual belief is powerless, he argues. Personal piety without ethical expression has no merit. James wants us to listen to our speech, look at our hands, watch our feet, study our pocketbooks. Of course, faith is essential; but if faith is real, it will show itself in works.

Presumption *Versus* Providence

In our world, we want to be in control, exercise freedom. We say boldly, "I'm going here; I'm going there." But the truth is, we do not know what tomorrow will bring. As believers, we understand we are under the gracious care of a loving God. For two reasons we should be cautious before boasting about tomorrow: First, each heartbeat, each breath is a gift of God's gracious providence. Second, we try to be led by the Spirit each step of the way. Therefore, we should say, "If the Lord wishes, we will live and do this or that" (James 4:15).

The Power

Notice how often the tongue is at work for good. Sing. When things are going well, sing praise (James 5:13). Pray. Pray for one another. Pray *for* the sick. Pray *with* the sick. Call in the elders to pray for them. Here is spiritual dynamite: "Confess your sins to one another . . . so that you may be healed" (5:16). Historians record that penance, confessing sin or wrongdoing, was not formalized as a sacrament (Sacrament of Penance in Roman Catholic practice) in the church until the thirteenth century A.D. But before then, Christians throughout the world practiced confession, confessing to one another. Who does not know the power of confessing wrongdoing directly to another person? Many Christians have found a world of guilt lifted from their shoulders when they have shared their experiences within a caring Christian fellowship.

What has been your experience of confession? How willing

DISCIPLE

are you to be open and vulnerable? How willing are the people in your group?

_____

_____

What makes confession both helpful and effective?

_____

_____

Rescue Others

Throughout the letter, James admonishes believers to avoid evil with their tongues and with their lives. His last words reach even further: If we see a fellow believer "wandering" from the truth, we should try, by prayer and gentle persuasion, to bring that person back (James 5:19-20). Instead of slander or backbiting, we are advised to give caring correction—a rather tricky business if not infused by love. The worldly will be defensive, but believers will accept reproof if it is truthful and caring.

Ezekiel ate the scroll of God's Word and offered reproof to the "house of Israel" (Ezekiel 3:1-11). Mosaic law mandated, "You shall reprove your neighbor, or you will incur guilt yourself" (Leviticus 19:17). That very law in Leviticus was the basis of Jesus' teaching and James's urging: "You shall love your neighbor as yourself" (19:18).

But how can rescuing others help overcome sin? In Proverbs, we learn that "love covers all offenses" (Proverbs 10:12). In First Peter we are told to "maintain constant love for one another, for love covers a multitude of sins" (1 Peter 4:8). The world tends to abandon the sin-sick; the Christian community comes together to pray over the afflicted. The world wants to write off the fallen; believers reach out a saving hand. The intentional Christ community desires to rescue the weak and alienated.

We should measure our churches by how well we care for the dispossessed, the distressed, the morally bankrupt. How does your congregation measure up?

_____

If love covers sins because it draws the sinner to repentance and manifests concern for neighbor, then we ought to increase in boldness. When we do so, we would be doing precisely what James has done for us, lovingly reproving us, challenging us to live simply and honestly, in prayer and in love, until the Lord comes.

Are our resources adequate? The world believes it never has enough. So the world frets, pushes others down, hoards against the future. Christians believe in abundance. Just as

Jesus fed the five thousand and had food left over, so, James insists, "God . . . gives to all generously and ungrudgingly" (James 1:5). We can give and we can love exuberantly because "every generous act of giving, with every perfect gift, is from above, coming down from the Father" (1:17). So we are not afraid to ask, nor are we afraid to give.

MARKS OF FAITHFUL COMMUNITY

"Wisdom from above is first pure, then peaceable, gentle, willing to yield, full of mercy and good fruits, without a trace of partiality or hypocrisy. And a harvest of righteousness is sown in peace for those who make peace" (James 3:17-18).

We seek to bridle our tongues, resisting the temptation to backbite, gossip, lie, grumble. We try to speak the truth, give words of encouragement, show compassion, offer prayers of praise.

Not taking lightly the use of the tongue includes recognizing the temptation to participate in convenient, culturally-sanctioned speech—trash talk and obscenities, verbal harassment, off-color jokes or jokes at others' expense. When do you find yourself taking up such speech habits and why?

_____

_____

How do we avoid participating in such speech?

_____

_____

Identify and reflect on your most serious speech struggles (lying? gossip? cursing? negative comments? belittling others? other?). What is helping you overcome these habits?

_____

_____

Describe ways you are growing more positive and bold in your speech (encouraging, praying, witnessing, bringing someone back to the faith).

_____

_____

IF YOU WANT TO KNOW MORE

Covenant as a group to use speech as an act of discipleship—to guard the tongue, speak truthfully and kindly, offer affirmation to others and praise to God—in other words, covenant together to clean up your speaking.

Being faithful community, we recognize words have power to build up or destroy. Therefore, we do not take lightly the use of our tongue.

APOCALYPSE

"Blessed is the one who reads aloud the words of the prophecy, and blessed are those who hear and who keep what is written in it; for the time is near."

—Revelation 1:3

27 Vision of End Time

OUR HUMAN CONDITION

The world has been here a long time, and it will continue for a long time. The world goes on. Life goes on. The end is nowhere in sight.

ASSIGNMENT

Stand up. Read The Revelation aloud. Why? Because John tells us to do so and promises a blessing (Revelation 1:3). Because the book is a vision, packed with imagery. Because reading it aloud in its entirety helps to keep the mystery and maintain the unity. Please obey and honor John. Read the book aloud.

Day 1 Read aloud Revelation 1–3 (John's vision, letters to the churches).
Day 2 Read aloud Revelation 4–11 (vision of God, seven seals, seven angels with trumpets, two witnesses, the beast from the pit).
Day 3 Read aloud Revelation 12–14 (the woman and the red dragon, two beasts, the Lamb, the redeemed).
Day 4 Read aloud Revelation 15–18 (seven bowls of God's wrath, the great whore and the beast, lament for fallen Babylon).
Day 5 Read aloud Revelation 19–22 (praises in heaven, end of Satan and death, new heaven and new earth, the new Jerusalem, the river and the tree of life).
Day 6 Read and respond to "Fruit From the Tree of Life" and "Marks of Faithful Community."
Day 7 Rest

PSALM OF THE WEEK

Follow each day's reading aloud of assigned Scripture with praying aloud Psalm 2. Think about how the psalm addresses each day's passages from Revelation.

PRAYER

Pray daily before study:
"You guide me with your instruction
and at the end you will receive me
with honor.
What else do I have in heaven but you?
Since I have you, what else could
I want on earth?" (Psalm 73:24-25, TEV)

Prayer concerns for this week:

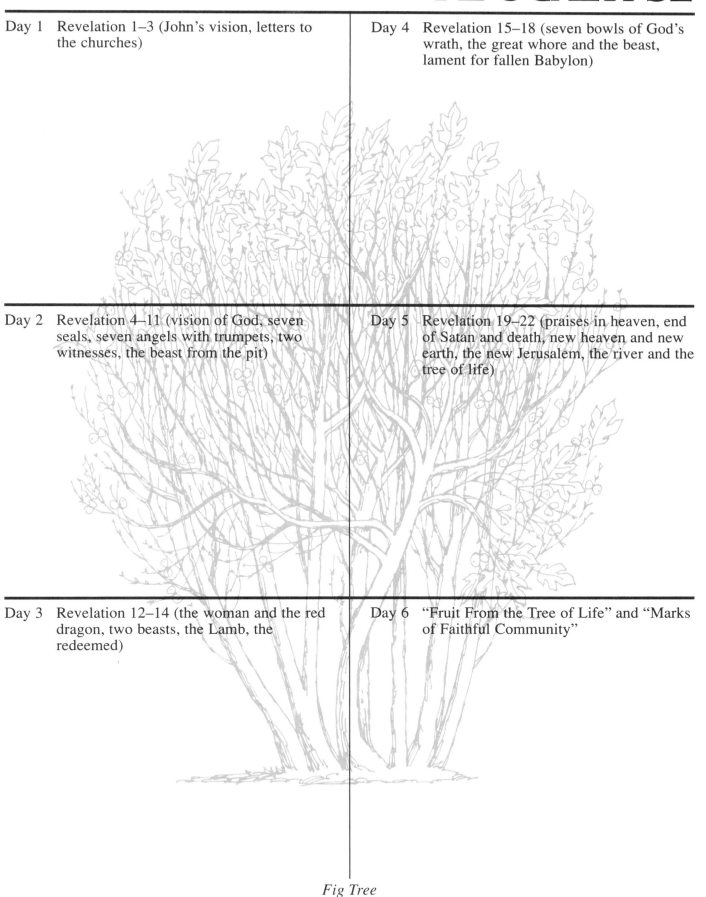

Day 1 Revelation 1–3 (John's vision, letters to the churches)

Day 4 Revelation 15–18 (seven bowls of God's wrath, the great whore and the beast, lament for fallen Babylon)

Day 2 Revelation 4–11 (vision of God, seven seals, seven angels with trumpets, two witnesses, the beast from the pit)

Day 5 Revelation 19–22 (praises in heaven, end of Satan and death, new heaven and new earth, the new Jerusalem, the river and the tree of life)

Day 3 Revelation 12–14 (the woman and the red dragon, two beasts, the Lamb, the redeemed)

Day 6 "Fruit From the Tree of Life" and "Marks of Faithful Community"

Fig Tree

DISCIPLE

FRUIT FROM THE TREE OF LIFE

I was in the spirit on the Lord's day" (Revelation 1:10). John had his vision, heard the voice, saw Christ on Sunday. Resurrection morn. Perhaps it was "early on the first day of the week, while it was still dark"—as when Mary Magdalene saw Jesus at the tomb (John 20:1). Perhaps John heard the waves splashing against the rocky shores of Patmos—as when Peter felt the waves on the Sea of Galilee and glimpsed the risen Christ "just after daybreak" (21:4-7).

Bible students are accustomed to prophets having visions. Ezekiel was "among the exiles by the river Chebar" when, in his words, "the heavens were opened, and I saw visions of God" (Ezekiel 1:1). As Ezekiel saw wheels within wheels and eyes on the wheels, John saw a rider on a white horse followed by the armies of heaven (Revelation 19:11, 14). As Daniel, after fasting for three weeks, "saw a man clothed in linen" with "arms and legs like the gleam of burnished bronze" (Daniel 10:5-6), John saw "one like the Son of Man, clothed with a long robe, . . . his feet were like burnished bronze" (Revelation 1:13-15).

John was in exile on Patmos, a small rocky island in the Aegean Sea seventy-five miles off the coast from Ephesus. Surrounded by salt water, punished by a blazing sun, life on the island was harsh; and there was little chance of escape. What's more, the sea symbolized chaos and evil. No wonder John, when he pictured heaven, saw a place where "the sea was no more" (21:1).

John knew persecution: "I, John, your brother . . . share with you in Jesus the persecution." He was exiled on "Patmos because of the word of God and the testimony of Jesus" (1:9). Faithfulness to this Jesus placed John in prison and gave him his vision. Whether he was the apostle John or an elder we do not know. He simply identified himself as "John, your brother."

The Apocalypse

The book is called "Apocalypse," which means revelation; but it is a revelation of end time—tough to comprehend. Countless people have been and still are bewildered, even intimidated, by this book. The reasons are many. Visions, by their very nature, are sometimes difficult to explain. But also, the document was deliberately coded. Only insiders would know the meaning of numbers like 666 and 42, names like Babylon and Jezebel. In addition, the setting—first-century politics, economics, and religion—is foreign to the modern reader. On top of it all, some interpreters misuse the book to frighten or confuse, or to profit from the unsuspecting.

But the major barrier to understanding the Revelation is that it was written by an exile to an oppressed minority. Believers in Jesus were hanging on to their faith at the risk of their lives. True, some Christians in some parts of the world today understand, because they too are suffering for their Lord. But

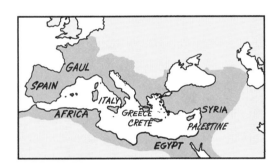

During the reign of the emperor Domitian (A.D. 81–96), when the book of Revelation was written, the Roman Empire extended west to east from the Atlantic Ocean to the Caspian Sea and included most of Europe in the north and the coastal lands of Africa and all Egypt in the south.

comfortable Christians in pleasant surroundings have difficulty comprehending the depth of pain or the darkness of despair experienced under the ever-present threat of persecution.

Late in the first century A.D., the Roman Empire took on a demonic character. The Flavian family—Vespasian, the father, and Titus and Domitian, the sons—used religious loyalty to their political advantage. With the Greek and Roman gods, people could ask their favor or not, could pick and choose their favorites. But when the emperors began to build temples honoring themselves, when the gods no longer were marble sculptures but carried the swords of the army, minted the coins of the realm, celebrated the festivals of the state, Jews and Christians were under great pressure to conform or to suffer. Some Christians were imprisoned, tortured, and killed when they refused to acknowledge emperors as gods. The persecution did not end with the Flavian emperors but continued into the second and third centuries A.D. Most scholars date John's Revelation to the reign of Domitian, perhaps A.D. 95 or 96.

A Sensory Experience

John knew the book would be read aloud, as were all New Testament writings. That practice was simply assumed, customary. John's letter, however, is different. The essence is in the hearing, in the feeling, in the seeing. John's Revelation is meant to be a sensory experience, not a closely reasoned argument. "Blessed is the one who *reads aloud* the words of the prophecy" (Revelation 1:3, *italics added*).

Much of the Bible appeals to the intellect, to the mind. The laws of Moses, the teachings of Ecclesiastes, the admonitions of Proverbs cause us to think. But some parts of the Bible, like the Song of Solomon, the Psalms, the narratives of Ruth and Esther, cause us to feel. The Revelation is a mighty burst of sensory experience. We hear trumpets, see the four horsemen, smell the burning sulfur, listen to the heavenly chorus, taste the fruit from the tree of life, and sense the serenity of the river of the water of life.

The God of the Bible

We can't mistake where John stands theologically. He does not worship some strange imported god. His God is the God of Abraham, Isaac, and Jacob; the God of Moses and the prophets; the One "who is and who was and who is to come" (Revelation 1:4). Almost every sentence of his writing is saturated with Old Testament themes and images. Of the 404 verses, 275 have some kind of Old Testament allusion. (Because John does not always quote Hebrew Scriptures word for word, but also alludes to them continually, he may have known them almost by heart.) Furthermore, John wants to make absolutely certain we know he has received his revelation from Jesus Christ, the Jesus Christ of Scripture. Watch as he establishes the central attributes of the Savior.

NOTES, REFLECTIONS, AND QUESTIONS

Roman Emperors

Augustus	27 B.C.–A.D. 14
Tiberius	14–37
Gaius (Caligula)	37–41
Claudius	41–54
Nero	54–68
Galba	68–69
Otho	69
Vitellius	69
Vespasian	69–79
Titus	79–81
Domitian	81–96
Nerva	96–98
Trajan	98–117
Hadrian	117–138

DISCIPLE

"Grace to you and peace . . . from Jesus Christ" (Revelation 1:4-6): "faithful witness" (1 John 1:9; John 18:37); "first born of the dead" (Acts 26:23); "ruler of the kings of the earth" (Colossians 2:10); "who loves us" (John 14:21); "freed us from our sins" (Acts 13:39; Hebrews 7:27); "by his blood" (1 John 1:7); "made us to be a kingdom, priests" (1 Peter 2:9); "serving his God and Father" (Matthew 20:28).

John holds to traditional faith. His bizarre apocalypse comes from the God of the Bible, the God of the prophets, the God of Ezekiel and Daniel; from the same Jesus Christ of the New Testament witness. Revelation brings to completion the biblical message of redemption.

Prophetic and Apocalyptic Contrasted

As interpreters of Scripture, we are learning to distinguish the prophetic from the apocalyptic. The prophetic handles real time and space. Jeremiah knew, like fire in his bones, that if the people did not repent and turn wholeheartedly to righteousness and compassion, punishment would come (Jeremiah 5:1, 29). Such is the nature of prophecy—prophets understand today and speak about tomorrow.

But apocalyptic writers "see" beyond tomorrow, beyond specific days and years into a reality not confined by geography or calendar. Apocalyptic visions contain truths bigger than our mental categories can contain. They discern spiritual reality outside of time and space.

Ezekiel, filled with a heavenly vision, started with prophecy, announcing that Zion would be restored, exiles would return, and the Temple would be rebuilt. But then his vision became apocalyptic. The Temple grew, large enough to hold the faithful from all the nations of the earth (Ezekiel 40–42).

Daniel read the words on the wall—"MENE, MENE, TEKEL, and PARSIN" (Daniel 5:25)—and knew the kingdom of Babylon was tottering. He wrote about the painful persecution under the Babylonians, the Persians, the Greeks. But then, he too became apocalyptic. While he was describing the beasts, he suddenly saw an Ancient One take his throne,
> "his clothing was white as snow,
>   and the hair of his head like pure wool" (7:9).

He foresaw a new kingdom, a final victorious kingdom. He saw "one like a son of man, coming with the clouds of heaven" (7:13, NIV). Warfare turned from earth to the heavenly realm. Even Daniel said, "I heard but could not understand" (12:8). Apocalypse deals with end time, last things, new creation breaking in upon us. We use our imaginations. We search for the overarching meaning. Apocalypse is not the same as prophecy, for it is even more real, more profound, more absolute. Those who treat apocalypse as if it were prophecy take dates and places literally, which means the symbolism is often misunderstood—and therefore the message in the symbolism is missed.

The Seven Churches

Because the churches are *seven*—seven meaning complete—and because the churches formed a geographical circle, they symbolize all Christian communities everywhere. The apocalyptic message is clear: Jesus Christ knows his people, intimately, thoroughly, better than they know themselves.

So John wrote down his Lord's day vision as a letter to seven churches, the seven lampstands. Under the authority of One who is "the first and the last," he wrote to them and to us the message he received (Revelation 1:20).

MARKS OF FAITHFUL COMMUNITY

We allow John's Revelation to jar us out of our complacency. We want to be fervent Christians. We want to live each day expectantly, eager to receive Christ's kingdom, doing the work of Christ so as to be ready, praying, "Come, Lord Jesus."

Knowing your time is limited, how can you be more intentional about being ready?

_____

_____

The world would have us believe we can live as the world lives and be ready for the next world. How are Christians tempted in small ways to live by the world's thinking?

_____

_____

What are the risks for the church and for Christians in taking a stand against the prevailing culture?

_____

_____

THE RADICAL DISCIPLE

While society in general thinks culture—behavior patterns, beliefs, arts, entertainment, products—is benign, the radical disciple resists the power of everyday culture, knowing it undermines the sovereignty of God.

IF YOU WANT TO KNOW MORE

Rome and its emperors are integral to the context and message of John's Revelation. Research Roman emperors from Augustus to Hadrian (see list, study manual page 211), giving particular attention to their attitudes toward Jews and Christians, and report briefly (two to three minutes) in the weekly group meeting.

NOTES, REFLECTIONS, AND QUESTIONS

Being faithful community, we live and work in the present, expecting God's victory in the future, secure in knowing the end—whenever it comes—is in God's hands.

LISTEN

"Let anyone who has an ear listen to what the Spirit is saying to the churches."

—Revelation 3:22

28 Letters to the Churches

OUR HUMAN CONDITION

That early zeal, commitment, dedication couldn't last. It demanded too much. Life has more to offer. We're compromised but comfortable.

ASSIGNMENT

Look for details—seven golden lampstands, seven stars, a two-edged sword, the first and the last, keys of Death and of Hades, an open door. Look for allusions—Old Testament echoes from Numbers, Daniel, First and Second Kings, Genesis. Identify problems in Paul's churches.

Day 1   Isaiah 6:1-7 (repentance and cleansing); 11:1-5 (the messianic king); 44:6-8 (the first and the last); Matthew 16:13-19 (the keys of the Kingdom); Revelation 1:9-20 (a vision of Christ)

Day 2   Revelation 2:1-7 (message to Ephesus); Acts 19:1-20 (Paul teaches in Ephesus); 20:17-38 (Paul's good-bye to Ephesian elders)

Day 3   Revelation 2:8-17 (messages to Smyrna and Pergamum); Matthew 10:26-28 (the secret will become known); Numbers 25:1-9; 31:16 (worship of false gods); Galatians 3–5 (purpose of the Law, Christian freedom)

Day 4   Revelation 2:18-29 (message to Thyatira); Acts 16:11-15, 35-40 (Lydia, dealer in purple); 1 Kings 16:29-34; 21:1-24 (Ahab, Naboth's vineyard, Jezebel, foreign gods); 2 Kings 9:29-37 (Jezebel's death)

Day 5   Revelation 3 (messages to Sardis, Philadelphia, and Laodicea); Colossians 1–2 (supremacy of Christ, warning against false teaching); 4:7-17 (Epaphras missioner to Laodicea)

Day 6   Read and respond to "Fruit From the Tree of Life" and "Marks of Faithful Community."

Day 7   Rest

PSALM OF THE WEEK

Pray Psalm 86:1-11 aloud daily, knowing that God hears and wants to give the undivided heart necessary for the church to listen to what the Spirit is saying.

PRAYER

Pray daily before study:
"None of us can see our own errors;
    deliver me, LORD, from hidden faults!
Keep me safe, also, from willful sins;
    don't let them rule over me" (Psalm 19:12-13, TEV).

Prayer concerns for this week:

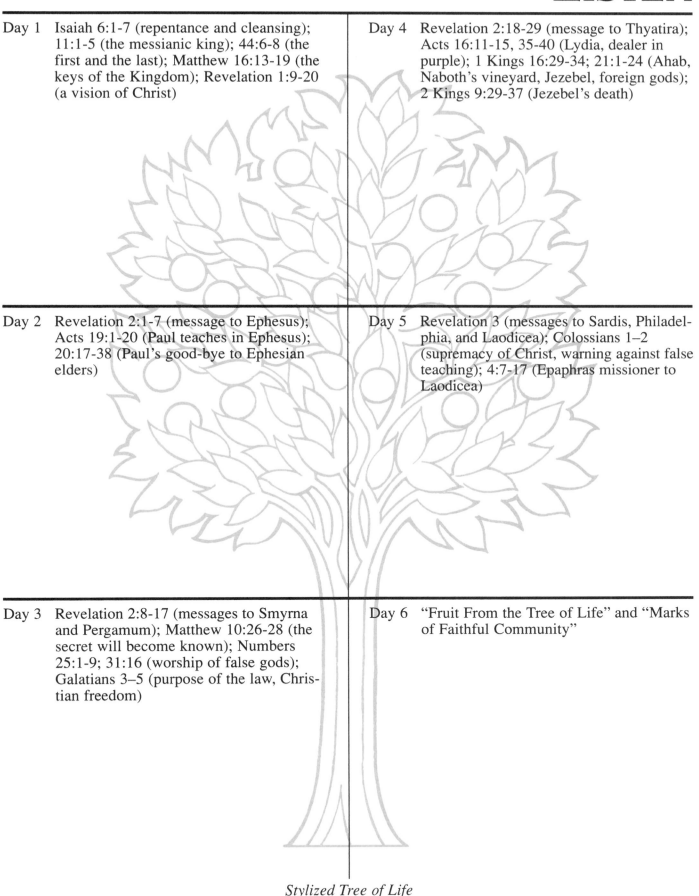

Day 1 Isaiah 6:1-7 (repentance and cleansing); 11:1-5 (the messianic king); 44:6-8 (the first and the last); Matthew 16:13-19 (the keys of the Kingdom); Revelation 1:9-20 (a vision of Christ)

Day 2 Revelation 2:1-7 (message to Ephesus); Acts 19:1-20 (Paul teaches in Ephesus); 20:17-38 (Paul's good-bye to Ephesian elders)

Day 3 Revelation 2:8-17 (messages to Smyrna and Pergamum); Matthew 10:26-28 (the secret will become known); Numbers 25:1-9; 31:16 (worship of false gods); Galatians 3–5 (purpose of the law, Christian freedom)

Day 4 Revelation 2:18-29 (message to Thyatira); Acts 16:11-15, 35-40 (Lydia, dealer in purple); 1 Kings 16:29-34; 21:1-24 (Ahab, Naboth's vineyard, Jezebel, foreign gods); 2 Kings 9:29-37 (Jezebel's death)

Day 5 Revelation 3 (messages to Sardis, Philadelphia, and Laodicea); Colossians 1–2 (supremacy of Christ, warning against false teaching); 4:7-17 (Epaphras missioner to Laodicea)

Day 6 "Fruit From the Tree of Life" and "Marks of Faithful Community"

Stylized Tree of Life

DISCIPLE

FRUIT FROM THE TREE OF LIFE

Ephesus

"These are the words of him who holds the seven stars in his right hand, who walks among the seven golden lampstands" (Revelation 2:1).

John named Ephesus first because it was preeminent among the cities of the province of Asia in the late first century A.D. The risen Christ holds "seven stars," the protective angels of the churches, "in his right hand." The right hand denotes power; holding the stars in the palm of his hand shows caring. The Lord Jesus does not stand among the churches. Rather, the caring Christ walks among the churches. "I will walk among you, and will be your God, and you shall be my people" (Leviticus 26:12).

In the Tabernacle in the wilderness, there had been a seven-branched golden lampstand with seven lamps. The gold honored God; the light revealed the presence of God; and the number seven meant completeness, even perfection.

"I know your works" (Revelation 2:2). Christ commends the Ephesian church for holding to faith and for resisting false teachers and their teachings. Decades earlier, Paul had taught the gospel every day in halls and synagogues there. He stayed longer in Ephesus than in any other missionary outpost. Colleagues like Priscilla and Aquila taught and preached in Ephesus. John's community of faith was there.

But a generation had passed. Where was the intimate caring for one another that characterized the Ephesians' earlier life? "You have abandoned the love you had at first" (2:4). Now the Spirit warns the church in Ephesus that if it did not "repent," turn about and reclaim the fervor of its first love, Christ would remove the lampstand—they would lose their identity as a Christian congregation.

Smyrna

"These are the words of the first and the last, who was dead and came to life" (Revelation 2:8).

The message came from "the first and the last," the Alpha and the Omega. The emperor might think he was first, but he was not. But why mention "who was dead and came to life"? Perhaps because the city itself had once been destroyed, abandoned for over two hundred years, gone from the map; then it came to life again.

The glorified Christ says, "I know" (2:9). In John's vision, Christ knew what was happening in the churches. You are "rich" in faith and spiritual blessings, but "I know your affliction and your poverty" (2:9). Political and economic oppression often meant unemployment, confiscation of property, even prison. The Christians of Smyrna were poor and insignificant in a rich society. Smyrna was a suffering church.

The church suffered slander from "those who say that they are Jews and are not." Were these Jewish Christians, like

The seven churches addressed in Revelation 2–3 were all in a relatively small area on the peninsula of the Roman province of Asia (Asia Minor) just east of the Aegean Sea.

Ephesus. Ephesus boasted a great library, an amphitheater built from Greek marble that seated 24,000 people, and the largest Greek temple ever built. The temple to Artemis was one of the seven wonders of the ancient world. It lasted over a thousand years. The many-breasted statue of Artemis was copied by artisans and silversmiths.

Mark Antony and Cleopatra anchored their ships side by side in the magnificent harbor. Caesar Augustus had relocated the capital from ancient Pergamum to Ephesus, declaring it "the capital city of the Roman province of Asia." Trade came by ship from Alexandria, Rome, Athens, and Syrian Antioch; by caravan from the east; and in carts from farmers in the fertile Meander River Valley.

Paul's adversaries in Galatia, who, though Christians, insisted on keeping the law of Moses as the road to righteousness (Galatians 1:6-9)? Perhaps they were Jews who simply did not accept Christian teaching. The question of who were true Jews touched also on the fact that Jewish people were not required to participate in emperor worship. Jewish Christians still related to Judaism benefited from the same protection. This meant that if Christians were considered separate from Judaism, they would lose both status and the protection of this exemption.

Christ promised Christians in Smyrna that if they were "faithful until death," he would give them "the crown of life" (Revelation 2:10). They would understand the reference, for the city was known for its great stone wall circling the citadel atop Mount Pagus. Sailors entering the harbor at night saw the wall, lighted by a thousand torches—the "Crown of Smyrna."

Pergamum

"These are the words of him who has the sharp two-edged sword" (Revelation 2:12).

The Lord said, "I know where you are living, where Satan's throne is" (2:13), a reference no doubt to the prevalence of pagan worship. Pergamum initiated emperor worship and built the first temple in Asia Minor to honor Caesar Augustus and Rome. With the addition of the temple of Emperor Trajan, the city was named "twice temple-warden of the Augusti." Satan sat on the throne. Yet Jesus comes with a sword—the word of God in his mouth—more powerful than the demands of the emperor. Christ will judge.

Two dangers are named—the teaching of the Nicolaitans and the teaching of Balaam. The Nicolaitans taught accommodation to the culture, and some in the church went along with the teaching. They thought that if they "believed right," they could do as they pleased. They separated faith from behavior, particularly in the realm of the body—food, drink, sex. The result was sexual immorality and participation in festivals that included food offered to pagan gods.

The actions of Balaam, the prophet, were remembered with disgust by the Jews. First, Balaam was willing to sell his divine word for a bribe (Numbers 22–24). The king of Moab wanted him to curse the Israelites. Though Balaam eventually blessed rather than cursed them, the Israelites did intermarry with the Moabites and participate in baal fertility worship. Israelites died of the plagues (25:9). Balaam represents compromise, selling out. For Pergamum Christians, "Balaam's" temptations were to eat meat from pagan sacrifices, participate in civil religion, and share in social excesses.

Christ will reward those who persevere. He will give "hidden manna," the food of the coming messianic banquet; and he will give "a white stone." In athletic events judges awarded white stones to the champions as trophies, often with

NOTES, REFLECTIONS, AND QUESTIONS

Smyrna. Smyrna, today's Izmir, is Turkey's third largest city. The poet Homer was born there. Smyrna was destroyed by Alyattes, the father of Croesus, in 600 B.C. and lay desolate for more than two centuries.

Alexander the Great awakened its glory and prosperity. By New Testament times, Smyrna had rebuilt the port city on the slopes of Mount Pagus and had become prosperous. Her patron deities, Poseidon, god of the sea, and Demeter, goddess of the earth, protected both sailors and farmers. Five Greek temples honored Cybele, Zeus, Apollo, Aesculapius, and Aphrodite.

Smyrna threw its full economic, political, and religious enthusiasm behind the Roman Empire. The *Pax Romana* stimulated a world trade that brought enormous income to this seaport city. Wealthy families throughout the area, in a fervent display of zeal toward Rome, poured money into new temple construction. They quickly fastened on to the imperial cult honoring the Flavian family. They built a great temple, first worshiping Vespasian, the father who fought the Jews in the sixties; then the eldest son, Titus, who destroyed Jerusalem in A.D. 70; and finally brother Domitian, who with a paranoid ego inscribed Roman coins with his own image and the words *Lord and God.*

Pergamum. On the bank of the Caicus River is today's Bergama, a corrupted form of the word *Pergamum*. Today's Bergama is on the plain, but ancient Pergamum was built one thousand feet higher atop a steep hill. It was the ancient capital of the region under Alexander the Great, with a mythology going back to the Trojan wars. The area was an independent country during the third and second centuries B.C., and the kings of that time allied themselves deeply with Rome. On his deathbed, King Attalus III bequeathed "the furnishings of my palace" to Rome; but Rome interpreted his will as meaning the entire kingdom, thereby inheriting a country of 66,750 square miles. Famous for its great altar to Zeus, Pergamum led the way into state religion.

DISCIPLE

the athlete's name inscribed on them. Christians will be given white stones for victory and purity with their new names carefully recorded. God will know their names.

Thyatira

"These are the words of the Son of God, who has eyes like a flame of fire, and whose feet are like burnished bronze" (Revelation 2:18).

John visualizes the workers at the furnaces making bronze and brass. Christ for them has "eyes like a flame of fire" and feet "like burnished bronze" (2:18). They are laborers, guild workers, so John commends their spiritual "works"—love, faith, service, endurance (2:19). Christ will give the workers —those who conquer and continue to do his works—"authority over the nations" so they can destroy evil the way they might take an iron rod and shatter clay pots (2:26-27).

But a woman, whom John labels "Jezebel," is misleading the church. Jezebel, in Israelite history, was King Ahab's queen. She brought baal religion with her to the Northern Kingdom, Israel. The baals were fertility gods, unencumbered by the Ten Commandments.

Thyatira's "Jezebel" undoubtedly taught blending Christianity with the sacred festivals of the guilds, for she was "beguiling" the faithful "to practice fornication and to eat food sacrificed to idols." Belonging to a guild was necessary if Christians were to have work. So the temptation to compromise their faith was strong. She must have taught that they could join the guilds and participate in the civil ceremonies if they believed Jesus "in their heart." Historically, Elijah had prophesied that Queen Jezebel and her heirs would be killed. (The queen was thrown from a window, and the dogs of the street ate her body.) John changes the forecast slightly. Thyatira's "Jezebel" will be "thrown" on a bed of adultery; and her "children," her followers, will be struck dead (2:22-23). She, like the old queen, will get what she deserves.

Sardis

"These are the words of him who has the seven spirits of God and the seven stars" (Revelation 3:1).

The exalted Christ saw through the busyness, the prestige, the complacency of the Sardis church. He pronounced them asleep, "on the point of death." Sardis had become a church just going through the motions of religion. The Lord said to Sardis, "You have a name of being alive, but you are dead" (3:1). Christ will come "like a thief" (3:3).

In 549 B.C. when Cyrus the Great's army approached Sardis, the Sardians thought the Persians would bypass Sardis because they thought the city to be impregnable. The city was built atop a one-thousand-foot hill surrounded by massive walls and fortifications. The citizens were self-assured, inattentive, even to the point of self-deception. One evening

Thyatira. Thyatira, on the border between the ancient kingdoms of Mysia and Lydia, was a thriving industrial city on the east-west and north-south trade routes. Flax from the farmers and wool from the shepherds provided materials for making the finest linen and wool fabrics in Asia Minor. Dye from shelled sea creatures made the city famous for its precious royal purple cloth. Lydia, Paul's first convert in Philippi and a trader in purple cloth, had come from Thyatira (Acts 16:14-40). The city also manufactured clothing, leather products, pottery, copper, and brass.

Textile workers organized into guilds or trade unions that provided social life, economic power, and political influence. Membership was compulsory, and members were under strict orders to attend meetings, learn the rules, participate in the state religion rituals. Each guild had its own deity, but each was careful to show enthusiastic religious and political support to the emperor.

Sardis. Have you heard the expression "as rich as Croesus"? Croesus was a king of ancient Lydia whose capital was Sardis. He owned the gold mines. Shepherds walked their sheep in the streams, and the gold dust washed from nearby mountains gathered on their wool. Wealth also came from trade because Sardis sat on the royal road from Smyrna to Philadelphia, where east met west. Sardis was a proud city—prosperous because of overland trade, self-satisfied because it was a city set on a hill, complacent because of its inland security.

at dusk a Persian soldier watched a Sardian soldier accidentally drop his helmet over the wall. The Persian watched the man retrieve his helmet by a secret pathway through cracks in the rock wall. In the night, a Persian unit followed that path and slipped into the city. The city fell within hours. Centuries later, in A.D. 17, an earthquake devastated Sardis when everyone was asleep. Sardis knew what it was like to be self-assured, then brought down quickly, as by "a thief."

Some persons in Sardis remained faithful, spiritually pure, and the promise to others was "If you conquer, you will be clothed . . . in white robes" (3:5). The temple of Artemis in Sardis was served by a host of priests dressed in white, symbolizing purity. Priests of Israel, called to be a "holy people," also wore white robes as a symbol of purity. Often Christian believers were baptized in white robes.

The Lord orders the nearly dead church to "wake up" and "conquer" so their names would not be blotted out of "the book of life." Roman cities kept an official ledger of citizens. If someone died or committed treason, that person's name was formally removed from the register. Christians who conquer, whose names are in "the book of life," are assured citizenship in God's kingdom.

The promise to "confess your name before my Father" (3:5) comes from Jesus' ministry. Including both promise and threat, Jesus said, "Everyone therefore who acknowledges me before others, I also will acknowledge before my Father in heaven; but whoever denies me before others, I also will deny before my Father in heaven" (Matthew 10:32-33).

Philadelphia

> *"These are the words of the holy one, the true one,*
>   *who has the key of David,*
> *who opens and no one will shut,*
> *who shuts and no one opens" (Revelation 3:7).*

"I know that you have but little power," says Christ (3:8). Philadelphia had no political clout. Its gods were mostly local Greek and Roman deities. Unlike the power cities, it had no Roman temples, little evidence of emperor worship.

Some members of the synagogue were saying the Philadelphian Christians were not true Jews. It was a family quarrel—Jewish brothers, sisters, and cousins against the Jewish Christians. John drew on the Jewish Scriptures to help the Jewish Christians hold steady. Isaiah prophesied,

> "Those who oppressed you
>   shall come bending low to you" (Isaiah 60:14).

What will they learn when they do that? "They will learn that I have loved you" (Revelation 3:9).

Why does the angel use the image of an "open door"? Because Philadelphia was the "open door" to the countries of the east. It was the passage for trade where east met west. So the door cannot be shut. What is this symbolic door? It is the

NOTES, REFLECTIONS, AND QUESTIONS

Philadelphia. The area is susceptible to earthquakes. Built on fertile but unstable volcanic soil washed down from the mountains, the city was built over huge fault lines and tectonic plates. Tremors were and still are recorded every few days. Philadelphia was destroyed by earthquake in A.D. 17, rebuilt, destroyed again in A.D. 23, rebuilt with the aid of Roman emperor Tiberius, destroyed again in A.D. 60, and rebuilt again.

In ancient days, kings of the region saw the need to establish communications from Pergamum to the tri-cities in the Lycus Valley—Colossae, Hierapolis, and Laodicea—and to open trade to the east. King Attalus II founded Philadelphia, "city of brotherly love," in honor of his beloved brother Eumenes. Not an elegant city, not a powerful Roman citadel, Philadelphia was a trade town, midway between Pergamum and Colossae. It was a doorway through which merchants from Pergamum, Smyrna, and Sardis poured into the narrow mountain pass made by the river Cogamus up onto the high plateau of Asia Minor called Phrygia.

DISCIPLE

door to God's kingdom; it is the passageway of salvation.

With the "key of David" Christ will unlock the door. Jesus Christ, descendant of King David, born in David's city, will open the way for those who have been rejected and excluded. He determines who can enter the Kingdom.

The Lord counsels, "Hold fast to what you have" (3:11). With little strength, they have held steady. They have kept Christ's word. They have not denied Christ's name. Amid earthquake-toppled pillars and stones in disarray, this weak band of Christians would be a permanent pillar in the new temple of God. They had grown accustomed to holding fast. In earthquakes entire households were buried. Cemeteries were obliterated. Family names were forgotten. God will write down their names and remember them forever. John has only words of consolation and encouragement for the suffering churches in Smyrna and Philadelphia.

Laodicea

"The words of the Amen, the faithful and true witness, the origin of God's creation" (Revelation 3:14).

Christ is the "Amen," the only time in Scripture *Amen* is used as a proper name.

In one of Scripture's most devastating denunciations, the church in Laodicea is accused of being "lukewarm, . . . neither cold nor hot" (3:16). The city of Laodicea had one major economic problem: It had no fresh drinking water. Engineers, financed by the wealthy city, built an elaborate stone aqueduct that stretched about ten miles to Hierapolis, tapping into that city's boiling mineral springs. The water started out steaming hot; but by the time it reached Laodicea, it was tepid and foul-tasting. Also, cold, clear mineral water was piped in from Colossae; but by the time it arrived, it was lukewarm too. The Laodiceans got only smelly, tepid water. John's description would have been easily understood. The church, like the water, was lukewarm.

The church was pompous and proud. Laodicea was a banking center (money), a regional capital (power and prestige), a medical center (noted for treatment of eye diseases), an industrial center (noted for fine wool clothing). Christ turns each point of pride upside down: You are wretched, not powerful; pitiable, not prestigious; poor, not rich; blind, not seeing; and naked, not clothed in fine garments (3:17).

What does Christ counsel? "Buy from me gold refined by fire"—faithfulness refined by suffering. Buy "white robes" of baptismal holiness to cover your spiritual nakedness. Buy "salve to anoint your eyes so that you may see." (Physicians who treated eyes used an ointment made from local volcanic ash and other chemicals.) Above all, "repent" (3:18-19).

Jesus stands at the door and knocks. This concluding word to the churches is meant for all people. Judgment is coming: "I am coming soon" (3:11). The entire Revelation was meant

Laodicea. Near the confluence of the Lycus and Meander rivers were the tri-cities, about ten miles apart. Colossae was famous for its black wool industry; Hierapolis was a trade town; Laodicea was a banking center and capital of the Phrygian region. Trade crossed to all directions. Paul skipped this region, but his converts and co-workers evangelized it. The key evangelist was Epaphras, who was from that region and "always wrestling in his prayers" on their behalf (Colossians 4:12-13). Missionaries and missionary letters flowed from Ephesus to these three important interior towns and back. Paul wrote to Philemon at Colossae asking for grace for Philemon's runaway slave Onesimus. Both men became key Christian converts and beloved church leaders. The Letter to the Colossians closes with crisp instructions: Have this letter "read also in the church of the Laodiceans" (4:16).

to give the churches and us a wake-up call. We have an opportunity to repent. Open the door, invite Christ in, and eat together the meal of reconciliation! Savor a foretaste of the messianic banquet! Do it now.

Which of the seven churches does your congregation most closely resemble? In what ways?

MARKS OF FAITHFUL COMMUNITY

As Christians, we experience tension with our culture because we want the teaching and example of Christ, not society, to determine our lifestyle. Our desire is to be faithful, not to "fit in," to be passionate, not lukewarm; for we know we will be held accountable.

Recall a time when you or your church were excited to the point of overflowing about your faith. What is the current state of that "first love"?

Compromise is so subtle. Describe ways you and your congregation compromise with the world.

Some churches, like Sardis, are so complacent they are embarrassed if someone has a life-changing religious experience. Describe your congregation.

THE RADICAL DISCIPLE

The radical disciple leads the way in calling the congregation to accountability and Christ-like faithfulness when the pull toward accommodation and compromise is strong.

IF YOU WANT TO KNOW MORE

If you are interested in history, geography, and archaeology, western Turkey, location of the seven cities, is a rich area for study. Consult Bible dictionaries, Bible atlases, and books on Mediterranean archaeology, as well as the internet.

Being faithful community, we listen to what the Spirit of God is saying to our congregation and strive to be faithful.

WOE WOE WOE

"After this I looked, and there in heaven a door stood open! And the first voice, which I had heard speaking to me like a trumpet, said, 'Come up here, and I will show you what must take place after this.'"

—Revelation 4:1

29 What Must Take Place

OUR HUMAN CONDITION

The clock rules. The calendar dictates. The car's waiting. Never enough hours in the day or days in the week. Have to stay focused on now. No time to think about what will take place after this.

ASSIGNMENT

The open door into heaven reveals a throne and one seated on the throne—and a Lamb standing. Imagine yourself entering the throne room of God. Look. Listen.

Day 1 Revelation 4–5 (vision of God on the throne, twenty-four elders, four living creatures, a scroll with seven seals, the Lamb); Ezekiel 1 (vision of the throne chariot, four living creatures)

Day 2 Revelation 6–7 (opening six seals, the four horsemen, martyrs, judgment, marked with God's seal, a multitude of the redeemed, songs of praise)

Day 3 Revelation 8–9 (the seventh seal, silence in heaven, seven angels with seven trumpets, plagues); Joel 2:28-32; Acts 2:17-21 (day of the Lord)

Day 4 Revelation 10–11 (angel with little scroll, measuring the Temple, two witnesses, the beast from the pit); Ezekiel 3:1-3 (eating the scroll); 40–41; 47:1-12 (vision of the new Temple)

Day 5 Revelation 12 (the woman, the child, and the red dragon)

Day 6 Read and respond to "Fruit From the Tree of Life" and "Marks of Faithful Community."

Day 7 Rest

PSALM OF THE WEEK

Combine praying Psalm 97 and writing a litany. Each day read the psalm aloud and write one sentence describing God, followed by *The LORD is king! Let the earth rejoice.* On the sixth day read the whole litany aloud after the psalm.

PRAYER

Pray daily before study:
"I thank you, LORD, with all my heart;
    I sing praise to you before the gods.
I face your holy Temple,
    bow down, and praise your name
because of your constant love and faithfulness,
    because you have shown that your name
        and your commands are supreme"
(Psalm 138:1-2, TEV).

Prayer concerns for this week:

WOE WOE WOE

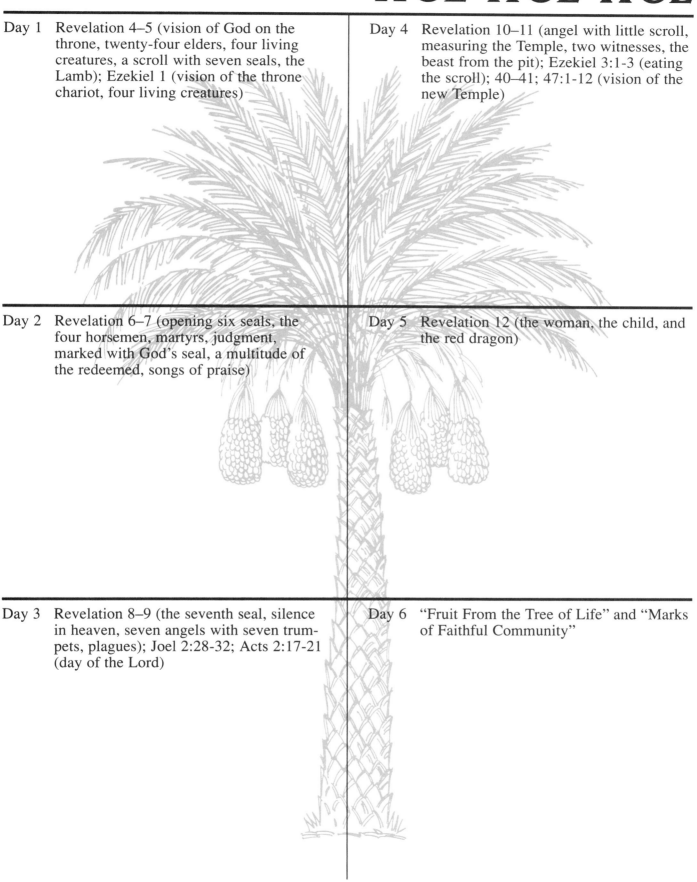

Day 1   Revelation 4–5 (vision of God on the throne, twenty-four elders, four living creatures, a scroll with seven seals, the Lamb); Ezekiel 1 (vision of the throne chariot, four living creatures)

Day 2   Revelation 6–7 (opening six seals, the four horsemen, martyrs, judgment, marked with God's seal, a multitude of the redeemed, songs of praise)

Day 3   Revelation 8–9 (the seventh seal, silence in heaven, seven angels with seven trumpets, plagues); Joel 2:28-32; Acts 2:17-21 (day of the Lord)

Day 4   Revelation 10–11 (angel with little scroll, measuring the Temple, two witnesses, the beast from the pit); Ezekiel 3:1-3 (eating the scroll); 40–41; 47:1-12 (vision of the new Temple)

Day 5   Revelation 12 (the woman, the child, and the red dragon)

Day 6   "Fruit From the Tree of Life" and "Marks of Faithful Community"

Date Palm Tree

DISCIPLE

FRUIT FROM THE TREE OF LIFE

The divine spotlight has been shining on earth. We have seen the condition of the churches in a world that asks accommodation, that asks compromise. Suddenly the scene shifts. The light moves heavenward. The door stands open! We can peer in! The radiance is nearly blinding!

John hears the invitation: "Come up here." Notice that John, in apocalyptic fashion, is in another "space," a different kind of time—"I was in the spirit" (Revelation 4:2). What is the point of this heavenly vision? To let John glimpse "what must take place after this" (4:1).

The Throne Room

God's throne is mysterious, fiery, glorious. We're awestruck. To appreciate the dazzling imagery, we, like John, must be immersed in past visions of the holy. Remember when Moses was summoned to the top of the mountain (Exodus 19)—the flashes of lightning, the peals of thunder, the blare of trumpet when Moses came near to God.

John's vision of the throne echoes Ezekiel's throne vision—sparkling jewels and fire. Both Ezekiel and John mention the rainbow, God's promise to Noah after the Flood. "Like the bow in a cloud on a rainy day, such was the appearance of the splendor all around" (Ezekiel 1:28).

Three jewels catch John's eye—jasper, carnelian, and emerald (Revelation 4:3), representations of the brilliance and the splendor of the divine presence. In early Israelite history those stones were among the stones on the breastplate of the high priest (Exodus 28:17-20). Later in John's vision, they adorn the foundations of the wall of the holy city.

Students of Ezekiel become alert when they read of "four living creatures" (Revelation 4:6). The number four stands for the four corners of the earth, meaning everywhere. The lion, the ox, the human, and the eagle came to be symbols for the four Gospels: Matthew, the lion of Israel; Mark, a calf of sacrifice; Luke, the Son of Man; John, an eagle, the Holy Spirit hovering over the church. With their eyes, like the eyes in Ezekiel's chariots, they see everything. All nature, animal and human, is praising God. "Bless the LORD, all his works, / in all places of his dominion" (Psalm 103:22). Music fills the throne room. The four creatures never stop singing a doxology (Revelation 4:8).

The twenty-four elders may stand for the priests of Israel. Because so many priests served the Temple, they were divided into twenty-four groups, each group to serve an appointed time. In total, they would represent the full praises of Israel. Or twenty-four may symbolize the twelve patriarchs plus the twelve apostles. For John's time, the double twelve may be a reminder that the church is composed of Jews and Gentiles. Certainly, the twenty-four elders represent the total unified people of God.

The Scroll

Who knows the future? Only God. When the scroll appears, it is "sealed with seven seals" like a king's edict or a valuable will. Who is worthy to break the seals, to open the scroll? John weeps bitterly, for no one was found worthy. But wait. An elder whispers there is one—the Lion of Judah who has triumphed, the Lamb who has been slain. He is worthy (Revelation 5:3-6). Suddenly all the angels in heaven, "myriads of myriads and thousands of thousands" (5:11), burst into song, "with full voice, 'Worthy is the Lamb that was slaughtered'" (5:12). Every creature—in heaven, on earth, in the sea—joins in a universe-deafening doxology "to the Lamb" (5:13). The Lamb will open the scroll that contains the meaning and dramatic conclusion of history.

The Seven Seals

What is coming? The opening of the *first seal* reveals a rider with a bow, mounted on a white horse (Revelation 6:2). This rider is not Christ as some suppose, for Christ has just opened the seal. Christ Jesus is the Lamb who does not defeat with bow and arrow. Later in the vision he will ride a white horse, but not at this time. This rider is conquest. He will ravage the earth.

From the opening of the *second seal* comes a rider on a blood-red horse (6:4). He will take away peace from the earth, causing people to slaughter one another in war.

The opening of the *third seal* shows a rider on a black horse, dark as depression, ugly as famine that follows war. The rich have manipulated the economy so the poor are starving. The scales in the rider's hand weigh unjustly.

"The LORD detests differing weights,
and dishonest scales do not please him" (Proverbs 20:23, NIV).

This horseman makes simple food too expensive for the working family. Inflation destroys the poor. Wine and olive oil, good sources of revenue, were protected by the powerful. Famine would ravage the land. Starvation occurs again and again in our greedy world.

The *fourth rider* rides a horse as green as decaying plants, awful as death (Revelation 6:8). By war, famine, disease, wild animals, Death along with Hades would sweep over a portion of the earth. Death doesn't deal the cards fairly. The powerful manipulate the market, confiscate property owned by Christians. Rulers throw millions of soldiers into bloody battle. Believers are clothed in animal skins and thrown before bulls, lions, and wild dogs in the public arenas while crowds cheer. Death is coming.

The *fifth seal* is opened. John sees the souls of martyrs under the altar like the sacrificial blood under the altar in Jerusalem's Temple, crying out, "How long?" How long will justice be perverted? People who reject the Revelation

DISCIPLE

because it is too violent, too vindictive, miss the point. The point is the evil. Wickedness, cruelty, oppression, starvation, and war must end if God's kingdom is to come in its fullness.

With the opening of the *sixth seal* comes a gigantic earthquake, more devastating than the quakes that often rocked Asia Minor (6:12). Creation turned to chaos. Joel 2:28-32 uses images similar to John's in depicting the coming judgment of the day of the Lord—the sun darkened and the moon turned to blood. In John's vision, who hid in the caves? Everyone—rich, powerful, slave, free, kings, generals, and business tycoons. They pleaded to be saved from the wrath of God and of the Lamb. Wrath is not capricious anger. Wrath is righteousness coming to the rescue, punishing wrong, rectifying the situation.

Opening of the seventh seal is delayed. We must hold our breath and wait. And not only wait but also resolve to be faithful. Repent while there is time. We have a moment of reprieve, an hour of possibility. Seize this moment!

"Wait," cried an angel, "until we have marked the servants of our God with a seal on their foreheads" (Revelation 7:3). In John's vision all are marked by their owner. Each person will have a mark—either the mark of the beast or the mark of God. It is the eleventh hour; each person must decide.

The twelve tribes of Israel are listed, beginning not with Reuben, the oldest, but with Judah, the tribe of David and Jesus. Twelve times twelve thousand—the perfected people of God—will be brought safely through God's wrath. The picture shifts. A multitude from every people and nation stands before the throne praising God in Christ for salvation. The angels sing praises. The people wear white robes washed in the blood of the Lamb. Though the image is mixed, the message is clear. Those who have yielded to the healing mercy of Christ, made pure by his blood, will sing the songs of salvation. Their robes will be spotless. Suffering will cease. "They will hunger no more" (7:16). Does this mean hunger for food or hunger for righteousness—or both? "God will wipe away every tear from their eyes" (7:17).

When the *seventh seal* is finally opened, the singing stops. Silence "for about half an hour" (8:1). A time to reflect, to repent. During this holy silence, the prayers of the saints, like heavy incense, are rising on our behalf.

Then everything breaks loose—trumpets and angels, fire and earthquake, hail mixed with blood. A great star falls. Every aspect of the universe feels the judgment—mountains, sea, rivers; even the sun, the moon, and the stars. Judgment comes.

Trumpets

Among the Jews, everything new is announced by the sound of the trumpet. Rosh Hashanah, the Feast of Trumpets, begins the religious new year in September-October. In the days of the Jerusalem Temple, a priest would climb to the pinnacle of the Temple, sound the trumpet to announce that at least three people had sighted the tiny sliver of the new moon. Each new moon, the trumpet was again sounded. Jews believed the age of messiah would be announced by the trumpet from the pinnacle of the Temple.

In John's Revelation, new happenings are signaled by the sound of trumpets. For six trumpet blasts visions of new and terrible destruction do not move the wicked to repent. But then comes the interlude with repentance and conversion, and finally the seventh trumpet.

> "The kingdom of the world has become the kingdom
> of our Lord
> and of his Messiah" (Revelation 11:15).

Three Woes

"Woe, woe, woe," cries the eagle, warning all to prepare for three awful plagues (Revelation 8:13). To understand the background imagery for the locust invasion (9:3-11), read of the locust plague in Egypt (Exodus 10:1-20) and the prophecy of Joel (Joel 1:1–2:27). Moses was foretelling a true plague of locusts; Joel may have been using a figure of speech to prophesy a horde of enemy soldiers. In John's vision of the first woe, the locusts are unbelievably ferocious, like scorpions whose sting is worse than death itself. Their king's name, Abaddon, means "Destruction."

The second woe focuses on the river Euphrates, ancient home of the Assyrian and Babylonian empires. In this plague Babylon symbolizes Rome. A gigantic force will attack. Normally, fifty thousand troops was a large army. Here the cavalry numbered two hundred million!

Those who survived "did not repent of the works of their hands or give up worshiping demons and idols. . . . And they did not repent of their murders or their sorceries or their fornication or their thefts" (Revelation 9:20-21). Amazing. All this wrath and no repentance!

A mighty angel held a small scroll in his hand. This angel stands, one foot on the sea and one on the land. Sea and land mean Roman ships and Asian authorities. Sea and land mean everywhere. The angel would speak to all.

No more delay. Time is up! "The mystery of God will be fulfilled" (10:7). John eats the scroll just as Ezekiel ate the scroll of the word of God (Ezekiel 3:1-3). Like Ezekiel, John ate a honey-tasting scroll; but for John the taste turned bitter. John must make fearful, "bitter" prophecies. Plagues will come, and famines, and awful wars.

The Temple

From the days of David the Jews could not get the Temple out of their minds. David had dreamed it; Solomon had built it. The exiles remembered its destruction:

DISCIPLE

"By the rivers of Babylon—
    there we sat down and there we wept
    when we remembered Zion" (Psalm 137:1).

Under the direction of Ezra and Nehemiah, the Judean exiles rebuilt the Temple and the city walls. Centuries later Herod would build a more magnificent Temple. But now the Temple was gone.

Now John sees a heavenly Temple. The Temple will be measured, but so will "those who worship there" (Revelation 11:1). Using Daniel's time period—forty-two months, the time Antiochus Epiphanes IV lived after the desecration of the Temple—John says there will be a time of suffering and sackcloth.

During these months of tribulation believers are given encouragement. Two olive trees and two lampstands keep the light burning. Two witnesses encourage testimony. Like Elijah, they have the power of prayer to stop the rain. When Satan, the beast, comes up from the bottomless pit, they will be killed; but after three and a half days they will live again, for the "breath" of God will enter them. God will say, "Come up here!" (Revelation 11:12). They will join loud voices in heaven singing,

"The kingdom of the world has become the kingdom
    of our Lord
    and of his Messiah,
and he will reign forever and ever" (11:15).

In the cosmic battle, the Lamb will be victorious, first in heaven, then on earth.

A Heavenly Battle

Revelation 12 concludes the first half of the Revelation by portraying a heavenly battle between Christ and Satan. The woman who gives birth could symbolize Mary, the mother of Jesus; Israel, the womb of Messiah; or the church. A "red dragon," evil personified, tries to devour the baby. Memories of Herod the Great, who slaughtered all the boy babies in Bethlehem, flood in upon us. In the garden of Eden, humankind was tempted by a serpent. Now in John's vision, Mary's Son will conquer the serpent dragon.

Then "war broke out in heaven" (12:7). When evil rebelled, heaven itself was infected. We recall the heavenly war depicted in Daniel. In both Daniel and Revelation, the dragon and his angels are defeated. In Revelation the archangel Michael throws Satan out of heaven. Evil will not exist in heaven. But Satan is hard to get rid of. The deceiver, the one Jesus called the "father of lies," continues to ravage the earth, even though he has been conquered "by the blood of the Lamb" and by people's testimony (12:11). Notice: The faithful witness of the church will help defeat Satan! The persecuted counterculture plays a role in the ultimate victory.

The war continues. The dragon, who could not win in

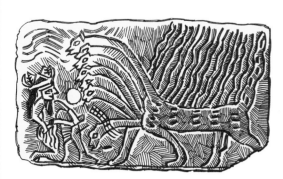

This Sumerian shell inlay, dating from 2600 B.C. and depicting a god fighting a lionlike monster with seven heads on long snakelike necks and flames rising from its back, reminds us of the great red dragon with seven heads in Revelation 12:3.

heaven, continues to tempt the faithful on earth. The demonic powers know they are losing the battle, but they struggle on, harder than ever. The angry dragon "went off to make war on the rest of her children, those who keep the commandments of God and hold the testimony of Jesus" (12:17). We recall when Jesus was tempted in the wilderness, Satan departed "until an opportune time" (Luke 4:13). The Letter to the Ephesians advises us to "put on the whole armor of God" because we struggle "against the cosmic powers of this present darkness, against the spiritual forces of evil in the heavenly places" (Ephesians 6:11-12). The final victory is certain, but the earthly struggle continues. We live in the heat of the battle.

MARKS OF FAITHFUL COMMUNITY

We are participating in a drama much larger than our own life story. We are not merely observers; we are actively engaged in a vast spiritual war. God and countless people are involved. Everything is at stake; a battle is being waged for the hearts and souls of human beings. The life of the community is a witness, but the saving Word must get out.

What is your understanding of the demonic powers with which we struggle?

_____

_____

In what ways does the cosmic battle affect your life? the life of your congregation?

_____

_____

When and in what ways are you tempted to betray your loyalty to Christ?

_____

_____

THE RADICAL DISCIPLE

The saints are praying continually; their prayers rise like incense. Perseverance makes praying radical. How might you become a more powerful person of prayer?

IF YOU WANT TO KNOW MORE

To get a sense of how John uses Old Testament themes, language, and images, look up cross-references to Old Testament passages in your study Bible. Work through Revelation a chapter at a time.

NOTES, REFLECTIONS, AND QUESTIONS

Being faithful community, we refuse to be defined and confined by the routine; we take our place in the universal struggle, knowing that victory is assured.

PERSECUTION

"Then I heard another voice from heaven saying,
'Come out of her, my people,
so that you do not take part in her sins,
and so that you do not share in her plagues;
for her sins are heaped high as heaven,
and God has remembered her iniquities.'"

—Revelation 18:4-5

30 The Power of Evil

OUR HUMAN CONDITION

We live in the real world. We have to make a living, get along with our neighbors, live in our culture. Compromise is the name of the game. People who insist on being different can expect to suffer.

ASSIGNMENT

After seven bowls of God's wrath, Rome (Babylon) with all its powerful economic systems, military structure, tentacles everywhere, is totally destroyed. The empire was full of the blood of the saints. Soon all heaven will rejoice.

Day 1   Revelation 13–14 (two beasts and a dragon, 666, the Lamb and the redeemed, messenger angels)
Day 2   Revelation 15 (seven angels with seven plagues, sea of glass)
Day 3   Revelation 16 (seven bowls of God's wrath)
Day 4   Revelation 17 (the great whore and the beast, the Lamb will conquer)
Day 5   Revelation 18 (lament for fallen Babylon; kings, merchants, seafarers mourn fall of city)
Day 6   Read and respond to "Fruit From the Tree of Life" and "Marks of Faithful Community."
Day 7   Rest

PSALM OF THE WEEK

As you pray Psalm 26 aloud daily, reflect on the struggle of Christians and the church to remain faithful to God while surrounded by evil.

PRAYER

Pray daily before study:
"Be merciful to me, O God, be merciful, because I come to you for safety.
In the shadow of your wings I find protection until the raging storms are over" (Psalm 57:1, TEV).

Prayer concerns for this week:

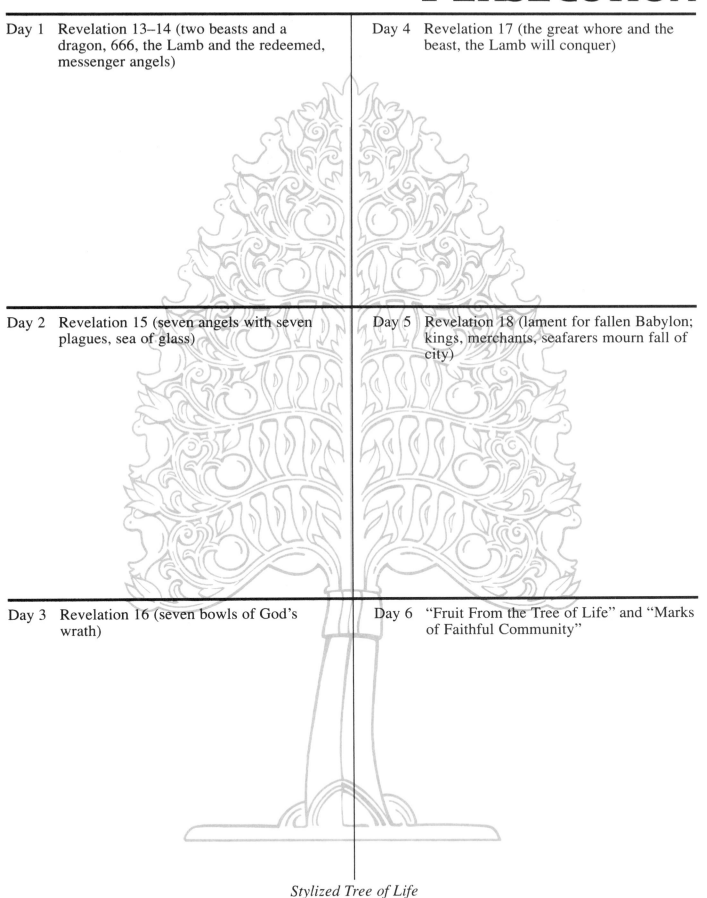

Day 1 Revelation 13–14 (two beasts and a dragon, 666, the Lamb and the redeemed, messenger angels)

Day 4 Revelation 17 (the great whore and the beast, the Lamb will conquer)

Day 2 Revelation 15 (seven angels with seven plagues, sea of glass)

Day 5 Revelation 18 (lament for fallen Babylon; kings, merchants, seafarers mourn fall of city)

Day 3 Revelation 16 (seven bowls of God's wrath)

Day 6 "Fruit From the Tree of Life" and "Marks of Faithful Community"

Stylized Tree of Life

DISCIPLE

FRUIT FROM THE TREE OF LIFE

If you were the Roman authorities, you would be mystified by the notion of warfare in heaven, with angels fighting a dragon. When the scene moves from heaven to earth, you would scarcely notice the change. The dragon provides the connection. The word *and* smoothly begins Revelation 13, the second half of the book. The language, grammar, and style are part of a careful disguise because John's eyes now stare at Rome.

Thrown from heaven, the dragon, Satan, stands on the seashore. Satan's power is everywhere, but the sea and the land are hints of things to come. The dragon controls the beast that comes from the sea and represents Rome. Satan controls Rome, empire of evil. Satan's evil is done on earth by and through Rome. Clothed in imagery from Daniel, the beast combines four ferocious animals—leopard, bear, lion, and a dragonlike creature. In John's mind, The Roman Empire is larger and more terrible than the kingdoms of the past.

The hostile authorities may have been confused by John's allusions, but the believers understood. Rome's representatives came to Asia Minor on ships, "out of the sea." Believers knew Rome was built on seven hills, the beast's "seven heads." They remembered Daniel used the "ten horns" to symbolize all the kingdoms under the control of the empire.

Civil Authority

Earlier, when Paul was preaching and writing letters, the Roman Empire was noted for its good roads and safe travel, a benefit to merchants, missionaries, and the military. Except for violent outbursts like Nero's, Roman law and Roman civil authorities tried to rule fairly and impartially over a kingdom crowded with diverse cultures, religions, and ethnic groups. Rome was famous for its legal system. Paul was saved from angry mobs by fair-minded, legally responsible Roman officials in Corinth, in Ephesus, and in Jerusalem. For a time the Roman Senate had even passed legislation giving privilege to Jews and Jewish Christians to practice their "peculiar" religion. Even in A.D. 70 when Titus sacked Jerusalem, the battle was seen by many as a political crackdown on rebellious zealots in Jerusalem.

Most New Testament literature assumes civil authority is both necessary and helpful, maintaining order and allowing Christians to live honorably and in peace. When Paul was in Greece, preparing to go to Rome as a Roman citizen, he wrote, "Let every person be subject to the governing authorities" (Romans 13:1). Rulers are "not a terror to good conduct, but to bad" (13:3). The same idea is expressed in the Letter to Timothy: "I urge that supplications, prayers, intercessions, and thanksgivings be made for everyone, for kings and all who are in high positions, so that we may lead a quiet and peaceable life in all godliness and dignity" (1 Timothy 2:1-2). Christians were urged to "accept the authority of every human institution. . . . Honor everyone. Love the family of believers. Fear God. Honor the emperor" (1 Peter 2:13, 17).

Rise of Emperor Worship

By the end of the first century A.D., times had changed. With the rise of imperial state religion—worship of the emperor and Roman gods—the Christians were vulnerable. While earlier caesars or emperors believed people with various allegiances could coexist under Roman law and order, worshiping a multitude of gods, the new caesars insisted the empire must be woven together by common political, religious, and cultural ties. Earlier, the Roman Senate had various degrees of power; now the Flavian caesars had become dictators. The emperor was not merely "divine" *after* his death but "divine" during his rule. Domitian, for example, placed his image and the words *Lord and God* on coins, combining the imperial economy and religion.

Not to burn incense to the emperor was like waving a red flag before a bull. Failure to eat the food offered in the Roman temples was an act of treason. Unwillingness to trade in the coin of the realm meant unemployment, boycott, or seizure of property as in the time before and during the Maccabean revolt.

The beast would have authority for "forty-two months" (Revelation 13:5). Rome was powerful; "If you are to be taken captive, / into captivity you go" (13:10). Christians were advised not to take up the sword: "If you kill with the sword, / with the sword you must be killed" (13:10). John calls the faithful to endure. Their resistance would be passive and painful.

Asia Minor

But wait. Still another beast comes, this one rising out of the earth (Revelation 13:11). The governors, the political supporters of Rome, the wealthy families of Pergamum and Ephesus were more zealous about emperor worship than those in Rome. They built the temples; they enforced the edicts. They too were under Satan's authority, for they "spoke like a dragon."

This beast exercises the authority of the first beast. The "number of the beast" is the worst number possible—six hundred sixty-six. Six stands for imperfection because it is the sacred number seven less one. Repeated three times, 666, it is really bad, a symbol of greatest possible imperfection. Irenaeus, student of Polycarp, disciple of John, said simply that 666 is the epitome of all rebellion against God.

But in Revelation, 666 is also a name, a human name. Whose? In both Greek and Hebrew, letters of the alphabet were used instead of Arabic numbers. If we add the numerical

DISCIPLE

values in Hebrew for the spelling of *Neron Caesar,* we get 666. In a few ancient manuscripts, the number is 616, which can be arrived at by the spelling *Nero Caesar*. But Nero was dead. The mad emperor, who burned two thirds of Rome in A.D. 64 and blamed it on the Christians, who probably martyred Paul and Peter and brought shame on the empire, killed himself in A.D. 68. His reign of terror was gone, much to the relief of the Romans and the Christians. So if officials even figured out that 666 meant Nero, they would still be confused. Apparently, the number 666 stands for Nero, Nero stands for caesar, and caesar stands for Rome—a beast under the dominating influence of Satan. Today in popular usage 666 often refers to evil personified, Satan himself.

Who stands against the beast? The Lamb! With his blood and his Word! Who stands with the Lamb? The redeemed, the first fruits for God and the Lamb, uncompromised by the idolatries of Rome. The Lamb will stand on Mount Zion surrounded by a 144,000-voice choir! They will sing; my, how they will sing! They will sing songs of redemption.

Angels—messengers from God—now speak in a flurry. One angel urges repentance and announces judgment (14:6-7). Still time to turn away from pagan practices. Another shouts, "Fallen, fallen is Babylon the great" (14:8). The great Roman Empire is tottering. A third angel cries out that "those who worship the beast and its image" will "drink the wine of God's wrath" (14:9-10). They will feel the fire and smell the burning sulfur without end. Those who worship the beast will have no rest, "day or night" (14:11). Yet, the faithful will not be spared persecution and suffering. An angel, the Spirit, and John himself plead for the church to "hold fast to the faith of Jesus" (14:12).

Angels arrive with sickles; harvest time has come: "Use your sickle and reap, for the hour to reap has come, because the harvest of the earth is fully ripe" (14:15).

Seven Bowls of God's Wrath

Then seven angels are sent with seven golden bowls "full of the wrath of God" (Revelation 15:7). The angels pour out plagues on the earth, on the sea, in the rivers, on the sun so that people were scorched with fire, on the throne of the beast—on Rome itself, on the river Euphrates where life purportedly began, and into the air causing hundred-pound hailstones to fall and the earth to quake. (These plagues hint of the imagery of the plagues Moses brought on Pharaoh—boils, a river of blood, frogs, gnats, flies, hail and thunder, darkness, and death; Exodus 7–11). The plagues in Egypt brought freedom to the people of God. "And a loud voice came out of the temple, from the throne, saying, 'It is done!' " (Revelation 16:17). The wrath of God has ended.

Notice: The angels continually give opportunity for repentance. But the final judgment, the threat of doom on land, sea, and air, does not frighten the wicked into faith. "They did not repent and give him glory" (16:9). Even plunged into total darkness, "people gnawed their tongues in agony, and cursed the God of heaven," but "they did not repent of their deeds" (16:10-11). Remember, repentance means to turn your life around, to become one of Christ's people.

How do you evaluate the power of fear to bring about repentance?

What do you think? Does "too late" ever come?

Armageddon

The kings of the world assemble "at the place that in Hebrew is called Harmagedon" (Revelation 16:16). Megiddo was the strategic military fortification that for centuries controlled the highway through the pass in the Mount Carmel range into the Plain of Esdraelon (Jezreel). From countless battles, the soil was soaked with blood. Deborah defeated Sisera there. King Josiah died there in the battle with Egypt's Pharaoh Neco. The great empires of the north—Assyria and Babylon, collided with the armies of Egypt at Megiddo. No wonder John picked this historic battleground as the place where good and evil would fight the final war. No wonder the world now speaks of Armageddon as the symbolic place of God's ultimate victory.

Judgment of the Great Whore

Earlier John envisioned "a woman clothed with the sun, with the moon under her feet, and on her head a crown of twelve stars" (Revelation 12:1). She represented Israel, mother of the Messiah, and the church. But Rome, who tried to kill her baby and did crucify her Son, is depicted now as an ornately dressed whore luring admirers into her chambers. She sits "on many waters" and "on a scarlet beast" (17:1, 3) that is full of blasphemous names—the names of emperors written on temples, idols, and coins. She is Rome; she sits on the seven hills, and she is "drunk with the blood of the saints" (17:6).

The main idea behind "the great whore" is not sexual but spiritual. Although the culture was permeated with sexual immorality, the real "fornication" was religious compromise, paying homage to the empire. Remember, the prophets of Israel often used the symbol of fornication or prostitution to mean serving false gods. Idolatry was often described as harlotry or adultery.

"The woman you saw is the great city that rules over the

DISCIPLE

kings of the earth" (17:18). But the kings and rulers who now admire Rome will soon strip her naked, "devour her flesh and burn her up with fire" (17:16). Now all heaven is rejoicing. A magnificent angel, having great authority, calls out "with a mighty voice, 'Fallen, fallen is Babylon the great' " (18:2). The whore carries the title of the traditional enemy of God's people—Babylon. Rome is finished. "The Lamb will conquer . . . for he is Lord of lords and King of kings" (17:14).

Kings, Merchants, Seafarers

The kings, the merchants, the seafarers have yielded their power and authority to Rome. Now as Rome burns, they weep. The kings weep because they "lived in luxury with her" (Revelation 18:9). The merchants of the earth mourn, "since no one buys their cargo anymore" (18:11). Observe the luxury items—fine cloth, costly furniture, expensive spices. The greed of the empire has ground out wealth from the backs of the poor. The rich have bartered for the best of everything. They have bought and sold human beings. Even the sailors weep. They too have grown rich on the injustices of the empire. But the saints rejoice!

John's image of fallen Rome recalls Jeremiah's description of doom for ancient Babylon—not fit for human habitation; a dwelling place for hyenas and ostriches, a den of jackals (Jeremiah 50:39; 51:37). John simply says that his "Babylon" will be

"a haunt of every foul bird,

a haunt of every foul and hateful beast" (Revelation 18:2). The emperors thought they would reign over the eternal city forever, but the empire is laid waste "in one hour" (18:10).

"Rejoice over her, O heaven, you saints and apostles and prophets" (18:20). Should we rejoice when an evil empire comes crashing down? Even when that empire is made up of people like you and me? When a yoke is lifted, the persecuted celebrate more exuberantly than the bystanders. Heaven is not rejoicing over human suffering or human tragedy. Heaven shouts "Hallelujah" when God metes out fairness, when divine justice is administered. In John's vision all heaven sings "Hallelujah" when evil is eradicated.

Meanwhile, believers are admonished to "come out of her . . . / so that you do not take part in her sins" (18:4). John's vision, experienced at the height of Rome's power, gave courage and assurance to the churches. The Lamb they love is the true and final authority, and the great whore who was squeezing their lives from them would soon perish.

Historically, the Roman Empire didn't fall quickly, and persecution persisted from time to time. A period of intense persecution occurred around A.D. 156 when Statius Quandratus was proconsul. He brought eleven Christians from Philadelphia and put them to death in the stadium at Smyrna during a festival. The crowd howled for more, including the blood of the beloved Polycarp, who had been bishop for over forty years. The proconsul refused and closed the games, but the crowd persisted, yelling, "This is the teacher of Asia; this is the destroyer of our gods; this is the father of the Christians." The proconsul relented. Polycarp was burned at the stake, refusing to recant his faith. His final words were, "Eighty-six years have I served him, and he has done me no wrong; how then can I blaspheme my King who saved me?" No doubt Polycarp had been inspired by the Revelation to be faithful unto death. Two centuries later the blood of the martyrs would prevail, and the Roman Empire would disintegrate.

List some places where people are suffering for their faith.

_____

_____

Evil holds within itself the seeds of its own destruction. What do you think?

_____

_____

MARKS OF FAITHFUL COMMUNITY

Every culture is, to some extent, alien to the ways of God. When the community of faith withdraws from those common practices that are foreign to Christ, the community is prepared to suffer. We try to be Christ's people. Sometimes that makes us different.

If we live lives faithful to the coming Kingdom, what kind of criticism, rebuke, or pressure might we receive from others?

_____

_____

Even from within the church?

_____

_____

THE RADICAL DISCIPLE

The radical disciple is willing to accept suffering but also knows how to give encouragement to others who are paying a price for their faith. Who needs your support?

IF YOU WANT TO KNOW MORE

To be reminded that faith in God is costly, research first-century to fifteenth-century Christian martyrdom.

Being faithful community, we choose to be faithful rather than fearful, bold in our witness whatever the cost.

HALLELUJAH

"Then I saw a new heaven and a new earth; for the first heaven and the first earth had passed away, and the sea was no more."

—Revelation 21:1

31 A New Heaven and a New Earth

OUR HUMAN CONDITION

Evil is loose in the world. Wars slaughter millions; economic systems squeeze the poor; diseases cause untold suffering. Arrogance and prejudice, violence and greed rule. And we accept things as they are. That's reality.

ASSIGNMENT

Our reading brings us to the climax of the biblical story. We read the last chapters of the Bible. High drama! Victory and defeat are juxtaposed. Read on, but with a backward glance. Imagine you are John. Look back over his vision—see the images; hear the words; experience the mystery. What brought him, and brings us, to Hallelujah?

Day 1   Revelation 19 (praises in heaven, rider Faithful and True, beast and false prophet thrown into lake of fire)
Day 2   Revelation 20 (binding of Satan, the first resurrection, overthrow of Satan, final judgment, the second death)
Day 3   Revelation 21 (vision of the new Jerusalem, renewal of creation)
Day 4   Revelation 22 (the river of the water of life and the tree of life, invitation and warning)
Day 5   Matthew 24–25 (be ready)
Day 6   Read and respond to "Fruit From the Tree of Life" and "Marks of Faithful Community."
Day 7   Rest

PSALM OF THE WEEK

Each day pray Psalm 148 in the midst of creation. Read it aloud under the moon and stars, in the bright sunlight, surrounded by hills and mountains, with ocean in view, in falling rain or snow, in the hearing of young people and old, with birds and animals in sight. Call on all created things to praise God.

PRAYER

Pray daily before study:
"O LORD, you live forever;
    long ago you created the earth,
    and with your own hands you made
        the heavens.
They will disappear, but you will remain;
    they will all wear out like clothes.
You will discard them like clothes,
    and they will vanish.
But you are always the same,
    and your life never ends" (Psalm
    102:24-27, TEV).

Prayer concerns for this week:

HALLELUJAH

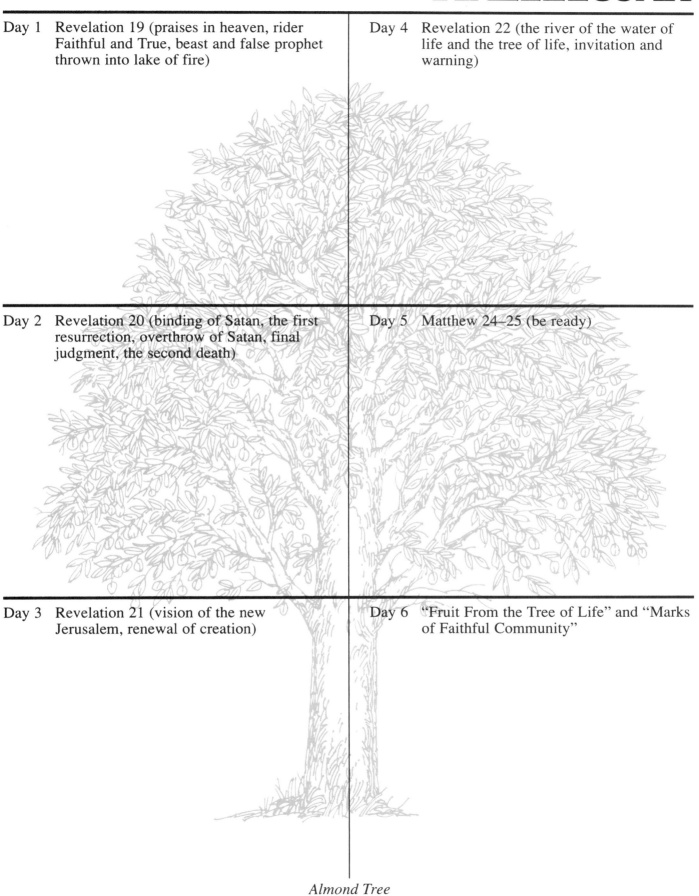

Day 1   Revelation 19 (praises in heaven, rider Faithful and True, beast and false prophet thrown into lake of fire)

Day 4   Revelation 22 (the river of the water of life and the tree of life, invitation and warning)

Day 2   Revelation 20 (binding of Satan, the first resurrection, overthrow of Satan, final judgment, the second death)

Day 5   Matthew 24–25 (be ready)

Day 3   Revelation 21 (vision of the new Jerusalem, renewal of creation)

Day 6   "Fruit From the Tree of Life" and "Marks of Faithful Community"

Almond Tree

Disciple

FRUIT FROM THE TREE OF LIFE

Celebration in heaven begins before the final victory is complete. The twenty-four elders and the four living creatures sing, "Hallelujah!" A "great multitude" shouts, "Hallelujah!" Not only will Rome fall, but the powers of evil—sin, death, hell—are doomed. The absolute certainty is cause for celebration. Let the invitations for the wedding of the Lamb and his people be sent out!

This time Jesus really is the one on the white horse. The earlier white horse, the first of the four horsemen, was ridden by a warrior with a bow, and his name was "Conquest." This rider's name is "Faithful and True" (Revelation 19:11). His robe is covered with blood before the battle begins. The blood is his; it is the blood of his sacrifice. His soldiers are not dressed in armor but wear the pure white robes of their baptism. The war is a strange war. After the violence is over, after judgment has been administered, the immeasurable love of God will prevail. But first, evil must be eradicated. Evil is embodied in systems and in human beings. Symbolically, birds of the air will eat the flesh of kings, the mighty, the servants of the beast. But the beast itself will be captured. So will the false prophet. All who worship the beast will be destroyed also. Imagine: The war will be won by Jesus Christ's blood (love) and his Word (truth).

Evil Is Eradicated

Meanwhile, life with its daily pressures goes on. John cannot get out of his mind the soul-wrenching temptations his readers are facing. When the judgment comes, who will be sent away? The cowardly—those who cannot stand firm under pressure of persecution. The faithless—those who decide the gospel is not true, at least not true enough to die for. The polluted—those believers who try to have it both ways, in the social customs and in the church, compromisers and collaborators, worshipers of other gods. Sorcerers—those who thought they had "special knowledge" from the stars, fortunetellers, practicers of magic and divination. Fornicators—likely both the sexually immoral and those who participated in sacred orgies or pagan idolatry. Murderers—certainly those who took the life of another, but possibly a reference to those who collaborated with a murderous regime. Liars—those who spoke false teachings as well as those whose word was not completely honest.

Students of the Bible misinterpret the "thousand years" if they take it literally. A "thousand years" is symbolic, just as "ten days" (Revelation 2:10) or "forty-two months" (11:2) is symbolic. It means a long time and a short time. A long time to weary persecuted saints, a short time to God,

> "For a thousand years in your sight
>   are like yesterday when it is past,
>   or like a watch in the night" (Psalm 90:4).

The angel will bind the dragon—Satan—in chains and seal him in the bottomless pit. Satan won't deceive for a while—a thousand years. But then, Satan will have power again for a little while, to prepare for the final battle. Satan is hard to get rid of. The martyrs will not need to undergo scrutiny: Their blood testifies for them. Theirs is the first resurrection, a reward for righteousness. They will reign with Christ. When released, Satan gathers all his henchmen, including Gog and Magog, apocalyptic enemies of God's people envisioned by Ezekiel (Ezekiel 38–39). The point is, every evil thing, real or mythological, will now finally be finished. The devil is thrown into the "lake of fire and sulfur." Even death—according to Paul, humankind's last great enemy (1 Corinthians 15:26)—and Hades (in the Septuagint *Sheol,* the abode of the dead; in the New Testament *hell,* a place of torture) are "thrown into the lake of fire" (Revelation 20:14). Evil is eradicated.

A second resurrection is for judgment (20:12). In John's vision, each person will stand before the throne. Alone and in silence. The trumpets, the angels, the elders, the choirs—all are gone. Even "the earth and the heaven fled from his presence" (20:11). Two books will be opened. The first is the complete account of each person's life—every thought and every action. The second is the book of life. It contains the names of the godly. Others, along with their names, will be thrown into the "lake of fire" (20:15), the "second death" from which there is no resurrection. What an imperative for evangelical zeal! Like the church at Ephesus, we are challenged to regain our first love of Jesus and our passion to help people know and love Christ.

New Heaven and New Earth

John's vision is not a Greek notion of a disembodied soul going to some idyllic location. Nor is it the pious idea of dying and going to heaven. The vision is much more comprehensive. John sees a new universe. God, who spoke creation into existence (Genesis 1–2), will create a new earth and a new heaven. The whole order will be different (Revelation 21:4). Do you remember when God questioned Job about Leviathan, the great sea monster, the symbol of chaos? Leviathan, who lives in the sea and causes the random accident, will exist no longer. "The sea was no more" (21:1). Tragedy will end.

Instead of people going to heaven, heaven will come to earth, beautiful as "a bride adorned for her husband" (21:2). The imagery of God as bridegroom and the people of God as bride runs throughout the Bible. Jeremiah says of Israel,

"Thus says the LORD:
I remember the devotion of your youth,
your love as a bride" (Jeremiah 2:2).

DISCIPLE

Isaiah writes,

"As the bridegroom rejoices over the bride,
so shall your God rejoice over you" (Isaiah 62:5).

Jesus told parables in which the kingdom of God was compared to a wedding feast (Matthew 25:1-13). His disciples would not fast "while the bridegroom is with them" (Mark 2:19). The Revelation is filled with this joyous image.

"The marriage of the Lamb has come,
and his bride has made herself ready"
(Revelation 19:7).

The Holy City

The last two chapters abound with Old Testament imagery. Do you recall when God "tabernacled" or "tented" with his people in the wilderness—a time kept alive in memory by Sukkoth, the festival of booths? Do you recall that, in John's Gospel, the Word became flesh and "tabernacled" among us (John 1:14)? Revelation declares, "I heard a loud voice from the throne saying,

'See, the home [the tabernacle] of God is among mortals.
He will dwell [will tabernacle] with them'"
(Revelation 21:3).

The walls of the New Jerusalem are higher and stronger than any wall Nehemiah ever built. On the twelve foundations of the wall are the names of the twelve apostles. The gates, inscribed with the names of the twelve tribes of Israel, open in all four directions. For as Isaiah said,

"Do not fear, for I am with you;
I will bring your offspring from the east,
and from the west I will gather you;
I will say to the north, 'Give them up,'
and to the south, 'Do not withhold;
bring my sons from far away
and my daughters from the end of the earth'"
(Isaiah 43:5-6).

And Jesus promised, "I tell you, many will come from east and west and will eat with Abraham and Isaac and Jacob in the kingdom of heaven" (Matthew 8:11). The doors are open to God's people everywhere.

Of what use is a gate to an earthly city? To keep out fearful beasts, evil people, enemy troops. But the gates of the New Jerusalem are wide open, all day; and because of the light of the glory of God, "there will be no night there" (Revelation 21:25). Jesus gave light to the man born blind and spoke the words, "I am the light of the world" (John 8:12). Because Jesus "the lamp" is there, the holy city needs neither sun nor moon. There is nothing to fear, ever again. "Do not let your hearts be troubled, and do not let them be afraid," said Jesus (14:27).

The city is immense, fifteen hundred miles square, room for a lot of people. But wait. It is also fifteen hundred miles high! The city is a cube, just like the Holy of Holies in the

"Blessed are those who are invited to the marriage supper of the Lamb" (Revelation 19:9). God's final act of restoration of creation is an invitation to a meal of celebration. This image of a marriage supper draws on meaning connected to eating throughout Scripture: covenant meals eaten before God, the Passover meal, the messianic banquet, Jesus eating with sinners, the Last Supper, the church in Acts eating together in homes. The word translated "supper" in Revelation 19:9 suggests the main meal of the day, enjoyed after sunset, after work was finished, when the entire household was present to share in an abundant meal. It is the same word found in John 13:2 to describe Jesus' last "supper" with his disciples.

The marriage supper in the Revelation is the ultimate meal, where previous promises associated with meals are fulfilled. The invited rejoice in the restoration of abundance, the consummation of God's purposes for creation, the unity of Christ and the church, the deliverance of the faithful, the assurance of God's defeat of sin and death, and the blessing of God's eternal presence.

Temple. A cube symbolizes perfection. Only the high priest could enter the Holy of Holies once a year. Now saints live in the Holy of Holies forever—a place of perfection. The jewels in the foundations and walls of the New Jerusalem are radiant, making an oriental king's treasury look like a child's toy box. (For other references to jewels, see Exodus 28:15-21; Isaiah 54:11-12; Ezekiel 28:13.) If Croesus, king of Lydia, thought he was rich, he should see the streets of gold! We don't need a Temple anymore, not even a vast apocalyptic Temple like Ezekiel's. A Temple is designed to help people find God, to help God reach people. Now the Lord God Almighty and the Lamb *are* the Temple. Their glory fills the city with light.

The River of the Water of Life and the Tree of Life

Throughout Scripture, the river and the tree are symbols rich with meaning. A tree is the symbol of life and health. "The righteous flourish like the palm tree" (Psalm 92:12). Those who delight in

"the law of the LORD . . . are like trees
    planted by streams of water,
which yield their fruit in its season,
    and their leaves do not wither" (1:2-3).

Wisdom, who was with God in Creation, is "a tree of life to those who lay hold of her" (Proverbs 3:18). Does First Peter have the tree of life in mind when the letter says literally that Jesus bore our sins "on the tree" (1 Peter 2:24, NIV)?

Two trees in Genesis capture our attention. One is "the tree of the knowledge of good and evil"—the forbidden tree (Genesis 2:16-17). When Adam and Eve ate of this tree, they disobeyed God, lost their innocence, and experienced guilt and shame. The other tree is "the tree of life" (2:9). To eat from this tree would be to live forever (3:22). When the Lord God sent Adam and Eve from Eden, he placed at the east of the garden "cherubim, and a sword flaming and turning to guard the way to the tree of life" (3:23-24).

In John's vision, the sins of Adam and Eve will be gone. The bliss intended by the original garden of Eden will be restored. Death will be no more, for now women and men will eat of the tree of life. No more tears. No more trauma such as Job experienced. The healing will be not only personal, but international, because "the leaves of the tree are for the healing of the nations" (Revelation 22:2). Notice that John, in order to maintain the Creation phrase *tree of life,* must have that tree grow on both sides of the river. The symbol was important to maintain. It is the tree of promise. Whoever eats of it will "live forever," even all of us who have sinned and eaten of the tree of the knowledge of good and evil.

The prophet Ezekiel moved the imagery beyond mere description into apocalyptic symbolism. The water of life that flows like a river from the throne of God in Ezekiel's visionary Temple gets deeper and deeper as it flows to the Dead

DISCIPLE

Sea. It brings healing and health along its way. "I saw on the bank of the river a great many trees on the one side and on the other" (Ezekiel 47:7). "Everything will live where the river goes" (47:9). "On the banks, on both sides of the river, there will grow all kinds of trees for food." Ezekiel provides the basis for the picture language in Revelation. "Their leaves will not wither nor their fruit fail, but they will bear fresh fruit every month. . . . Their fruit will be for food, and their leaves for healing" (47:12).

God promises to give water to the thirsty. Isaiah had cried out,

> "Ho, everyone who thirsts,
> come to the waters" (Isaiah 55:1).

Jesus said to the Samaritan woman at Jacob's well, "those who drink of the water that I will give them will never be thirsty. The water that I will give will become in them a spring of water gushing up to eternal life" (John 4:13-14). Now the faithful drink of the pure, cool water from the "water of life, bright as crystal, flowing from the throne of God" (Revelation 22:1). John's throat was parched on Patmos. "Let everyone who is thirsty come" (22:17). The water, the grace of God, is "a gift" (21:6).

When the seven angels had poured out their seven bowls of wrath, a loud voice from the throne said, "It is done" (16:17). The moment of judgment has arrived. All is ready for the events that will bring the end. Later, with divine justice meted out, Babylon the great whore fallen, Satan and death thrown into the lake of fire, the new heaven and the new earth established, the one on the throne announces the final words of victory, "It is done!" (21:6). God's purposes have been accomplished.

Death

Human beings have been drawn to some concept of life beyond the grave in almost every civilization. The teacher in Ecclesiastes, who saw no reason to believe in life after death, still wrote that God has "set eternity" in the hearts of people (Ecclesiastes 3:11, NIV).

Israel's messianic dream will be fulfilled. One day "they shall beat their swords into plowshares, . . . / and no one shall make them afraid" (Micah 4:3-4). In the new heaven and the new earth, "the wolf shall live with the lamb, . . . / and a little child shall lead them" (Isaiah 11:6). All the pain and suffering of this life will disappear. "Sorrow and sighing shall flee away" (35:10). "No more shall the sound of weeping be heard" (65:19). God will put on our heads a crown of beauty instead of a heap of ashes, "the oil of gladness instead of mourning, / and a garment of praise instead of a spirit of despair" (61:3, NIV).

The crying will stop because suffering and death will be over. The psalmist, in making the point that death has the last word, said, "Death will feed on them" (Psalm 49:14, NIV). But Paul, drawing on Isaiah and Hosea, reversed the image: "Death has been swallowed up in victory" (1 Corinthians 15:54). What a comfort to hear John's Revelation declare, "He will wipe every tear from their eyes. Death will be no more" (Revelation 21:4; see also Isaiah 25:8).

Presumption

John of Patmos surely knew the teachings of Jesus about the end of the age. Notice how closely John's vision conforms to Jesus' guidance. On the Mount of Olives the disciples asked Jesus to tell them about end times (Matthew 24:3). Jesus said, "Watch out that no one deceives you. For many will come in my name" (24:4-5, NIV). John's vision commended the church at Ephesus for weeding out false teachers (Revelation 2:2-6).

Jesus said wars, famines, earthquakes would come in various places, not as signs but as reality in the interim period (Matthew 24:6-7). So John's four horsemen will ride across the landscape bringing the tragedies of history (Revelation 6:1-8).

Beware of those who claim to know the time. "About that day and hour no one knows, neither the angels of heaven, nor the Son, but only the Father," said Jesus (Matthew 24:36). In John's vision, the scroll is sealed. No one, no one can open it until the Father gives permission to the Son, the only one who is worthy to unfold the meaning of history and announce its final chapter.

When that moment happens, it will be no secret, not hidden as the Kingdom is now. When lightning flashes across the night sky, everyone can see it. When vultures circle, everyone knows they fly above a dead carcass. When the fig tree begins to blossom in late spring, everyone knows summer is soon. The coming will be obvious, taught Jesus.

And sudden. Like a thief in the night. Without warning. Like the Flood in Noah's day. Presumptuous are those who claim to be wiser than angels, more knowledgeable than Jesus. They point to a war and say "here," to an earthquake and say "there." But they are false prophets.

Equally presumptuous are those who say, "He is not coming." Like the folks carrying on normal life—eating and drinking—when the Flood came. Or like the wicked servant who thought his master wasn't coming home, so he got drunk and beat his fellow servants. They will be like the five virgins who went to sleep, letting the oil in their lamps burn out. In John's vision, there is time for repentance, even time when floods and famine come. Invitations to the marriage supper of the Lamb will be extended even when Rome crashes. But when the Alpha and Omega says "It is done," it will be done, complete (Revelation 21:6).

The presumptuous say "today" or "not today." Both are in error. The faithful know these truths:

DISCIPLE

• The victory has been won on the cross of sacrificial love. That victory will be declared in its fullness.

• Suffering in the interim is likely. Jesus said, "They will hand you over to be tortured" (Matthew 24:9). John saw, near the throne, "the souls of those who had been beheaded for their testimony to Jesus and for the word of God" (Revelation 20:4).

• The faithful will remain faithful and will be hard at work in Kingdom business. They will not turn aside when someone says, "Look! Here is the Messiah!" (Matthew 24:23). "Be faithful until death, and I will give you the crown of life" (Revelation 2:10). The apocalyptic images—the light of the sun darkened, the stars fallen from their places—are not simply signs of the end. They are pictures of God's reordering the universe with justice and redemption.

• The oil in the lamps carries deep meaning. Oil symbolizes healing as well as light. Just as the Samaritan in Jesus' parable poured oil on the wounds of the man (Luke 10:29-37), so believers go about the compassionate work of ministry. Oil in the lamps of the five faithful virgins represents the well-prepared, those who are caring for the tasks at hand. When Jesus comes, disciples are found feeding the hungry, giving water to the thirsty, welcoming the stranger, clothing the naked, visiting the prisoner (Matthew 25:31-46).

Tradition remembers Francis of Assisi, hoeing his garden, raising vegetables for the poor. Someone interrupted him and asked, "What would you do if you knew Christ were coming this afternoon?" Francis replied, "I'd finish hoeing the row."

• Both Jesus and John stress vigilance. "Keep awake," said Jesus, "for you do not know on what day your Lord is coming" (24:42). "I know your works," wrote John to Thyatira, "your love, faith, service, and patient enturance" (Revelation 2:19).

John understood who is coming. Jesus. In blood-stained robe with the Word of truth in his mouth. He is not to be feared; he is to be welcomed, yearned for. For his coming completes the covenant begun in Abraham and Sarah, manifested in the cross. God will live with the covenant people in harmony forever.

"The Spirit and the bride say, 'Come.'

And let everyone who hears say, 'Come'" (22:17).

John hears the Savior say, "Surely I am coming soon." He and the whole church respond, "Amen. Come, Lord Jesus!" (22:20).

The Revelation was written amid persecution. What meaning does it have for your faith now?

MARKS OF FAITHFUL COMMUNITY

Someday Satan will be destroyed. Someday death will die. Someday weeping will cease. Remember, the essence of John's Revelation is this: God wins!

If we believe God wins, what is required of us in a world filled with evil? Where do you see evil?

_____

_____

How does your belief in life beyond death affect the way you live each day?

_____

_____

What difference does it make in day-to-day living if you believe your name is written in the book of life?

_____

_____

How would you answer a question like that asked of Francis of Assisi, What would you do if you knew Christ were coming today?

_____

_____

We can already taste the victory. We will not quit or become discouraged. If the Lord delays, we will not falter. If the Lord comes, we will be found doing his work. Hallelujah is in our hearts and on our lips.

THE RADICAL DISCIPLE

The radical disciple acknowledges the reality of evil and calls it what it is, sees evil and confronts it, decides what action is necessary in the face of evil and proceeds with active hope.

IF YOU WANT TO KNOW MORE

Enjoy a great work of art that illustrates themes from the Revelation. Listen to a recording of George Frederick Handel's _Messiah_. Most public libraries have collections of art books. Check for books of art on the Apocalypse or the Revelation. Read hymns in your church's hymnal to discover allusions and quotations from the Revelation. Usually hymnals have an index of Scripture that identifies hymns related to particular Scripture.

NOTES, REFLECTIONS, AND QUESTIONS

Being faithful community, we live fully in the present, confronting the evil that surrounds us, and fully in the promise of God's new heaven and new earth.

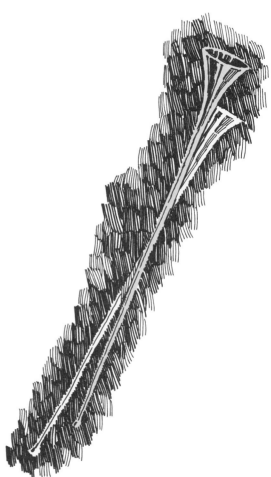

"Hallelujah!
For the Lord our God
the Almighty reigns"
(Revelation 19:6).

FOREVER

"It is done! I am the Alpha and the Omega, the beginning and the end. To the thirsty I will give water as a gift from the spring of the water of life."

—Revelation 21:6

32 Under the Tree of Life

OUR HUMAN CONDITION

Control. We spend our lives trying to stay in control. We resist admitting need or want. Risk. We avoid risk if it means trusting something beyond ourselves, if it means becoming vulnerable to anything or anyone. We're in charge.

ASSIGNMENT

We have read these passages before, so we read not for knowledge but for introspection. The issue is this: How might God's revelation in Scripture become revelation to us? What would it take for us to yield our hearts to those things that lead to life, abundant and eternal?

Day 1 *Caring*—Ruth 1:8-18; 2:8-20; 4:14-17 (caring for family); Esther 4 (caring for one's people); James 2:14-26 (caring for the needy); 1 John 3:14-24 (caring for the community)
Day 2 *Guidance*—Proverbs 2:1-12; 4 (instruction); 1 Chronicles 17; 2 Chronicles 6:12-42 (prayer); John 8:12-36 (light)
Day 3 *Building*—Nehemiah 4:1–6:15 (a wall restored); John 15 (a fruitful fellowship); Revelation 3:7-13 (a faithful church)
Day 4 *Humility*—Ecclesiastes 3:1-15; 12:1-8 (the seasons of life); Job 29–30 (the human condition); James 4:1-10 (humble in spirit)
Day 5 *Hope*—Psalm 146 (praise); Job 38; 41:1–42:11 (God's greatness); John 20:19-31 (Lord and God); Revelation 21:1-14, 22-27; 22:1-5 (no tears, no death, no night)
Day 6 Read and respond to "Fruit From the Tree of Life" and "Marks of Faithful Community."
Day 7 Rest

PSALM OF THE WEEK

Pray Psalm 96 aloud daily. Choose a different recording of instrumental music to accompany your reading of the psalm each day. If you are able, consider praying the psalm on your knees.

PRAYER

Pray daily before study:
"Your mighty deeds, O LORD, make me glad; because of what you have done, I sing for joy" (Psalm 92:4, TEV).

Prayer concerns for this week:

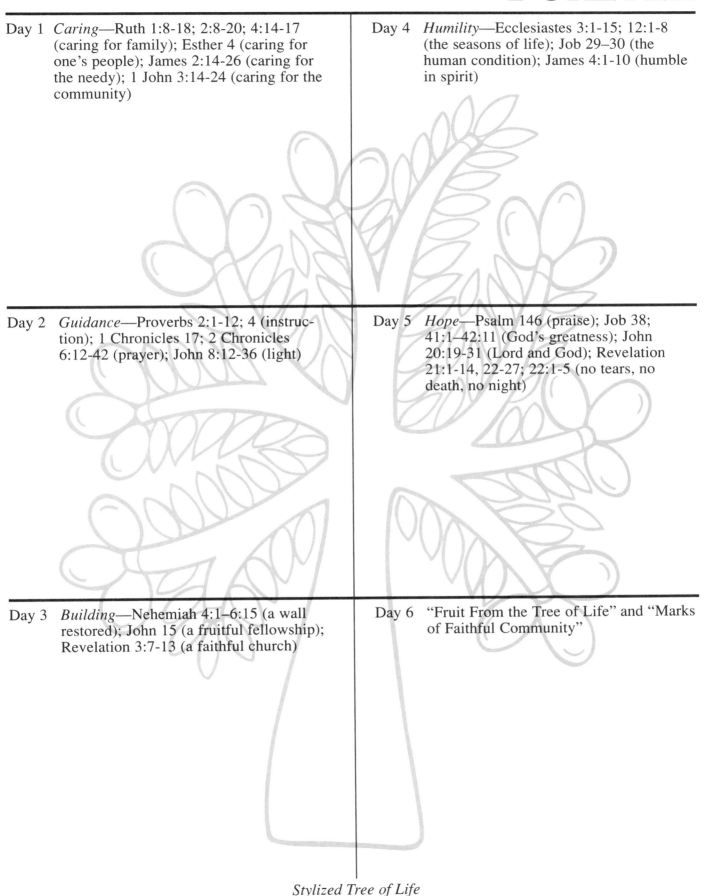

Day 1 *Caring*—Ruth 1:8-18; 2:8-20; 4:14-17 (caring for family); Esther 4 (caring for one's people); James 2:14-26 (caring for the needy); 1 John 3:14-24 (caring for the community)

Day 2 *Guidance*—Proverbs 2:1-12; 4 (instruction); 1 Chronicles 17; 2 Chronicles 6:12-42 (prayer); John 8:12-36 (light)

Day 3 *Building*—Nehemiah 4:1–6:15 (a wall restored); John 15 (a fruitful fellowship); Revelation 3:7-13 (a faithful church)

Day 4 *Humility*—Ecclesiastes 3:1-15; 12:1-8 (the seasons of life); Job 29–30 (the human condition); James 4:1-10 (humble in spirit)

Day 5 *Hope*—Psalm 146 (praise); Job 38; 41:1–42:11 (God's greatness); John 20:19-31 (Lord and God); Revelation 21:1-14, 22-27; 22:1-5 (no tears, no death, no night)

Day 6 "Fruit From the Tree of Life" and "Marks of Faithful Community"

Stylized Tree of Life

DISCIPLE

FRUIT FROM THE TREE OF LIFE

Caring
  When Ruth, the young Moabite widow, gave loyalty and love to Naomi, her Israelite mother-in-law, she took hold of life. She helped establish family continuity, which led not only to survival for widows but lineage for King David. When Boaz obeyed the Mosaic laws to allow the poor to glean in the fields and when he fulfilled the intent of the levirate marriage, he found family for himself and others. Ruth and Naomi survived hardship and found life. Bethlehem again became the "house of bread," and Naomi again meant "pleasant."

What act of caring might you perform that would strengthen your family?

_____

_____

When Queen Esther listened to her cousin Mordecai, she knew her people needed her. It was her moment. With incredible courage (and cleverness), she turned her back on self-interest and did the deed of brave love that saved her people. Most moments in our lives are not so dramatic. Yet by what act of courage and caring have you assisted or could you assist your congregation, your community, your country?

_____

_____

James insists we put our faith into action, particularly as we care for the poor. In what ways are you presently assisting the hungry, the needy, the feeble, the widowed, and the orphan?

_____

_____

We learned from the letters of John that love within the fellowship is the heartbeat of Christianity. What are you doing "in truth and action" to express concern for sisters and brothers in the faith?

_____

_____

Guidance

As we walk the path of life, we receive help. We gain guidance from pastors and teachers, from fellow disciples. We are taught by Scripture.

What insights into life have you gained from this study?

How did you learn them?

_____

_____

How are you incorporating these insights into daily living?

_____

_____

David, through Nathan's prayers and his own, learned he was not to build the Temple. Solomon offered his prayers at the altar of the Temple, dedicating it as a house of prayer where all people could gain forgiveness and a sense of direction.

In your prayer life during this DISCIPLE study, what guidance have you received?

_____

_____

Jesus said, "I am the light." Describe any specific way his light is guiding your steps right now.

_____

_____

Building

Everyone would like to build, create, or restore something. Everyone would like to be productive, creative, even as God, in whose image we are made, is creative. We want to build a house, write a book, bake a cake, teach a child, plant a tree, raise a crop, fix a motor, operate a computer. Nehemiah, by sheer determination and dedication, rebuilt the Jerusalem wall.

What creative activity are you engaged in right now that gives your life purpose and meaning?

_____

_____

Jesus said we must live in him if our lives are to bear fruit. Bearing fruit means training disciples. Whom are you currently mentoring, teaching, guiding?

_____

_____

The message to the Philadelphia church offered no criticism, only encouragement. One great contribution lifegivers

DISCIPLE

make is to keep open the door of faith—in the home, in the church, in the community.

How does your church regularly extend the invitation to faith both within and beyond the congregation?

_____

_____

What do you hear in the words "I am coming soon; hold fast to what you have" (Revelation 3:10-11)?

_____

_____

Humility

Humility is not thinking too little of ourselves, nor is it thinking too highly of ourselves. Humility rejoices in being a child of God and a neighbor with others. Being human, we are subject to the changing circumstances of life (Ecclesiastes 3) and, if we avoid an early death, to the relinquishing of powers that comes with growing old (Ecclesiastes 12).

How are you handling the ups and downs of life?

_____

_____

Job was a wealthy patriarch before he was brought low. People deferred to him, listened when he spoke, stood when he entered the room. They asked him for money for the poor, and he was glad to oblige. But when he lost his herds, had deaths in his family, became sick, he got no respect—as most people get little respect. When has some misfortune, accident, mistake, or illness humbled you?

_____

How has that experience helped you "join the human race," see yourself as human like everyone else?

_____

_____

James cautions against worldly pride. He warns against arrogance that covets and craves, that creates conflict. How are you becoming humble in spirit without putting yourself down or becoming weak?

_____

_____

What servant tasks do you regularly perform?

_____

_____

Hope

The Psalms inspire hope in our hearts. God seems so majestic, yet so willing to lift us up. As we sing and pray psalms, the community of faith, across the centuries and around the world, surrounds us. Even the "communion of saints" joins in. In this study we have prayed the psalms daily and weekly. In what ways have the psalms given you hope?

_____

_____

Many people find hope in Job—in Job's persistence with his friends and with God, in God's awesome speeches, in Job's new view of the world and life. Some find hope when Job is restored and when his friends help put him back on his feet. In tough times, what has given you hope to pull through?

_____

_____

Although John's Gospel insists Jesus was glorified on the cross, the resurrection of Jesus is still the great symbol of victory to believers. Thomas doubted until he could touch the wounds. When Jesus appeared to the disciples, Thomas cried out, "My Lord and my God!" (John 20:28).
Describe your experience of the risen Christ.

_____

_____

What continuing impact does Jesus' resurrection have on your life and on your hope for life eternal?

_____

_____

John's Revelation encouraged a struggling and threatened church to hold on. Describe how the vision of a new heaven and a new earth gives meaning and hope to you in this world and hope and assurance for the world to come.

_____

_____

NOTES, REFLECTIONS, AND QUESTIONS

Being faithful community, we rest in the knowledge that God is in control; we yield our lives in obedience to a God who stooped to wash feet and calls us to do the same for others.

DISCIPLE

THE LOVE FEAST

The love feast is a celebration of Christ's community. Through its three expressions of worship—footwashing, fellowship meal, and Holy Communion—we affirm and renew our covenant relationship as Christ's community. Whenever we gather around the love feast tables, we are reminded of the relationship of all disciples to one another and to the Christ we serve.

Footwashing. We ponder the powerful meanings in Jesus' washing the disciples' feet—God's cleansing and forgiveness and our need to give and receive service. Jesus' command to wash one another's feet is a clear warning that if we do not live in the spirit of footwashing, we have no part in him.

Fellowship meal. The love feast meal recalls the meal Jesus shared with his disciples, and the unique character of the relationship envisioned for those who are members together in Christ's body. Christ is the center, the source of our unity. The sharing of food symbolizes the sharing of life and looks toward the messianic banquet of the future.

Holy Communion. We share the bread and cup, remembering Christ's supreme gift of life and renewing our commitment to embody Christ, to follow his path of sacrificial love for the world.

ORDER OF THE LOVE FEAST

GREETING
The grace of the Lord Jesus Christ be with you.
And also with you.

Taste and see the goodness of the Lord.
Christ has prepared a feast of love.

INVITATION
The great truths of the faith need to be said, but they must not be fenced in by the limitation of words. They demand something more. By enacting our faith through symbols, we not only confess that they stand for the truth, but by our participation in them, the truth is experienced anew. We meet today not only for a drama that allows us to proclaim our faith but also for involvement and participation that opens the door for the Holy Spirit to communicate the gospel in fresh and vivid experience.

HYMN
"O Master, Let Me Walk With Thee" **or**
"Have Thine Own Way, Lord"

SCRIPTURE READING
John 13:20-25

LITANY OF SELF-EXAMINATION AND CONFESSION
Lord, we confess that we who call ourselves your children sometimes betray you. Some of us are unwilling to see those around us who are hurting.

Lord, is it I?

Some of us run after the things of this world
rather than seek the things of your kingdom.

Lord, is it I?

Some of us insist on our own way, unwilling to listen
and discuss openly with our brothers and sisters
who have different opinions.

Lord, is it I?

Some of us have neglected opportunities
you have given us to be your witnesses.

Lord, is it I?

Some of us have failed to use the gifts and talents
you have given us to serve your church.

Lord, is it I?

Some of us have not kept a place in our busy daily schedules
to be with you in prayer, Bible reading, and meditation.

Lord, is it I?

Some of us have said and done things to hurt others,
and have not worked to heal the brokenness.

Lord, is it I?

All of us have failed in many times and ways to be your people,
to be your church.

Forgive us, Lord.

SILENCE

WORDS OF PARDON
In the name of Jesus Christ, you are forgiven.
In the name of Jesus Christ, you are forgiven.

PRAYER OF PREPARATION
**Lord of hosts, preparer of this table;
prepare us.
The feast is ready. Make us ready.
Enable us to come to this banquet rejoicing,
Knowing we are clothed in forgiveness and mercy
And gifted with the joy of your salvation.
Amen.**

THE SYMBOL OF SERVANTHOOD: FOOTWASHING

SCRIPTURE READING
John 13:1-17

HYMN
"Jesu, Jesu" **or**
"Just as I Am, Without One Plea," **or**
"Jesus, United by Thy Grace"

INVITATION

Some will say that to wash another's feet is an outdated act, that the symbol is no longer common in our time. We are not seeking to learn a common lesson, but rather, a deep one. The servanthood assumed by Jesus in this act is eternally bound to the cause for which he came and died. As the bread and cup are symbols of the sacrifice and giving of his life, so the kneeling to wash another's feet is the symbol of the purpose and the living of his life.

By demonstrating the servanthood of his life, Christ called all disciples to be servants.

PRAYER BEFORE FOOTWASHING

Eternal Creator and Loving God,
In the act of kneeling to wash one another's feet,
   may we kneel also in our hearts
   so that our lives may bow in service
   to your will and not our own.

In allowing our feet to be washed,
   may our lives be cleansed with your forgiveness
   so that we may go forth
   freed from the bonds of guilt and despair
   to live in freedom and hope.

O Lord,
In our washing of feet,
   cleanse our relationships with one another as well.

May we, in washing one another's feet,
   forgive and accept forgiveness from one another
   for any hurts or wrongs or misunderstandings
   that have passed between us,
   so that we may rise to sit together at your table
   in a renewed and strengthened fellowship in your love.
     Amen.

THE FOOTWASHING

The leader will give whatever instructions necessary for all to participate comfortably. During the footwashing, participants may sing hymns, or appropriate music may be played ("Lord, I Want to Be a Christian," "Trust and Obey," "Sweet, Sweet Spirit," "Breathe on Me, Breath of God"). After the footwashing is complete, participants may wash their hands and prepare the table for the fellowship meal.

THE SYMBOL OF COMMUNITY: FELLOWSHIP MEAL

SCRIPTURE READING
John 15:9-17

PRAYER
Offer prayers of petition for the needs of others.

INVITATION

Jesus lifted up for us two great commandments. First, that we should love the Lord our God with heart, mind, soul, and strength. And the second, that we should love neighbor as self.

Whom shall we love? Who is our neighbor? Sometimes those close, whom we know well, are the hardest to love. Jesus ate with those very near to him. He ate, knowing Thomas; he ate, knowing Peter; he ate, knowing Judas.

As we eat together, we recall that through Christ, God's love reached out to make us acceptable. We remember that through Christ, God's love makes us acceptable to one another and empowers us to be in community, beginning in this room and extending to the far reaches of the world.

HYMN
"Blest Be the Tie That Binds"

PRAYER OF THANKSGIVING

O God, when Jesus was in this world, he ate and drank with sinners and outcasts, welcoming them, enjoying them. For the hungering, Jesus was food and the people ate and were full.

O God, as we eat the bread of fellowship and are sufficiently fed, we pray that you make out of us something of nourishment. Enable us to be bread for our sisters and brothers who are starved for gladness and hope. And may we, by feeding them, be ourselves made full of rejoicing. Amen.

THE FELLOWSHIP MEAL
After the prayer of thanksgiving, the group will eat together as instructed by the leader. When the meal is concluded, everyone participates in making the table ready for Holy Communion.

THE SYMBOL OF REDEMPTION: HOLY COMMUNION

SCRIPTURE READING
Revelation 3:20-21
1 John 4:7-12

HYMN
"Let Us Break Bread Together"

INVITATION

Let all who are in love and community with your brothers and sisters, who do truly and earnestly repent of your sins, who humbly put your trust in Christ and desire his help that you may lead a holy life, draw nigh to God and receive these sacred symbols to your comfort, through Jesus Christ our Lord.

On the night in which he gave himself up for us,
Jesus took bread, gave thanks to God,
broke the bread, gave it to his disciples, and said:
"Take, eat; this is my body which is given for you.
Do this in remembrance of me."
When the supper was over, he took a cup, gave thanks
to God, gave it to his disciples and said:
"Drink from this, all of you; this is the new covenant,
poured out for you and for many for the forgiveness of sins.
Do this, as often as you drink it, in remembrance of me."

DECLARATION OF FAITH
And so, as we prepare to break the bread and share the cup, we join in this declaration of faith :

The bread which we break is a sharing in the body of Christ.
The cup which we drink is a sharing in the blood of Christ.
Thanks be to God.

BREAKING THE BREAD
The bread is broken in silence.
The cup is lifted in silence.

PARTAKING OF THE BREAD AND THE CUP
As the bread and cup are passed, participants exchange words of blessing:
The body of Christ given for you. **Amen.**
The blood of Christ given for you. **Amen.**

PRAYER AFTER COMMUNION
Almighty and loving God,
we thank you that through your great love
you have fed us from our Lord's table,
and have assured us that your goodness to us never fails.
We give you thanks that we are members of the body of Christ,
heirs with Christ, and brothers and sisters in your family.
By your grace assist us in our pilgrimage that we may go forth
strong and faithful in our witness,
through Jesus Christ our Lord. Amen.

SCRIPTURAL RESPONSE
"See, I am coming soon; my reward is with me, to repay according to everyone's work. I am the Alpha and the Omega, the first and the last, the beginning and the end."
Blessed are those who wash their robes, so that they will have the right to the tree of life and may enter the city by the gates.
"It is I, Jesus, who sent my angel to you with this testimony for the churches. I am the root and the descendant of David, the bright morning star."
The Spirit and the bride say, "Come."
And let everyone who hears say, "Come."
And let everyone who is thirsty come.
Let anyone who wishes take the water of life as a gift.
(Revelation 22:12-14, 16-17)

HYMN
"Soon and Very Soon" **or**
"This Is the Day of New Beginnings" **or**
"Marching to Zion"

SENDING FORTH
Go now:
Go in safety,
for you cannot go where God is not.
Go in love,
for love alone endures.
Go with purpose,
and God will honor your dedication.
Go in peace,
for it is the gift of God to those whose hearts and minds
are in Christ Jesus. **Amen.**

The Love Feast introduction and service are adapted from *For All Who Minister: A Worship Manual for the Church of the Brethren;* pages 183–230, incorporating litany by Larry M. Dentler (pages 221–222) and prayers by Judith G. Kipp (pages 190, 194) and Larry M. Dentler (page 197). Copyright © 1993 by Brethren Press.